GLITTERING
VICES

GLITTERING
VICES

A NEW LOOK AT THE SEVEN DEADLY
SINS AND THEIR REMEDIES

REBECCA KONYNDYK DEYOUNG

BrazosPress

a division of Baker Publishing Group
Grand Rapids, Michigan

Published by Brazos Press
a division of Baker Publishing Group
P.O. Box 6287, Grand Rapids, MI 49516-6287
www.brazospress.com

Printed in the United States of America

Library of Congress Cataloging-in-Publication Data
DeYoung, Rebecca Konyndyk.
    Glittering vices : a new look at the seven deadly sins and their remedies /
Rebecca Konyndyk DeYoung.
        p.   cm.
    Includes bibliographical references (p.   ) and index.
    ISBN 978-1-58743-232-3 (pbk.)
    1. Deadly sins. I. Title.
BV4626.D49 2009
241'.3—dc22   2009005330

17   18   19   20   21   22   23   16   15   14   13   12   11   10

CONTENTS

ACKNOWLEDGMENTS

I would like to acknowledge the generous support of Calvin College in granting me sabbatical leave in 2005 to work on this manuscript, as well as a grant from the Calvin Center for Christian Scholarship in the fall of 2007 to revise it. I am also grateful for a grant from the National Endowment for the Humanities to attend a summer seminar on the topic in 2006. Their research support has been invaluable. Thanks also to Rodney Clapp and Lisa Ann Cockrel for their help polishing the manuscript in its final stages, and to Mary VandenBerg for her prayers.

This book has its roots in my teaching. It is, in many significant respects, both for and by my students at Calvin College. The ideas contained here came to fruition in classes on the virtues and vices I taught between 2002 and 2008. I sought to help students understand the Christian moral tradition as expressed in the work of figures like Thomas Aquinas but soon realized how impressed they were by its practical value as well. Their examples, analyses, questions, and insights therefore prompted many of my own reflections here. One student nicknamed the course "Spiritual Formation 101," a testimony to the way the tradition came alive for them and fed them moral and spiritual guidance in their walk with Christ. They were, and still are, the deepest inspiration for my work. These reflections on the vices, therefore, are dedicated to them.

INTRODUCTION

To flee vice is the beginning of virtue.—Horace

Several years ago I found myself in my first year of graduate school, wishing I were somewhere else. Everyone in my classes seemed so smart, so witty, so well read, so eager and able to ask brilliant and insightful questions. I felt like an impostor. How did I—obviously so inferior—ever get admitted with *these* people? How soon would they find out who I really was (or wasn't), and quietly shoo me out the back door in disgrace? Partly I struggled with genuinely difficult philosophical texts; mostly, however, I struggled with my own sense of inadequacy. So instead of engaging in class discussions and seeking out opportunities to improve myself, I spent that first year of graduate school pulling back into the shadows, believing I had nothing much to contribute, hoping no one would notice when I wrote something stupid.[1]

A few years later, reading Thomas Aquinas (1224–74) on the virtue of courage, I happened across a vice he called pusillanimity, which means "smallness of soul." Those afflicted by this vice, wrote Aquinas, shrink back from all that God has called them to be. When faced with the effort and difficulty of stretching themselves to the great things of which they are capable, they cringe and say, "I can't." In short, the pusillanimous rely on their own puny powers and focus on their own potential for failure, rather than counting on God's grace to equip them for great work in his kingdom—work beyond anything they might have dreamed of for themselves. Picture Moses at the burning bush, said Aquinas. The future leader of Israel in one of the greatest episodes of its history—the exodus from Egypt— stands there stuttering that he's not qualified, and asks God to send Aaron instead.

Reading Aquinas's account of the vice of pusillanimity was like looking at myself in the mirror for the first time. I had a name for my problem, one that made sense of my anxieties and struggles. At the same time, the biblical portrait of Moses presented inspiring evidence that God's power and grace can transform even—or especially—the weakest and most fearful of us:[2] Moses's pusillanimity did not have the last word in his life; God did.

It's a bit ironic, I suppose, that the discovery of this *vice* in myself turned out to be not only illuminating, but also liberating. Finally I understood what held me back, and calling it by name was a small yet significant step toward gradually wresting free of its grip. That I shrank back from all God called me to be and that I judged my own abilities as inadequate because I was not relying on God's grace to grant me strength—these perhaps are insights so obvious I should have seen them for myself. Yet seeing ourselves clearly is often difficult. Sometimes we need to hear a precise diagnosis from someone else, and to hear it at a particular time.

I have often joked that every time I read Aquinas I find another vice I never realized I had. My sense, however, is that whether or not we run the risk of becoming moral hypochondriacs, finding ourselves guilty of a new sin every day, most of us would benefit from some deeper moral reflection and self-examination—as I did in graduate school.

A study of personal vices can be a catalyst for spiritual growth, if it is done within the context of spiritual formation. This project of spiritual formation finds a natural home in the work of Thomas Aquinas, since Aquinas does not organize his major text on the moral life around the vices, but rather around the virtues and spiritual gifts. His central focus and framework is the people of good character we are meant to become. The pursuit of righteousness and moral excellence is the primary task—not obsession with the sins that so often entangle. So, along with Aquinas and many others in the Christian tradition, the present study will examine the vices within the context of spiritual formation. This book, based on his inspiration and insights, offers the conceptual tools to illuminate our personal stories, enable penetrating diagnoses of our struggles, and—more importantly—give us a glimpse of life beyond the entrapments of sin.

Contemporary Treatments of the Seven Deadly Sins

Reading Aquinas, I found the vices to have revealing and illuminating power. By contrast, many voices in contemporary culture, unfortunately, dismiss, redefine, psychologize, or trivialize them.

Some dismiss the vices on the grounds that they are not moral problems at all. In a tract recently republished by NavPress, the Reverend James Stalker proclaims, "On the whole, I should be inclined to say, gluttony is a sin which the civilized man has outgrown; and there is not much need for referring to it in the pulpit."[3] Francine Prose, likewise, confuses gluttony with feasting in her chapter "Great Moments of Gluttony,"[4] and Robert Solomon questions "why God would bother to raise a celestial eyebrow about [the vices]" given that "the 'deadly sins' barely jiggle the scales of justice"—as if sloth were nothing more than "a bloke who can't get out of bed," lust were nothing more than "one too many peeks at a *Playboy* pictorial," and gluttony were nothing more than "scarf[ing] down three extra jelly doughnuts."[5] These dismissals of the vices as irrelevant or trivial would be easier to swallow if they had anything much to do with the traditional conceptions of sloth, lust, gluttony, and the others.

Other authors attempt to redefine the seven vices as virtues—and to recommend them as such. In most of these cases too, what they are talking about has no clear relation to the original vice at all. For example, Michael Eric Dyson celebrates "black pride" in his book on the vice of pride; Wendy Wasserstein's parody of sloth offers a detailed "self-improvement plan" for becoming lazier;[6] and Simon Blackburn rejects the notion of disordered sexual desire altogether in his book on lust. "Everything is all right," he reassures us. "By understanding it for what it is, we can reclaim lust for humanity, and we can learn that lust flourishes best when it is unencumbered by bad philosophy and ideology, by falsities, by controls . . . which prevent its freedom of flow."[7]

Elsewhere, the vices are psychologized: gluttony becomes a quaint name for various eating disorders, wrath is wholly treatable in anger management seminars, and pride is replaced by talk about self-esteem. Psychologist Solomon Schimmel recounts a session with one Catho-

lic patient who was struggling with lust: "What were the effects of
therapy? My client overcame unpleasant feelings about premarital sex
with an affectionate companion who was also a marriage prospect . . .
Therapy made her much happier."[8] The general implication of all
this psychologizing is that just as we have abandoned the spiritual
counsel of benighted Christian monks, we can leave safely behind
any notion of the danger or seriousness of these "vices" as genuine
moral problems.

The vices are most often treated as a matter of lighthearted humor.
Evelyn Waugh remarks that the term *sloth,* is "seldom on modern lips.
When it is used, it is a mildly facetious variant on 'indolence,' and
indolence, surely, so far from being a deadly sin, is one of the world's
most amiable of weaknesses. Most of the world's troubles seem to
come from people who are too busy. If only politicians and scientists
were lazier, how much happier we should all be"—in part, he goes
on to argue, because then one wouldn't make the effort to commit
any of the really bad sins, such as pride.[9] Martin Marty reports that
the French have sent a delegation to the Vatican to get gluttony off
the list, because *la gourmandise* (the French term usually translated
as "gluttony") connotes not gluttony but "a warmhearted approach
to the table, to receiving and giving pleasure through good company
and food."[10] And in 1987, *Harper's* magazine ran a feature called
"You Can Have It All! Seven Campaigns for Deadly Sin," in which
seven Madison Avenue advertising agencies each created a print ad
"selling" one of the seven vices. Sloth's tagline reads, "If the original
sin had been sloth, we'd still be in Paradise."[11]

Most contemporary approaches to the vices, therefore, neither recognize nor respect the centuries of Christian teaching on the subject.
If all we know about the vices comes from contemporary sources, we
will probably oversimplify, stereotype, and scoff at moral problems or
rationalize them away. It is easy, especially now, to substitute silly or
shallow parodies for the actual content of centuries of moral reflection by philosophers and theologians. But if contemporary voices
do indeed misunderstand the tradition or present only a shallow and
dismissive reading of it, then in following them, we risk misunderstanding both our past and ourselves. If we were to go back to the
tradition and learn what gluttony was and the kind of power it can
wield in us, would we find it so natural and unproblematic that vastly
more Christians today are dieting than fasting? Could we be missing
something here?

An honest look at our own intellectual history requires that we listen carefully to the wisdom of the past. Unless we have some sense of what our own tradition has to say on the subject, Christians will not know how to engage contemporary challenges to historical conceptions of the vices. What is worth keeping and defending from the past? What insights might enrich our own spiritual formation and confessional practices? What concepts and definitions will enable us to recognize and restore broken aspects of our world and culture? Most fundamentally, of course, a Christian understanding of these seven vices requires taking sin and vice to be genuine moral categories. This book aims both to take sin and moral formation seriously and to take centuries of Christian wisdom on the subject seriously as well.

Vices and Virtues

In a book on the vices, we ought to be clear what a vice is. How are vices and virtues distinguished? How is a vice different from sin? Understanding these terms will give us a foundation to explore the tradition and its history in chapter 1, where we will answer questions such as: Where did the list of vices come from? What does it mean to call a set of them "capital vices" or "deadly sins"? Which ones should we single out as "capital," which as "deadly," and why? We begin here, however, with the concept of vice itself.

Although most references to the lists of seven use "vice" and "sin" in a roughly synonymous way, distinguishing the two turns out to be important. A vice (or its counterpart, a virtue), first of all, is a habit or a character trait. Unlike something we are born with—such as an outgoing personality or a predisposition to have high cholesterol levels—virtues and vices are acquired moral qualities. We can cultivate habits or break them down over time through our repeated actions, and thus we are ultimately responsible for our character.

By way of an analogy, think of a winter sledding party, in which a group of people head out to smooth a path through freshly fallen snow. The first sled goes down slowly, carving out a rut. Other sleds follow, over and over, down the same path, smoothing and packing down the snow. After many trips a well-worn groove develops, a path out of which it is hard to steer. The groove enables sleds to stay aligned and on course, gliding rapidly, smoothly, and easily on their way. Character traits are like that: the first run down, which required some effort and tough going, gradually becomes a smooth track that one glides down without further intentional steering.[12] Of course, a rider can always stick out a boot and throw the sled off course, usually damaging the track as well. So too we can act out of character, even after being "in the groove" for a long time. In general, however, habits incline us swiftly, smoothly, and reliably toward certain types of action.

Virtues are "excellences" of character, habits or dispositions of character that help us live well as human beings. So, for example, having the virtue of courage enables us to stand firm in a good purpose in the midst of pain or difficulty, when someone without the virtue would run away or give up. A courageous friend stands up for us when our reputation is unfairly maligned, despite risk to his own personal or professional reputation; a courageous mother cares for her sick child through inconvenience, sleepless nights, and exposure to disease. Courage enables us be faithful to other people and our commitments when the going gets rough and so enables the loving, trusting, and secure human relationships that are essential to a good human life.

Courageous individuals are still admirable people even when their good purposes are thwarted: when the friend's reputation becomes unfairly tarnished or when the sick child does not recover. We think it is better to be the sort of parent who suffers for and with her sick child than to be the sort of parent who can't handle sacrifice and leaves the hard work of caregiving to others. So virtue helps us both to live and act well *and* to be good people, as Aristotle once famously wrote.[13] Similarly, the vices are corruptive and destructive habits. They undermine both our goodness of character and our living and acting well. In the chapters that follow, we will explain how wrath, lust, gluttony, and the rest have a corrosive effect on our lives—how they eat away at our ability to see things clearly, appreciate things as we ought, live in healthy relationships with others, and refrain from self-destructive patterns of behavior.

Virtues and vices are gradually internalized and become firm and settled through years of formation. Often we develop habits by imitating those around us or following their instruction. We may or may not be intentional about all of our habit formation. For example, most children develop habits by imitating their parents, and in this way both virtues and vices can "rub off," so to speak. Other times, habit formation is the cumulative effect of many small, casual choices, similar to developing a smoking habit. Someone who wants to quit smoking after many years, or break any habit, needs serious deliberation and self-discipline. Sometimes we have a crisis that brings a new perspective. We see ourselves as if for the first time and want to change. But to make good on that desire to change, we have to wrestle daily against a deeply ingrained habit—and wrestle, perhaps, for the rest of our lives.

Very simply, a virtue (or vice) is acquired through practice—repeated activity that increases our proficiency at the activity and gradually forms our character. Alasdair MacIntyre describes a child learning to play chess to illustrate the process of habit formation.[14] Imagine, writes MacIntyre, that in hopes of teaching an uninterested seven-year-old to play chess, you offer the child candy—one piece to play, and another piece if the child wins the game. Motivated by his sweet tooth, the child agrees. At first, he plays for the candy alone. (And he will cheat to win, in order to get more candy.) But the more the child plays, the better at chess he gets. And the better at chess he gets, the more he enjoys the game, eventually coming to enjoy the game for itself. At this point in the process, he is no longer playing for the candy; now the child is playing because he enjoys chess and wants to play well. And he understands both the intrinsic value of the game and the way cheating will now rob him of that value. He has become a chess player. Moral formation in virtue works much the same way. We often need external incentives and sanctions to get us through the initial stages of the process, when our old, entrenched desires still pull us toward the opposite behavior. But with encouragement, discipline, and often a role model or mentor, practice can make things feel more natural and enjoyable as we gradually develop the internal values and desires corresponding to our outward behavior. Virtue often develops, that is, from the outside in. This is why, when we want to re-form our character from vice to virtue, we often need to practice and persevere in regular spiritual disciplines and formational practices for a lengthy period of time. There is no quick and easy substitute for daily repetition over the long haul. First we have to pull the sled out of the old rut, and then gradually build up a new track.

As with most human endeavors, we usually do not do this alone. Our parents, most obviously and deeply, contribute to our character formation, but so do friends, mentors, historical figures, and the community of saints past and present. If we marry, our spouse will shape our character, as will our teachers, and the fictional characters we read about and find inspiring. Our coworkers influence our habit formation, and so do the friends with whom we spend the most time—which is why good parents care so much about their children's friends. When we make a new resolution or try to cultivate a new habit, having a community back us, or even a single partner with whom to practice or from whom to learn, can make all the difference.

In the end, both virtues and vices are habits that can eventually become "natural" to us. Philosophers describe the perfect achievement of virtue as yielding internal harmony and integrity. Compare, for example, the following two married persons: The first, let's call Jane. Although she resists them, Jane regularly struggles with sexual feelings for men other than her husband. The second, call him Joe, enjoys an ardent affection for his wife throughout the ups and downs of thirty years of marriage. Are they both faithful? In a technical sense, at least, yes. Jane successfully exercises self-control over her wayward desires. But only Joe embodies fidelity as a *virtue*. His faithfulness is deeply rooted in who he is. While we can give her moral credit for her efforts, Jane's faithfulness stays on the surface; it is the uncomfortable voice of conscience countering her adulterous inclinations and keeping her actions in check.[15] By contrast, Joe's desires are in harmony with his considered judgment.[16] Who wouldn't rather have a spouse with Joe's fidelity than Jane's self-control?

The ancient Greek philosopher Aristotle called this the difference between acting *according* to virtue—that is, according to an external standard which tells us what we ought to do whether we feel like it or not—and acting *from* the virtue—that is, from the internalized disposition which naturally yields its corresponding action.[17] The person who acts *from* virtue performs actions that fit seamlessly with his or her inward character. Thus, the telltale sign of virtue is doing the right thing with a sense of peace and pleasure. What feels like "second nature" to you?[18] These are the marks of your character.

Virtues and Virtuous Character

As the previous examples make clear, it is not enough merely to *want* to be virtuous, or to wish we had greater harmony between our motivation and our action. One can aspire to be a better person, or want not to be corrupt or weak, but not yet have a clear sense of how to achieve those goals. "Cultivate good character" is a useless prescription if we don't know what good character amounts to and how to cultivate it. We need to be able to pinpoint our shortcomings and set our sights on specific objectives. If cultivating virtue and avoiding vice is the key to moral formation, then we need to know first of all what the particular virtues and vices are.

When I ask my students and friends to list various virtues, they invariably name things like honesty, courage, kindness, loyalty, and fidelity; for the vices, the list usually includes qualities like cowardice, greed, and selfishness. A *Newsweek* article on character education came up with this list of virtues: "prudence, respect, loyalty, love, justice, courage, hope, honesty, compassion, fairness, and self-control."[19] Answers like these are generally on the right track. Despite our distance from traditions of ethics that focus on the virtues and vices, we retain a sense of what should count. But why privilege one list of vices over another? What makes one list a random collection and another an ordered set?

Contemporary lists given by my students usually share an important feature with those of the Christian virtue tradition. The process of compiling lists of virtues and vices implicitly starts with thinking about moral ideals, embodied in heroes or saints or cultural icons (or villains). That is, we implicitly draw our lists from a mental picture of someone we admire (or despise) as a model of moral excellence (or corruption). Role models who embody a moral ideal are anchors for moral education into the virtues (or vices), since we learn and acquire character traits by observing and imitating role models. From this model or ideal, we can then analyze more specifically what we find admirable or dishonorable about that person's character. A United States Marine embodies honor, courage, and fidelity; an Olympic athlete embodies perseverance and hope; a family practice doctor embodies compassion and wisdom; saints such as Mother Teresa are a model of kindness and mercy; heroes such as Martin Luther King Jr. are a picture of steadfastness and courage.

The Christian tradition is also explicit about its role model, a picture of perfected human nature, the image of God redeemed and restored, the one to be emulated by all human beings. As Aquinas writes, "Our Savior the Lord Jesus Christ . . . showed unto us *in His own self* the way of truth."[20] Christ's life and ministry model the virtues for us, and we must rely on the grace and power of the Holy Spirit to make progress in our imitation of him.[21]

How do Christ's example and the work of grace affect a Christian view of virtues and vices?[22] A Christian understanding of temperance, for example, will have to include not only moderating our desire for food, but also fasting and feasting. Likewise, the virtue of courage challenges us to endure suffering for the sake of love, relying on God's strength, even to the point of martyrdom—this in contrast to contemporary portraits that show us a brave individual charging the enemy alone with guns ablaze. Christ teaches us too how gentleness and humility ground righteous anger, enabling us both to turn over tables of injustice and to turn the other cheek.

The tradition eventually singled out seven virtues—three theological virtues (faith, hope, and love) and four cardinal virtues (practical wisdom, justice, courage, and temperance). These are the qualities of character that *everyone* who wants to become Christlike must seek to cultivate, whatever his or her culture and calling. At the same time, these virtues are the foundation of human perfection for all human beings. They are meant to comprise a holistic picture of the human person—that is, to cover every aspect of our nature, from our mind to our will to our emotions, and to direct them all toward God.[23] According to the Christian tradition, everyone needs faith, hope, and love, as well as practical wisdom, justice, courage, and temperance in order to become all God intended him or her to be as a human being. Of course, courage can be manifested in different ways at different times—on a battlefield or a sickbed—but no one can hold firmly to the good in the face of pain and difficulty without it. Chastity, a part of temperance, can be fulfilled through marriage, celibacy, or seasons of singleness, but the married and the celibate alike are called to order sexual desire rightly. In a parallel way, the seven vices depict for us the traits of character to which we must die in order to live as people with Christlike character.

Why Study the Vices Today?

Other than piquing our historical interests, is there a good reason to try to recover the traditional Christian view of the vices? For Christians, there is both intellectual and practical payoff—in the way we understand ourselves and our world, and in the way our practices and prayers are reshaped. But for non-Christians as well, it is worth grasping the traditional view of the vices. This tradition has deeply shaped our culture, and it is worth understanding its influence—whether we accept or reject it—in order to better understand ourselves. I'll begin in what follows with several reasons that should appeal to both believers and nonbelievers.

First, we can find a wealth of references to the seven in films, books, and art. Studying the vices can help us uncover layers of depth and significance in contemporary stories and culture that trade on human weaknesses and temptations. For example, when we read *Brideshead Revisited* by Evelyn Waugh, we see a portrait of the vice of sloth in explicitly religious terms (although narrated by an agnostic character) and can recognize points of contact with the traditional, Christian conception of this vice. We also pick up on additional cues, for example, that the family name Waugh chooses in the novel—Flyte—stands for one of sloth's most common symptoms, escapism or flight. Likewise, many viewers could recognize the portrait of envy in the film *Amadeus*, even if few catch the equally acute depiction of vainglory in Salieri's need for public affirmation and acclaim. The film's opening scene, in which Salieri quizzes a priest to see if he recognizes any of Salieri's compositions, reveals a need for recognition and approval from others as deep as his envy of Mozart's musical gifts. It's a perfect illustration of Gregory the Great's claim that the two vices are intimately related. The film also links hatred of neighbor to hatred of God. Thus it shows how envy violates both aspects of charity—love of God and love of neighbor—the virtue to which it is opposed, in Aquinas's account. And long before today's abundant testimonies of the addictive power of pornography, Alan Paton's story *Too Late the Phalarope* offered a haunting case study of the binding and blinding power of lust and its power to destroy human relationships.

The vices also offer us a framework for explaining and evaluating common cultural practices. Envy and its offspring vice, *Schadenfreude*—joy at another's misfortune—go a long way to explaining the popularity of tabloids exposing and trumpeting the cellulite and poor fashion of the rich and famous. Reality shows of the makeover variety, which spawned a boom in cosmetic surgery, are a tribute to the power of vainglory and the image-driven advertising industry that requires it. Action–adventure films' formula for box office success depends on the celebration of wrathful revenge in the guise of righteous anger. Corporate workaholic culture depends on a secularized notion of sloth and mistakenly glorifies frantic industriousness as its opposing virtue. Modern-day gluttony drives inventions like diet sodas and specially manufactured potato chips that give us the pleasures of eating and drinking without caloric consequences.

Most importantly, however, understanding the vices can yield spiritual rewards. Most historical Christian figures treated in this book—Evagrius, Cassian, Gregory, Aquinas—wrote with a life of intentional Christian discipleship in mind. Aquinas, for example, makes the virtues the key building blocks of a Christian life, while the vices describe our greatest moral and spiritual pitfalls. Becoming holy involves "putting away" the sinful nature—the vices—and "clothing ourselves" with the character of Christ, the only human being who perfectly exemplifies the virtues.[24] The Christian tradition follows the apostle Paul's old-self/new-self distinction when it describes how our character is transformed from vice to virtue:

> You were taught to put away your former way of life, your old self, corrupt and deluded by its lusts, and to be renewed in the spirit of your minds, and to clothe yourselves with the new self, created according to the likeness of God in true righteousness and holiness. (Eph. 4:22–24)

> Put to death, therefore, whatever in you is earthly: fornication, impurity, passion, evil desire, and greed (which is idolatry) . . . These are the ways you also once followed, when you were living that life . . . Do not lie to one another, seeing that you have stripped off the old self with its practices and have clothed yourselves with the new self, which is being renewed in knowledge according to the image of its creator . . . As God's chosen ones, holy and beloved, clothe yourselves with compassion, kindness, humility, meekness, and patience . . . Above all, clothe yourselves with love, which binds everything together in perfect harmony. (Col. 3:5–14)

In other words, *the* moral project for a Christian is to die to the old self and rise to new life in Christ. This dying and rising is the rhythm of a life of discipleship, a life devoted to becoming more and more like Christ. Centuries before the advent of Christianity, the Greek philosopher Aristotle wrote that virtues and vices describe aspects of our character that become "second nature" to us. This makes the vices especially apt for describing our old sinful nature, and the virtues, for our new nature in Christ. Thus, Christian thinkers from Augustine through Aquinas overwhelmingly adopted the Greek conception of virtue and vice to describe the moral life and the development of Christian character.[25] We are to shed the old nature—described in terms of the vices—and put on Christlikeness—the virtues. The model of character change or moral formation therefore neatly fits the theological idea of transformation from the "old self" into a renewed and sanctified person.

One of the movements in the rhythm of discipleship and sanctification is the movement of dying. The practice of confession is where the "dying" of conversion repeatedly occurs. We come as though to the edge of our own graves and renounce our old self and its habits and practices. Yet that renunciation, as a preface to new life, requires knowing our sin. This is just how the tradition of the seven vices got started. The desert fathers' classification of seven vices began as a Christian system of self-examination in the fourth century and continued to provide an almost ubiquitous rubric for confession in penitential manuals up until the fifteenth century—an endurance that testifies to their power as a spiritual tool for confession and repentance. When we study the vices, we can better articulate for ourselves what parts of our sinful nature we are grappling with and trying to put to death, and learn how one vice might variously reveal itself in feelings and actions. We can use the list of vices to recognize and identify networks of sin in our lives and discover layers of sin of which we were previously unaware. In this way, our confession can be fine-tuned. Rather than praying in general for forgiveness of sin, or reducing all our sin to pride or generic selfishness, we can lay specific sins before God, ask for the grace to root them out, and engage in daily disciplines—both individually and communally—that help us target them. Naming our sins is the confessional counterpart to counting our blessings. Naming them can enrich and refresh our practices of prayer and confession and our engagement in the spiritual disciplines.

Reaching back to the tradition of virtues and vices can also give us fresh eyes and expose new layers of meaning in our reading of scripture. Before I read Aquinas on sloth, I would have associated it with only a few proverbs about sluggards and perhaps the parable of the talents with this vice. A closer study of sloth helped me to see it in the Israelites' resistance to embracing their new home in the promised land, and in Lot's wife turning back to the familiarity of Sodom while angels attempted to rescue her. Similarly, understanding the distinction between wrath and righteous anger helps us understand how Jesus integrated justice and love—how he could burn with anger against Pharisees who would deny a man healing on the Sabbath and then forgive those who crucify him. Studying avarice leads us to see connections between the story of the widow of Zarephath and the prodigal son. Once we grasp the envy–charity link, we gain new insight into the depths of the brothers' antipathy toward Joseph, Jacob's favorite son.

Finally, if we're able to identify our own sins more carefully, we'll be better equipped to reflect on and engage with the world around us. Are there areas of moral complicity or compromise in our own lives of which we are not even aware? Consider contemporary American culture, torn between relentless workaholism on the one hand and an obsession with maximizing leisure on the other. What lies behind this cultural ethos? Should Christians endorse the limitless pursuit of work as selfless diligence and godly industriousness? Or might they find in these lifestyles evidence of cravings for control, self-sufficiency, and a refusal to depend on God? Perhaps our drivenness, even more than our pursuit of leisure, is closer to vice than virtue.

Perhaps. Human culture and motivations are notoriously difficult to penetrate, even—or especially—when they have become our own. Why not, then, avail ourselves of the historical perspective and collective wisdom of the Christian tradition to help us see and know ourselves more truly? The project of becoming like Christ is our life's most important task. It makes sense to use every resource we can find to help us do it well. The whole story of human sin and failure cannot be told by our contemporaries or invented anew by our own imaginations. There is often value in contemporary reflection and our own insight. But when we seek moral advice, we need also to listen to the experienced, the devout, those saints and sages of past centuries whose insights often still ring true today.

C. S. Lewis once said, "We are half-hearted creatures, fooling about with drink and sex and ambition when infinite joy is offered us, like an ignorant child who wants to go on making mud pies in a slum because he cannot imagine what is meant by the offer of a holiday at the sea."[26] When we recognize our vices for what they are, we take a first step toward turning to the sea. When we understand the slum for what it really is, we can countenance preferring the seashore. Once we see the mud of our moral corruption, we are faced with the challenge of re-forming our habits from vice into virtue, a process that immediately confronts us with the need for grace. Dante Alighieri outlines the same movement in his *Divine Comedy*. Through remedial punishments, sinners come to grasp the true nature of their offenses and can be gradually weaned from their distorted desires. The fruit of this process is the full joy of a life in loving relationship with God.[27]

In the next chapter, we turn to the history and origins of both lists. This history reveals why certain vices made the infamous list of seven, why they are better called "capital" than "deadly," and what common theme explains their twisted but seductive search for happiness. Most importantly, this intriguing story shows us how the vices tradition was linked from the start to a Christian tradition of discipleship and spiritual formation, and how it can still serve those ends today.

1

GIFTS FROM THE DESERT

The Origins and History
of the Vices Tradition

A Short History of the Virtues and Vices

The seven capital vices as we know them evolved from a tradition—a tradition interwoven with Christian moral reflection, and one that any serious study of the vices cannot afford to ignore. Unfortunately, much of the confusion and ignorance (both willful and accidental) that characterizes many contemporary treatments of the vices results from a neglect of the history or an unwillingness to take it seriously. G. K. Chesterton once said, "Defending any of the cardinal virtues has today all the exhilaration of a vice," in part because serious defenses of the virtues, and serious condemnations of the vices, are in terribly short supply. Commenting on a collection of articles on the seven deadly sins in the London *Sunday Times* by the likes of W. H. Auden and Evelyn Waugh, Henry Fairlie observed that even the editor of the collection found it striking that "in a series of articles such as I am introducing, passionate denunciations and threats of brimstone would be out of place . . . The mildness with which on the whole [the authors] regard the deadly sins may be thought surprising and significant."[1] At the same time, many contemporary sermons and Christian reflections on the sins fail to acknowledge, much less draw on, any ideas about the sins in their own tradition.[2]

Before considering each individual vice in the following chapters, then, I will seek to remedy these defects by revisiting the long tradition of thought that gave rise to the list of seven. Being explicit about our historical and cultural inheritance can often significantly enrich our ability to understand—or even more basically, to recognize—our own moral predicament. This book's approach seeks to give due weight to both the historical contexts and traditions in which the vices arose *and* the Christian moral and theological categories in which the vices make the most sense.

Contrasting the origins of the lists of virtues and vices will give us a better sense of the fluidity of the vices tradition, which goes some way to explain our confused inheritance of it. The seven principal virtues, unlike the list of the seven vices, claim both explicit biblical and weighty philosophical sources. Probably for this reason, the list of virtues fluctuated little over much of its history. The list of three theological virtues (faith, hope, and love) comes from the apostle Paul's famous hymn of love in 1 Corinthians 13. However, Paul does not use the Greek term for virtue (*aretê*) to describe faith, hope, and love, either in the 1 Corinthians passage or in Colossians 3:14, where love is said to "bind . . . together in perfect harmony" a list of virtue-like qualities, including patience, kindness, and so on.

The four cardinal virtues (practical wisdom, justice, courage, and temperance) are mentioned in Wisdom 8:7. This book was likely written for Jews in the Diaspora about 300 BC, the same era that the four cardinal virtues were prominent in Greek philosophical ethics. Chapter 8 of the book of Wisdom in the Septuagint does use the Greek term *aretê*, which the Latin Vulgate translates *virtus*. It is likely that biblical writers, like later church fathers, found the classical Greek concept a convenient category for the excellences of moral character they wanted to describe. This is to be expected: all ancient and medieval ethical systems framed questions about morality in terms of the perfection of character or human nature over a lifetime. Such a framework made the virtues—as the building blocks of good character—the central ethical category for centuries.

Whatever the ultimate sources of their lists—philosophical or scriptural—the church fathers explicitly endorsed the list of the four cardinal virtues and integrated them into a Christian ethic. Augustine, for example, did so by reconceptualizing them as forms of love for God. In his book *On the Morals of the Catholic Church* (15.25), he wrote:

> I hold that virtue is nothing other than the perfect love of God. Now, when it is said that virtue has a fourfold division, as I understand it, this is said according to the various movements of love . . . We may, therefore, define these virtues as follows: temperance is love preserving itself entire and incorrupt for God; courage is love readily bearing all things for the sake of God; justice is love serving only God, and therefore ruling well everything else that is subject to the human person; prudence is love discerning well between what helps it toward God and what hinders it.

By making them all forms of Christian love, Augustine intentionally transformed this philosophical set of virtues, which were part of a Greek ethic of self-perfection, into Christian virtues dependent on God's grace.

Given its origins in Christian practice and reflection—not scripture or philosophy—the list of vices presents a contrast to that of the list of seven virtues in its variation over several centuries. As far as historians can tell, this list of vices was first put in writing by Evagrius of Pontus (346–399 AD), one of the desert fathers in the early centuries of the Christian church. These monks deliberately withdrew into the desert to face temptation and sin head-on and to cultivate a contemplative spirit through prayer, following the example of Christ in his wilderness temptations.[3] Culling wisdom from the oral traditions and disciplines of these ascetics who sought spiritual progress in desert solitude, Evagrius set down a list of eight "thoughts" or "demons" that typically beset the desert hermit: "gluttony, then impurity [i.e., lust], avarice, sadness, anger, *acedia* [later called sloth], vainglory, and last of all, pride."[4] In Evagrius's texts, the vices were not systematically ordered, although later authors, most notably Cassian and Gregory, placed the seven on a continuum from carnal vices to spiritual ones—gluttony, lust, avarice, wrath, sadness, sloth, vainglory, and pride.[5]

Evagrius had a flair for the practical: he was more interested in describing the guises of the demons and how to fight against them than in developing a comprehensive theoretical system. His portrayals of the demons remind one of C. S. Lewis's *The Screwtape Letters*. For example, the "noonday demon" of sloth attacks in the heat of midday, appearing to make the sun stand still and filling one's mind with tempting rationalizations:

> This demon drives [the monk] along to desire other places where he can more easily procure life's necessities, more readily find work and make a real success of himself. He goes on to suggest that, after all, it is not the place that is the basis of pleasing the Lord. God is to be adored everywhere. He joins to those reflections the memory of [the monk's] dear ones and of his former way of life. He depicts life as stretching out for a long period of time, and brings before the mind's eye the toil of the ascetic struggle, and, as the saying has it, leaves no leaf unturned to induce the monk to forsake his [desert] cell and drop out of the fight.[6]

Evagrius's disciple, John Cassian (360–430), introduced the Western church to the list and its accompanying ascetic practices with his *Institutes*[7] and *Conferences*. From there the set of vices became more or less an institutional fixture within the monastic tradition. From the solitary life of the desert monks, Cassian's account of the vices was adapted to the shape of a communal monastic life. So, in the tradition of Cassian and as an antidote to the vice of pride, St. Benedict's Rule of monastic life (written in the sixth century) gave monks positive instruction concerning how to live virtuously with each other. For example, the Rule lists twelve ways to cultivate humility, including the spiritual disciplines of silence and submission to one's spiritual directors, all as part of the "common rule of the monastery."[8]

A few centuries after Evagrius and Cassian, Pope Gregory I ("the Great," 540–604) pared the list of capital vices down from eight to seven, the biblical number symbolizing completeness, by subsuming sloth under sadness, making envy a standard member, and separating pride out as their root. (Changes are marked with italics in the chart below.)

Evagrius's List (8)	Cassian's List (8)	Gregory's List (7)	Aquinas's List (7)
The same as Cassian's, but not ordered from carnal to spiritual.	Gluttony, lust, avarice, wrath, sadness, sloth, vainglory, pride.	Vainglory, *envy*, *sadness*, avarice, wrath, lust, gluttony. *Pride* = root	Vainglory, envy, *sloth*, avarice, wrath, lust, gluttony. Pride = root

In his *Moralia*, which became the standard for moral and theological reflection for at least the next six hundred years, Gregory sets

out the seven virtues and the seven vices with their progeny, and the
seven gifts of the Holy Spirit. It is Gregory who makes pride the root
of the seven capital vices, a list that now includes vainglory, rather than
counting pride as a member of the former list of eight, as Evagrius
and Cassian did. He writes:

> For the tempting vices, which fight against us in invisible contest on
> behalf of pride which reigns over them, some of them go first, like
> captains; others follow, after the manner of an army . . . For when
> pride, the queen of sins, has fully possessed a conquered heart, she
> surrenders it immediately to seven principal sins, as if to some of her
> generals, to lay it waste . . . For pride is the root of all evil . . . but
> seven principal vices, as its first progeny, no doubt spring from this
> poisonous root: namely vain glory, envy, anger, melancholy, avarice,
> gluttony, and lust.[9]

In addition to adopting Cassian's organic metaphor of the root and
offshoots, Gregory frames his account in the imagery of a spiritual
battle; the offspring vices of each capital vice are like the foot soldiers
of the generals, with pride as their commander-in-chief.[10]

By the time we get to Thomas Aquinas in the thirteenth century, we
find him synthesizing the wisdom of an amazing variety of predeces-
sors in both philosophy and theology. When it comes to describing
the vices, he quotes everyone from Aristotle, the Neoplatonists, and
the Stoics to Augustine, Gregory, and other church fathers. He defers
especially to Gregory's *Moralia* as his primary theological source
for the definitive *lists* of seven virtues and vices. However, whereas
Gregory's enumerations were part of a commentary on scripture that
was widely appreciated for its practical counsel, Aquinas's descriptions
formed a highly systematic and philosophically sophisticated account.
As a result, his treatment has a more theoretical, and less pastoral,
feel than Gregory's does. His *Summa theologiae*, written as a school
text for the instruction of his fellow Dominicans, stands as one of
the greatest pieces of moral theology in the Christian tradition. The
extensive section on the virtues and vices circulated independently, and
it quickly became the most-used part of the *Summa* in the centuries
immediately following Aquinas's death.[11]

The vice lists were not found solely in theological and moral trea-
tises. They also appeared in texts guiding the practices of confession
and penance. One edition of William Peraldus's *Summa of Virtues
and Vices* has no fewer than twenty-seven chapters on the single vice

of sloth![12] Like other penitential manuals, Peraldus's had a clerical, not an academic audience; it was written to aid priests and preachers in writing sermons and hearing confessions structured around the sins, as mandated by the Fourth Lateran Council (1215 AD). By the thirteenth century, therefore, not only theologians and clerics, but laypeople too, knew the vices. Confessional manuals and guides like Peraldus's typically listed each of the vices, along with "reasons for shunning the vice, specific vices that spring from it, and remedies for it."[13] The list of vices had become primarily a practical and pastoral tool, not a theoretical construct. If it had not been for this usefulness, the list might never have attained such popularity.

Our inheritance of it, however, comes only after several further turns of history. Later scholastics were dissatisfied with the list's unsystematic nature, and later Reformers with its lack of scriptural basis. Aquinas's own argument to explain why these seven and not others were counted as capital lacks compelling consistency. Cassian had tried to use the account of the seven nations of Canaan to be conquered as a metaphorical basis of the sins, but this also seemed inadequate.[14] Although they had the authority of thinkers like Gregory the Great and Peter Lombard (1100–1160), whose *Sentences* containing the list of vices was the theology textbook of the day, the seven vices are not found *as a list* in scripture, and thus the list of seven lacked credibility. As confessional practices of self-examination extended more widely outside the intentional, ascetic communities in which the rubric of vices was originally anchored, accounts of the moral life shifted toward ways of thinking that were more systematically satisfying or directly scripturally based—for example, the Ten Commandments or the fruits of the Spirit.[15] Moreover, although priests continued to use the list of seven for pastoral and confessional purposes, theories of ethics gradually shifted away from an emphasis on virtue and vice, and more toward law and casuistry, obligation and obedience.[16]

After the Reformation, Protestants who worried about "works righteousness" were wary of exhortations to practice the virtues; similarly, their emphasis on justification by faith and grace alone made them suspect efforts to purge one's life of the vices.[17] How could Protestants appropriate the vices tradition without compromising this essential tenet of Reformation theology? Framing the role of the vices and virtues in terms of the lifelong process of sanctification is the most obvious way. Cultivating virtue requires our effort, to be sure, but every effort we make is empowered by grace, as 2 Peter 1:3

states, "His divine power has given us everything we need for life and godliness" (NIV).

In the last few decades, with the revival of interest in the spiritual disciplines as lifelong practices of those who imitate Christ,[18] Protestants have begun to recover an appreciation of spiritual formation. There is a new and fruitful opportunity today to bring virtue-and-vice talk back into the Christian life of discipleship, properly embedded, as it was from the beginning, in the context of grace.[19] As Evagrius wrote, "As for those who have received from grace the strength for ascetic labors, let them not think that they possess this [strength] from their own power."[20]

Encouraging Christians to take spiritual discipline seriously again, Dallas Willard argues:

> We are saved by grace of course, and by it alone, and not because we deserve it. That is the basis of God's acceptance of us. But grace does *not* mean that sufficient strength and insight will be automatically "infused" into our being in the moment of need . . . A baseball player who expects to excel in the game without adequate exercise of his body is no more ridiculous than the Christian who hopes to be able to act in the manner of Christ when put to the test without the appropriate exercise in godly living.[21]

Willard's point, meant for Protestants suspicious of works-righteousness talk, is that when we receive saving or justifying grace, this should be only the beginning, not the finale, of our Christian story. Living as a Christian takes discipline and practice, but these activities are enabled by Christ's saving work, rather than replacing it.

Lost in Translation

The next chapter of the story of the vices tradition, after the Middle Ages and the Reformation, traces their fate as the Western world continued to move toward modernity. In this movement—most obviously manifested in the Enlightenment and the period of increasing industrialization following it—the vices were even more radically marginalized. Vices were not only abstracted from their place in Christian confessional practices, but purged of their theological context and secularized. David Hume (1711–76) offered a notably modern-sounding list of virtues—"discretion, caution, enterprise, industry,

assiduity, frugality, economy, good-sense, prudence, discernment"—
and extolled them solely on the grounds of their social "utility."[22]
Likewise, in his treatment of the vices, he recommended restraining
vainglory on the grounds that others find it disagreeable.[23] Marking
his views as a deliberate departure from traditional Christian conceptions, he defined "pride" as "that agreeable impression, which arises in
the mind, when the view either of our virtue, beauty, riches or power
makes us satisfy'd with ourselves: And . . . by humility I mean the
opposite impression. 'Tis evident the former impression is not always
vicious, nor the latter virtuous."[24] In the twentieth century, serving as
a spokesperson for the triumphs of modern industrialization, Henry
Ford interpreted sloth as "idleness," opposing it to the virtue of industriousness, on the grounds that not in God, but in "work is our
sanity, our self-respect, our salvation." He concludes that "through
work and work alone may health, wealth, and happiness inevitably be
secured."[25] And several decades after the sexual revolution, William
Gass freely comments:

> So what about lust? Let's compare it with gluttony. That will get us off
> to a good start. Satisfied lust isn't fattening. Satisfied lust may mean
> two people are happy . . . It improves the skin, all that blood rising to
> the top like cream. It detenses the limbs so that all one's aches feel far
> away and in the past. Common courtship costs. You take one another
> to dinner, gluttonize, pay up, the heart burns. But lust is easily relieved
> without any outlay.[26]

Like Gass's riff on lust, many contemporary treatments of the list
have lost touch almost entirely with the religious and philosophical
traditions behind the seven, and certainly with the notion of sin. As
attention to the vices has been recently revived, the list has quickly
been reduced to a convenient and catchy rhetorical device for popular
books, films, and advertisements. A quick survey of television and film
treatments of the vices turns up an MTV special on the seven, including an interview with Queen Latifah, depictions of the seven deadly
Santas (a collection of film clips of Santa committing all seven sins),
a 20/20 series on the seven, and a feature-length film starring Brad Pitt
and Morgan Freeman. Vices aficionados can purchase rubber wrist-
bands in the Archie McFee catalog color-coded for each deadly sin or
T-shirts for each vice, available at a variety of websites. A small cottage
industry of books cashed in on the theme "The Seven Deadly Sins of

[Fill in the Blank]." A small sample: obesity, small-group ministry, Ivy League schools, home remodeling, gardening, and apologetics. *Harper's* magazine ran a series of advertising spoofs on the seven for the high-brow; and for the lowbrow, Robin Wasserman wrote a smutty series for teens ("The Seven Deadly Sins: Commit Them All!"). On specific sins, we find YouTube clips of Gordon Gecko's famous "greed is good" speech from *Wall Street*; and a website that advocates buying more "sloth" apparel for those too lazy to do laundry.[27] Most contemporary references to the list of seven deadly sins use them for their symbolic power and rhetorical appeal, disregarding any claims they might have to being a genuine moral or theological classification.

The Capital Vices: Sources of Sin

For the first millennia of their use, then, the seven vices were at the heart of a process of self-examination and moral re-formation. If we are still interested in that project, either for historical or practical reasons, it is worth investigating why these seven vices, and not others, made the official list. The seven vices are not just any seven bad habits. Nor are they the worst possible or most frequent vices, although some critics mistakenly think this, complaining that surely cruelty and murder should have made the list (as the worst) or drunkenness and lying (as the most frequent).[28] The labels for the lists lend a clue as to why these seven were chosen: "the seven capital vices" or the "seven deadly sins."

Each label means something quite different from the other. And each is easily misunderstood. The Latin *caput* or *capitis* means "head," so we might initially assume that "capital" in "capital vice" means the same thing it does in the phrase "capital punishment." In certain methods of execution, capital punishment literally cuts off one's head and is therefore deadly. In the case of the capital vices, however, "head" indicates not the uppermost bit of human anatomy but rather a source or "fountainhead," as it were. Traditionally, the capital vices are singled out because they are "source vices," vices that serve as an ever-bubbling wellspring of many others.

To use another picture, more common in the Middle Ages, we can think of pride as the root and trunk of a tree, which extends upward into seven main branches, each of which represents one capital vice. From those vices, in turn, grow many other branches, each of which bears poisonous fruit. Cassian uses both metaphors:

> For a tall and spreading tree of a noxious kind will the more easily be
> made to wither if the roots on which it depends have first been laid
> bare or cut; and a pond of water which is dangerous will be dried up
> at once if the spring and flowing channel which produce it are care-
> fully stopped up.[29]

The seven capital vices are the set of vices that grow out of pride
and tend to proliferate additional sin. Thus, in the works of church
fathers like Cassian and Gregory the Great, as well as thirteenth- and
fourteenth-century guides for confession based on them, each vice
would be listed along with its "offspring" vices—with five to twenty
or even more vices sprouting out from the main branches.[30]

The tree metaphor yields a picture of moral education in which
the goal is to get to the problem's source, and root *it* out, thereby
eliminating a whole host of related vices. Moreover, it suggests that
merely pruning the new shoots and twigs at the end of the branches is
a bit like giving aspirin to an AIDS victim. It asks, are you interested
in temporary relief of symptoms or a cure that gets to the source of
the disease? The tree metaphor encourages people to see certain sins
as likely indicators of deeper moral problems and to see their connection to that great original sin, pride.[31]

Deadly Sins or Capital Vices?

As such a metaphor implies, the label "capital vices" has a significantly different meaning than its alternative, "the seven deadly sins."
Notice first the difference between *sin* and *vice*. *Sin* has a broader
scope, since it can include patterns of sinfulness in our behavior, our
fallen condition or nature in general, or a single act of disobedience.
The term *vice* is more specific: vices concern deeply rooted patterns
in our character, patterns broader than a single act but narrower
than our sinful human condition in general. The category "vice"
also makes better sense of the link between poisoned fruits, offshoot
vices, and their seven sources. For example, sixteen offshoot *vices* for
sloth might appear too overblown an estimate of the damage done
by a *single act* of sin (although in certain cases, perhaps not!).[32] So
many specific offshoot vices better describe the typical impact on our
character made over time by an embedded addiction to something
we mistake for happiness.

An even more important difference between the two labels "capital vices" and "deadly sins" lies in the meaning of *deadly*. The "deadliness" of the seven deadly sins refers to the distinction between mortal and venial sins. In Catholic moral theology, mortal sins are so-called because they cause *spiritual* death. They cut us off from God's grace when we reject the source of our spiritual life, the indwelling of the Holy Spirit. Aquinas calls this gift of the Holy Spirit's indwelling the virtue of charity: love of God and neighbor, the love that is the perfect fulfillment of the law (Matt. 22:37–40; Rom. 13:10). So he defines mortal sins as sins against charity. In this picture, to commit a deadly or mortal sin is to lose the grace of the Holy Spirit by rejecting God as one's highest good and refusing to put love of God and neighbor first in one's actions. The decision effectively shows that one prefers committing the sin—obtaining whatever good it promises—to having a relationship with God. Venial sins, on the other hand, may dispose us to mortal sin but do not themselves sever our union with God.

Many strands of Protestant theology deny the possibility that one can commit mortal sin after one receives saving grace. According to the doctrine of the perseverance of the saints, "the wages" of *all* sin is death (Rom. 6:23), because every sin separates us from God. However, once we are justified, nothing can separate us from the love of God (Rom. 8:38–39). Those who hold this doctrine, or those who deny the traditional Catholic distinction between mortal and venial sin on other grounds, would be more faithful to their own theological commitments by using the label "capital vices." Ironically, most Protestants tend to call them "the seven deadly sins."

There are still other important reasons to prefer the title "capital vices" to "deadly sins." Aquinas argues that not all acts of vice are necessarily (or even usually) mortal sins. Many instances of lust and gluttony, for example, seem better explained by weakness or impulsiveness than by an entrenched or willful preference for pleasure over a relationship with God, although they might well tend in that direction over time. Moreover, the conception of the sins as "deadly" does not explain their association with specific offspring vices. From the beginning of the history of the list, the vices were explicitly called *principia vitia* ("principal vices") and enumerated together with certain specific progeny. Again, here is Cassian:

> And though these [offspring vices] are far more numerous than the virtues are, yet if those eight principal sins, from which we know that

these naturally proceed, are first overcome, all these at once sink down, and are destroyed together with them with a lasting destruction. For from gluttony proceed surfeiting and drunkenness. From fornication filthy conversation, scurrility, buffoonery and foolish talking. From covetousness, lying, deceit, theft, perjury, the desire of filthy lucre, false witness, violence, inhumanity, and greed. From anger, murders, clamour and indignation. From dejection, rancor, cowardice, bitterness, despair. From accidie, laziness, sleepiness, rudeness, restlessness, wandering about, instability both of mind and body, chattering, inquisitiveness. From vainglory, contention, heresies, boasting and confidence in novelties. From pride, contempt, envy, disobedience, blasphemy, murmuring, backbiting.[33]

Aquinas, in turn, offers a detailed explanation of the name "capital vices," which is the only label he uses to describe the list of seven. The list was in use for centuries before Christian theology articulated the distinction between mortal and venial sin and applied the label "deadly." For all these reasons, then, whether one accepts the category of mortal sin or not, "the seven capital vices" seems to be a better label by which to refer to the great list of seven.

The List of Seven

So what *are* the capital vices? As we know from their history, there was disagreement about this. The original Evagrian list consisted of eight members. "All the generic types of [evil] thoughts fall into eight categories in which every sort of thought is included. First is that of gluttony, then fornication, third avarice, fourth sadness, fifth anger, sixth acedia, seventh vainglory, eighth pride."[34] In his systematization of the wisdom of the desert fathers, Cassian says, "There are eight principal faults which attack mankind; viz., first *gastrimargia*, which means gluttony, secondly fornication, thirdly *philargyria*, i.e., avarice or the love of money, fourthly anger, fifthly dejection, sixthly *acedia*, i.e., listlessness or low spirits, seventhly *cenodoxia*, i.e., boasting or vain glory, and eighthly pride."[35] (Envy, the only vice missing from these lists, is added later.)

We have seen that Gregory pared the list down to seven by designating pride, traditionally understood as *the* original sin, as the originator or root of all other vices. Even Gregory's authority, however, did not finally settle the issue of whether pride was the root of seven other sins or itself a member of the list. Most recent versions of the seven, for example, include pride rather than vainglory, perhaps because it is not easy to see, on first glance, the difference between them, and vainglory is the less familiar term of the two. This book will follow the earlier, Gregorian tradition and give pride a role as the source of the seven vices. In one sense this includes the best of both traditions, since making pride the root of the seven "source" vices implicitly counts it as a source vice itself, just a more ultimate one. I will also, however, replace Gregorian sadness with sloth, following Aquinas.[36] The list of seven used here thus includes vainglory, along with envy, sloth, avarice, wrath, lust, and gluttony, as well as pride, which is their root.[37]

Since each of them will receive individual treatment in a chapter later, I will not describe each of them here. For now, we should note that the list of seven vices does *not* directly correlate with the seven principal virtues—faith, hope, charity, practical wisdom, justice, courage, and temperance. Historically, the seven vices were sometimes paired with a list of opposing virtues; for example, in Prudentius's *Psychomachia*, anger is overcome by patience, pride by humility, lust by chastity, and so on.[38] Or one was to counter the vices not with virtues per se but with spiritual disciplines like fasting, psalmody, prayer, and vigils, as Evagrius suggests in his *Praktikos*. The seven vices were also viewed as a standard part of a larger system of "sevens," which includes the seven virtues, the seven petitions of the Lord's Prayer, the seven beatitudes, the seven corporal works of mercy, the seven gifts of the Holy Spirit, and so on.

In his *Summa theologiae*, Aquinas follows the Aristotelian pattern of opposing each virtue to its own pair of vices. Every virtue, in his account, lies on a continuum between two opposing vices, one on each extreme.[39] So generosity is a virtue characterized by a love of giving and an appropriate freedom from attachment to money. Avarice or stinginess, on the one extreme, names an *excessive* attachment to money, so that one hoards money for oneself rather than giving it away when one ought. On the other extreme is the vice of *deficiency*—prodigality or spendthriftiness—a habit of not being attached enough to money, to the point of carelessness and wastefulness. The virtue, therefore, lies somewhere between the two extremes, in what philosophers call "the golden mean." Because Aquinas organizes his *Summa theologiae* around the seven virtues and his structure requires more than seven opposing vices, it is difficult for him to retain much sense of the order or importance of the traditional seven. In the *Disputed Questions on Evil*, however, he retains both the Gregorian list and order and does not oppose each vice to a particular virtue.[40] So, for example, avarice in this work is opposed not to the virtue of generosity (as just described), but instead is considered an offense against justice.

Glittering Vices: The Misguided Pursuit of Happiness

What Aquinas's formulation in the *Summa* does reveal more clearly, though, are the goods at stake in the case of each vice. A glance at the virtues with which he associates the seven vices yields the following conclusions: charity is about love of God and neighbor, while sloth and envy oppose and undercut this; justice and generosity are about money and security, while avarice craves and pursues them excessively; magnanimity is about honor and respect, while vainglory is the twisted pursuit of them; and temperance is usually about pleasures associated with eating and sex—lust and gluttony, each in their own way, are a kind of selfish seeking of these goods. In other words, the title of Richard Foster's book on the three great temptations—*Money, Sex, and Power*—about sums up sin for most of us.[41]

Why count these seven as the main sources and most fruitful of the vices? Aquinas's explanation is that they aim at the things that most attract human beings, the goods which we most long to possess.[42] Because each good on the list above holds a close affinity to human fulfillment, we are tempted to substitute them for true fulfillment as the goal of our lives. The vices offer subtle and deceptive imitations of the fullness of the human good, what we often simply call "happiness." Lust offers pleasure; avarice promises self-sufficiency. In the words of one contemporary author, "The simplest definition of an addiction is anything we use to fill the empty place inside of us that belongs to God alone."[43] Augustine too refers to this substitute-fulfillment pattern of sin in his *Confessions*: "My sin was this, that I looked for pleasure, beauty, and truth not in [God] but in myself and in his other creatures, and the search led me instead to pain, confusion, and error."[44]

The vices have such attractive power because they promise a good that seems like true human perfection and complete happiness. As Augustine says, "Specious vices have a flawed reflection of beauty."[45] They promise us a shortcut and a recipe for self-made satisfaction. In their own twisted way the vices are our attempts to attain goods like love and friendship, provision and security, recognition and approval, comfort and pleasure, status and worth, all by ourselves.

When our character is distorted by vice, we seek these goods—and they *are* genuinely good things—in a misguided or even idolatrous manner: in the wrong way, at the wrong times and wrong places, too intensely, or at the expense of other things of greater value. That's what makes the vices evil. Our values are out of whack—or in Aquinas's Augustinian terms, our loves are "disordered." Our desire for and pursuit of these goods does not respect the right ordering of values. When children start grabbing fistfuls of cookies off the serving plate, their desire for the pleasure of sweets trumps their desire for others to have their fair share. Love of pleasure trumps love of neighbor. Yet most of us would concede that food and pleasure are genuine goods, in their due place and appropriately sought. When an employee tells subtle untruths to make himself look good to his coworkers, he values the approval of others more than truth or trust. Respect and acceptance from others is a genuine good within human social relationships. The problem is his manner of pursuing it, which subverts other goods in order to achieve it (or a semblance of it). When good things are wrongly pursued, sin happens.[46] And when sin accumulates, our character becomes warped and misshapen as well.

A New Look at the Seven Deadly Sins

After all the twists and turns of history, all the disputes over which vices are on the list and why, and all the wrangling between religious and nonreligious conceptions of the vices, the list of seven is still with us, in popular culture as well as in academic and pastoral contexts. What explains the vices' abiding power to captivate the human imagination? Why do people continue to be fascinated by them?

My own observation—based on the reactions of those I teach, and my own experience in graduate school with which this book began—is that the list of vices maintains its appeal because we recognize the way the vices powerfully articulate distortions of deeply human desires. As the ancient philosophical schools understood, and as our contemporary therapeutic culture also knows, humans seem to yearn to understand themselves better. The ancients and medievals sought this sort of self-knowledge as part of the ethical life, as is clear from the inscription at Delphi, "Know Thyself," and the mission of Aquinas's Dominican order, namely, the "care of souls."[47] Contemporary fascinations with the self might perhaps be more shallow and narcissistic, but they are still ostensibly oriented toward self-improvement of some sort or another, and sometimes born of a vague sense that something deeper is wrong with us. Given the ubiquity of this basic human instinct, the tradition of vices serves as a rich and still relevant frame for better understanding ourselves and our motivations today.

The reason it is crucial to recover the vices' tradition and history as well, however, is that they developed in a community of Christians seeking to live out their discipleship through daily disciplines and by the grace of God. Identifying and struggling against vice is not a purely human endeavor, and it is not an individualistic, psychological self-help program. It was and is the graced and disciplined formation of the body of believers seeking to become more and more like Jesus Christ. Like Cassian's monks, self-knowledge is sought in this way and for this end:

> Looking at [their struggles] as in a mirror and having been taught the causes of and the remedies for the vices by which they are troubled, they will also learn about future contests before they occur, and they will be instructed as to how they should watch out for them, meet them, and fight against them.
>
> As is the case with the most skilled physicians, who not only heal present ills but also confront future ones with shrewd expertise and forestall them with prescriptions and salutary potions, so also these true physicians of souls destroy, with a spiritual conference as with some heavenly medicine, maladies of the heart just as they are about to emerge, not allowing them to grow in the minds of young men but disclosing to them both the causes of the passions that threaten them and the means of acquiring health.[48]

For the next seven chapters, we will examine each of the capital vices in turn, expecting that as we learn about them, we will also learn about ourselves. Ideally, looking at our character in the mirror offered by the Christian tradition will better enable us, as Cassian intends, to make progress in spiritual formation and to turn from vice to greater virtue.

2

ENVY

Feeling Bitter When Others Have It Better

Of all the deadly sins, only envy is no fun at all.—Joseph Epstein

The film *Amadeus* is set in eighteenth-century Vienna and chronicles the relationship between court composer Antonio Salieri and his famous rival, Wolfgang Amadeus Mozart.[1] As a young man, Salieri prayed for musical talent, promising God his devotion and chastity if only God would make him a great composer. When Mozart burst in on the scene with his astounding talent and destroyed Salieri's dreams of greatness, Salieri was enraged. How could God lavish such amazing musical gifts on such an arrogant, shallow buffoon? From their first meeting, Salieri was envious of Mozart, and he nurtured his envy long after Mozart was dead. As an old man, Salieri makes a fascinating character study—still yearning for greatness, but also knowing that Mozart's music will outshine his own forever.

In the film's opening scene, Salieri tries to commit suicide, guilt-stricken over his complicity in hastening Mozart's death. A priest visits Salieri to hear his confession, a confession the rest of the film recounts.

When the priest arrives, the aged Salieri is playing the piano from his wheelchair. Salieri identifies himself as a composer and asks his confessor if he has any musical training. The priest admits to learning a little as a young boy in Vienna, and Salieri seizes the opportunity to test his reputation. He plays tune after tune he has written, expecting that one of them will be familiar to his listener. "This one was very popular in its day," he insists, but the priest shakes his head, embarrassed that he does not recognize any of them and exasperated that Salieri persists, exposing his ignorance. Then there is a pause. "Wait!" Salieri says, with a gleam in his eye. "What about *this* one?" He plays the opening measures of a sparkling little tune. The priest lights up almost immediately—"Yes, yes, I know it!"—and he continues humming it even after Salieri lifts his hands from the keyboard. He smiles at Salieri, visibly relieved. "Oh, that's nice! That's very nice. I'm sorry, I didn't know you wrote that." Salieri's faces darkens with malice and his eyes narrow.

"I didn't," he replies. "*That* was Mozart."

His experience with the priest has only confirmed the truth that Salieri cannot bear to admit to himself but also cannot escape: his own musical talent will always be second-rate and second-best compared to Mozart's God-given gifts. The priest tries to console him: "All men are equal in God's eyes." Salieri arches his eyebrows skeptically. "*Are* they?" After his rivalry with Mozart, he cannot, and will not, let himself believe it.

Amadeus is a portrait of the vice of envy and its destructive power. Why are we envious? Whom do we envy? And why does envy lead to such destructive impulses? While there is something ugly and malicious about envy—Gregory the Great lists hatred as a vice that arises from it—there is also something obviously *self*-destructive, self-hating about envy too. A poem by Victor Hugo recounts an opportunity granted to Envy and Avarice to receive whatever they wished, on the condition that the other receive a double portion. Envy replied, "I wish to be blind in one eye."[2] The envious person resents another person's good gifts because they are superior to his or her own. It's not just that the other person is better; it is that by comparison their superiority makes you feel your own lack, your own inferiority, more acutely.

Envy and Its Ugly Cousins

Envy in the technical sense we are speaking of it here needs to be distinguished from the everyday ways we use the word, especially since in ordinary language it is treated as synonymous with terms like *jealousy*, *covetousness*, and *greed*. For example: "I'm so jealous that you got to go on a cruise!" or "I am so envious of that great new purse you have. Where did you get it? I'm going to buy one too."

Envy is similar to covetousness in that both involve wanting something that belongs to another, something we ourselves lack.[3] The envious and the covetous are "have-nots." If they were greedy, they would want something *like* what the other has, or perhaps want more of it than another. If they were greedy, they could say, "I want that too." But the envious and the covetous don't want to "have one too." They want the very thing the rival has—"I want *that* one, the one *she* has." While the covetous person's desires are focused on having an object, however, the envier is at least as concerned that her rival not have it. The covetous person delights in acquiring the thing itself, while the envier delights in the way the redistribution of goods affects her and her rival's respective positions. Thus, it gives the envier satisfaction to see her rival's good taken away, even if she herself does not acquire it as a result.

Covetousness, like greed, tends to be more focused on possessions—things we *have* or own—than envy does. Ahab covets Naboth's vineyard (1 Kings 21). (If we think of people in terms of something we can own, like property, then this sense of covetousness can be extended to coveting people, as King David coveted Uriah's wife. Note that his wish was to have Bathsheba himself, not primarily the delight in taking her away from Uriah.) Envy, on the other hand, is typically more concerned with who we *are*. Envy targets the internal qualities of another person, qualities that give a person worth, honor, standing, or status. If the envious do desire an external thing, it is because that object symbolizes or signifies its owner's high position or greatness. There is a difference, for example, between wanting a BMW because we are car aficionados and love the driving performance of a particular model, and wanting a BMW because it will make us feel superior to our neighbor, who just bought a new Camry. Anything but to be the only ones in the neighborhood still driving a Taurus! But it's not the car that makes us green with envy, so much as what being the owner of such a car says about who we are, the personal respect and admiration that we command when we drive up in it. We envy not the car but the superiority, the classiness, of the person driving it. Getting the right car is just a means to that end of being the right person. Not to have the car is not just to lack that thing, but to be less of a person, to be deficient or defective. His or her lack makes the envier feel less loveable, less admirable, less worthy as a person.

In this way, envy—like jealousy—concerns love, between persons and for ourselves. (We see this most clearly in Aquinas's account, where envy is about love for the neighbor, but also love for God and proper self-love.) Although we commonly use *jealousy* and *envy* synonymously, jealousy is the condition of loving something and possessing it, and then feeling threatened because the loved thing or person might be taken away. For example, God is described as a "jealous" God in Deuteronomy 5, because the love he commands from his people can be lost when they run after idols instead. As we see in the most common examples of jealousy—the love triangle and the jealous lover—jealousy is most properly and paradigmatically linked to a love relationship, one in which a person considers another person his or her own. It is interesting that God describes himself as jealous (if *jealousy* is indeed the best English word to translate the Hebrew here), so that we cannot say that every instance of jealousy is sinful, the way every instance of envy is, according to the tradition. Perhaps sometimes jealousy is protective and therefore good. But the term is usually used pejoratively, to indicate a twisted or disordered claim to possession, not a righteous claim to hold on to what is our own. Human jealousy, in the bad sense, stems from a selfish or inappropriate claim to possess another, as when a jealous spouse claims the other as his property, or as something wholly under her control. Since only God can make a fully possessive claim toward another person—"You are mine!"—it is not clear that human claims to jealousy about another can be right and good.

Whether righteous or sinful, however, jealousy is like envy in the sense that it is personal and related to love. The jealous are those who "have" something they love which they might lose. The envious, by contrast, are the "have-nots"—they do not have the good their rival does, and they do not have self-love. Thus, they have nothing to lose and everything to gain from another's loss.

The Comparison Game

The bottom line for the envious is how they stack up against others, because they measure their self-worth comparatively. The envious sorrow over another's good because it excels their own,[4] and because the comparison reveals not only their lack of that particular good but also their consequent lack of worth. Unlike the possession of goodness ("*I* am good/this is good"), "to excel" is a two-term relation, implying a comparative ranking: "I excel *you*." All of us need to be loved and found worthy, but the envier makes attaining this love and worth a comparative game. As the stories of Jacob favoring Joseph over his brothers, and Rachel over Leah illustrate, the envious believe not all are loved fully or equally or unconditionally. There are winners and losers, the superior and the inferior, the more worthy and the less worthy. As Francis Bacon put it, "Envy is ever joined to the comparing of a man's self; and where there is no comparison, no envy."[5] Thus, envy is at least as much about the envier's lack of worth that the comparative ranking exposes as it is about any particular good they have or lack. Envy involves a sense of inferiority, which breeds a lack of self-love.

In *Amadeus*, what Salieri really envies is Mozart's musical genius. This is not something Salieri can buy or attain with more hard work. Mozart's musicianship is a gift, a personal quality, something unique and internal to who he is. It is the talent Salieri thinks should and could have been his, but which now lies impossibly out of reach. Since Salieri's envy targets another's personal quality or talent, qualities that define who that person is, however, he can't destroy what Mozart *has* without in some sense destroying Mozart himself. It is not enough for Salieri, consequently, to become more *like* Mozart. He cannot but think comparatively, so being superior to Mozart is the only way he thinks he can cure his envy. This is why Salieri's strategy—typical of those consumed by envy—is to take Mozart down, to ruin him, rather than emulate him. Envy's ruinous impulses are always personal.

When the envious are forced to confront a self they judge lacking in worth, their unhappiness and grief can be unbearable. They feel compelled to do something—anything—to get themselves out from under it. Usually this means sabotaging the rival, but even this cannot rescue the envier from stewing in her or his own self-made resentments.

According to one confessional manual,[6] envy can show itself in the following ways: feeling offended at the talents, successes, or good fortune of others; selfish or unnecessary rivalry and competition; pleasure at other's difficulties or distress; ill will; reading false motives into others' behavior; belittling others; false accusations; backbiting (saying something bad, even if true, behind another's back); slander (saying something bad, even if true, in the open about someone); initiation, collection, or retelling of gossip; arousing, fostering, or organizing antagonism against others; scorn of another's abilities or failures; teasing or bullying; ridicule of persons, institutions, or ideals; and prejudice against those we consider inferior, who consider us inferior, or who seem to threaten our security or position.

There is often a progression in these envious symptoms from thought and feeling to words to deeds, and from secret and underhanded to open and forceful. According to Aquinas, envy typically starts with "detraction," more commonly known as backstabbing, for instance, a little murmuring in the shadows about the book's weaknesses and the author's somewhat shoddy research. The envier's negative comments may come out in the open, as "reviling," but the envious usually prefer deceitful or underhanded strategies, like Epstein's suggestion of the time-honored ploy of "damn[ing] . . . with faint praise."[7] If these methods of trying to detract from their rival's excellence are successful, and the rival's reputation is damaged, the envious rejoice at the other's downfall (*Schadenfreude*). Of course, they can also revel in their rival's misfortune even if it happened by accident or by another's agency. But there can be something more satisfying for the envious about engineering it, a fact that betrays envy's real malicious intent.

If the envious try to undermine their rival and are *not* successful, then their bitterness intensifies and they resent the other person's good even more. If unassuaged, envy can even lead to a full-scale hatred of a rival. Hatred's object is whatever blocks our own happiness. Naturally, we have a strong aversion to such things as evil, because we see them as harmful or damaging to our good. For the envious, however, the hated obstacle to their own good is the rival's possession of the good, or more precisely, the rival himself who is identified as superior because of the good he possesses. Thus, the envious end up hating another and his good, because of the damage they see done to their own. Envy's view of the world is essentially antagonistic: it's me-versus-you, my good *or* your good—never both. In this zero-sum game, in which they lack the good they need, the natural reaction of the envious is to undermine and destroy the good of their rival.

Finally, if the envy that fuels these strategies becomes entrenched over time, the relationship to the rival becomes one of open malice, where one wills the other's evil without qualification, and one's hatred of one's neighbor spills over into hatred of the one who stacked the

deck against one. God (or fate, or whatever implacable force allo-
cated the goods at stake) gets the ultimate blame for what the envier
perceives is the unjust distribution of excellence those goods bring.
We see in Salieri's case that it is God whom he holds responsible for
giving some the short end of the stick and for helping others flourish.
So Salieri takes down his crucifix—the one before which he prayed
for the talent to become a great composer—and burns it in the fire,
vowing to "destroy Your incarnation" in Mozart.

It is notable that the envier does not typically advertise his envy
out in the open; he tends toward passive-aggressive stabs in the back,
as in the prayer found in Langland's *Piers Plowman*:

> I have a neighbor near me whom I annoy often,
> And belie him to lords to make him lose silver,
> And to make his friends foes through my false speaking.
> His gain and good luck grieve me sorely.
> Between house and house I sow hatred,
> So that life and limb are lost through my whispers.
> When I meet at market the man whom I envy
> I greet him graciously or with friendly manners
> And fear to offend him, for he is the stronger.
> If I had might and mastery, God knows my wishes! . . .
> So I live without love, like a low mongrel,
> And all my body bursts from the bitterness of my anger.[8]

Why does the envier shun open warfare? I contend that envy generally
comes with a sense of powerlessness, which accompanies one's sense
of inferiority. If one really were worth something and had the power
one needed to be greater, then one would already have outranked
and outstripped one's rival. To come out in the open and declare
one's envy is to admit and display one's inferiority. This sense of
inferiority is essential to envy. And even though envy is premised on
her own acknowledgement (at some level) that her rival excels her,
the envier is pained to admit this to herself and even more pained to
admit it to others.[9] Her envy silently eats her up from the inside. As
John Chrysostom writes, "As a moth gnaws a garment, so doth envy
consume a man."[10]

Not only is their self-worth measured from the perspective of inferiority, which breeds a certain feeling of helplessness, but the envious
also typically think passively about their relationship to the situation:
the world, God, fate, society, or some other force external to their own

sense of control has dealt them a bad hand. They feel cheated, but their own efforts against such a great, distant, and alien force seem doomed. The deck has been stacked. Salieri prays for musical talent and acclaim, vowing to dedicate himself to God in return for his answered prayer. God does not answer his prayer. Instead he doles out talent in spades to Salieri's undeserving rival. Who can win against God? When even an appeal to divine intervention fails him, Salieri's only remaining option is to strike out at Mozart himself, albeit with the usual stratagems of deceit characteristic of those who perceive themselves as weaker or inferior, or the guerilla-warfare-and-retreat tactics of those who know they cannot win an open battle.

Joseph Epstein tells a joke that illustrates envy's malicious and impotent character well. Once there was an Englishwoman, a Frenchman, and a Russian:

> Each [was] given a single wish by one of those genies whose almost relentless habit is to pop out of bottles. The Englishwoman says that a friend of hers has a cottage in the Cotswolds, and that she would like a similar cottage, with the addition of two extra bedrooms and a second bath and a brook running in front of it. The Frenchman says that his best friend has a beautiful blonde mistress, and he would like such a mistress himself, but a redhead instead of a blonde and with longer legs and a bit more in the way of culture and *chic*. The Russian, when asked what he would like, tells of a neighbor who has a cow that gives a vast quantity of the richest milk, which yields the heaviest cream and the purest butter. 'I vant dat cow," the Russian tells the genie, "*dead*."[11]

As Buechner says, envy's trademark is to desire that "everyone else [be] as unsuccessful as you are."[12] Just how to secure the satisfaction of that desire is the problem.

Syndrome (formerly called Incrediboy) in the film *The Incredibles* is one example of envy's futility and the envier's inferiority, which together secure the inevitable lack of success in besting one's rival to which the envier feels doomed.[13] Early in the film, Incrediboy is an ardent but annoying admirer of the superhero Mr. Incredible. Having been spurned and his inferiority openly acknowledged, he launches on a lifetime's work of killing off superheroes while at the same time creating a machine that only he, with his superior technological props, can defeat. He spends all his energy trying to make himself into an imitation-superhero. His plan, as revealed to Mr. Incredible, is simple:

perfect the machine, defeat it in a mock battle to win acclaim, and then sell his technology to the masses. His rationale? If *everyone* can be "super," then *no one will be*. His efforts are shown to be a pathetic failure when he sends his machine to wreak havoc in the city, and his charade of "defeating" it with pseudo-superpowers is exploded for the second-rate fakery it is. No technological imitation can be a real superpower. His position of inferiority cannot be changed, despite his best efforts. His inferiority can only be exposed even more painfully for all to see.

The Rivalry

It is also instructive to think about why Salieri envies *Mozart*, and not someone else. If we think about the people we envy, and why we envy them in particular, a pattern emerges. Enviers don't usually envy those who are far removed from their lives and lifestyles, or who are vastly more talented or successful than they are. They tend to envy people to whom they might actually be compared unfavorably, that is, those who are just like them—only better. A writer couldn't care less if an Olympic athlete wins gold in the 5,000-meter run, while she can barely finish a local 5K road race. But she burns when her colleague gets a rave review on his new novel, while her own published work gets only half-hearted notice. For the person who defines himself by his career status and earning power, success is not defined in comparison to Bill Gates or Donald Trump, but rather by "making $10 a month more than [his] brother-in-law."[14] As Aquinas puts it, we envy only those whom we wish to rival or surpass in reputation.[15] It is another paradox of the envious that they characteristically envy only those in whose place they can picture themselves—those whom they "might have been" were it not for the cruel twists of fate. Yet at the same time they find themselves feeling as though that possibility is so far removed from them as to be impossible. The envied one is paradoxically both too close for comfort *and* completely out of reach.

The envious want to be superior, for their self-esteem depends on outranking others in the relevant field of comparison. Their own identity hangs on excelling others, but only those others who threaten that identity, that is, those close enough to be compared as rivals.[16] If we reflect on whom we envy, we are likely to discover how we define our own identity and where we see that identity as most vulnerable.

Envy generally strikes in areas where another's superiority seems to threaten or lessen our own excellence and where that comparison leaves us feeling inferior in a way close to our identity.

Reflecting on the different ways we can experience competition and rivalry gives us some insight into the envier's perspective. How and why do we strive for excellence, and do so in competitive venues? In the film *Chariots of Fire*, we get a character portrait of two different men with diametrically opposed views of competition.[17] Eric Liddell and Harold Abrams are rivals in the 100-yard dash. Harold is driven to excellence and devoted to winning, because he is afraid to lose. This is the envier's mentality. After the first race in which he failed to win, Harold sits in the stands with his head in his hands, his whole self-image dashed to pieces. He is not someone who runs and sometimes wins; he *is* a winner. "If I can't win, I won't run!" he says vehemently to the woman he loves. Exasperated, she responds, "Well, if you won't run, you can't win." Harold's attitude is like the envier's: he is defensive, afraid of being shown inferior, happy with himself only when he outranks all his competition in excellence. His identity and worth depend on his being better than another.

Eric Liddell, in turn, tries to explain to his sister that his desire to run comes not from a restless desire to prove something, but from an already possessed sense of rest in God. "When I run," he tells her passionately, "I feel God's pleasure." When I *run*—not when I *win*. Eric is already sure of God's favor. He does not strive to run well or to win in order to earn favor, but rather to revel in it. He loves competition not because he needs to win, but because he loves to run well. His competitors are valued because they are his partners in seeking excellence, not rivals who would strip him of all excellence should they best him in the race.

Each man is equally intense about his running. But Harold has the fearful edge of the envier, the one who can never be good or good enough unless he is the winner. Harold's love for himself is contingent on his performance. Eric has the calm confidence of one who knows he is worth something, whatever place he finishes. He runs with joy and freedom, not fear.

Thomas Williams has argued that the envious are in fact very astute judges of excellence and how they measure up against others.[18] The distorting effects of the vice are instead expressed in how and why they seek that excellence and how their self-worth is grounded in it (or its lack). Their perception of inferiority, of their own lack of some quality they value highly, something in terms of which they define their own worth, leaves the envious feeling bad about themselves. When their rivals outshine the envious, it is not over something negligible or trivial; rather, their rivals' success threatens the best part of themselves—the part they take pride in, something on which their self-affirmation depends. Those who envy acknowledge and internally chafe at their judgment that they are worth less because someone else is better. When we envy, our love for ourselves is conditional on excelling our rival. This is why Aquinas locates the vice of envy in the *will*—the same place he locates the virtue of love.

Envy: The Enemy of Love

It's obvious by now how the fundamental attitude of the envious is directly opposed to love. To love is to seek others' good and rejoice when they have it.[19] To envy is to seek to destroy others' good and sorrow over their having it. The "greatest commandment" instructs us to love God above all and our neighbors as ourselves (Matt. 22:37–39). Envy directly undercuts love of our neighbor. In *Amadeus*, Salieri's envy drives him to plan Mozart's downfall and, ultimately, to plot his death. *The Incredibles* gives us a slightly more comic take on the same theme. In all of these cases, the chain of psychological causes is clear: envy gives rise to hatred, and murder is hatred's bitter fruit. The same is true in the story of Joseph and his brothers in Genesis: "Now [Jacob] loved Joseph more than any other of his children, because he was the son of his old age; and he had made him a long robe with sleeves. But when his brothers saw that their father loved him more than all his brothers, they hated him, and could not speak peaceably to him" (Gen. 37:3–4). Soon after, they devise a plan to kill him. What the analysis of envy so far suggests, however, is that hatred of the rival is an elaborate cover-up, ultimately, for the envier's sense of rejection and unworthiness—his own self-hatred. The commandment is to love your *neighbor* as you love *yourself*. The envier can do neither.

    Amadeus also illustrates how Salieri's hatred of Mozart is linked to hatred of God. The film's title plays on the idea that God plays favorites: Amadeus means "loved by God," as in, Mozart is loved and therefore Salieri is hated. A contemporary confessional manual picks up on this idea, defining envy as "dissatisfaction with our place in God's order of creation, manifested in begrudging his gifts to others."[20]

Salieri's ultimate gripe is not with Mozart, but with God, for giving Mozart greater talent than he gave Salieri. In Salieri's judgment, that he had asked for talent and dedicated his chastity to God in return for God's favor on his musical career, and that Mozart was an immature, irreverent, unworthy recipient, only confirmed the injustice of God's choice to favor Mozart at Salieri's expense. Salieri's retaliation against God is to destroy Mozart. Aquinas argues that this opposition to love of God and neighbor (the virtue of *caritas*) makes envy a mortal or deadly sin, in the sense of making one worthy of damnation,[21] so that the envious reject God's love, hate others, and condemn themselves to a hell of their own making already on earth.

The envier's solution to her predicament is to try to rearrange the rankings so that she comes out excelling her rival. Even if she could be successful in bringing her rival down and establishing her own superiority, however, her self-worth is still a fragile and temporary thing. That's why those who are prone to envy—like Harold Abrams— are still fearful *even when they win*. Their hold on their position is tenuous and easily lost. And when their position of excellence is lost, so is their sense of self-worth. Like being the "number one Proust scholar" for one of the characters in the film *Little Miss Sunshine*, to lose one's place in the ranking is to lose everything.[22] This means even when the envier achieves her goal, she still does not have what she really desires or needs, namely, a secure, noncontingent, uncon- ditional sense of her own worth. Some secular philosophers declare envy to be naturally human and incurable, and recommend trying to channel envy's discontent into self-improving strategies.[23] What they do not see, however, is that the cure for envy requires getting out of the comparative game of engineering self-worth altogether.

The vice of envy is rooted in pride, because the envier takes it to be her prerogative and responsibility to make her own place in the ranking and manufacture her own worth by excelling the relevant rivals. The envious thus expend all their efforts usurping God's role: founding their self-worth on their own claims to excellence, creating their own superior status by engineering the downfall of their competitors, and deciding for themselves who is and who is not worthy of the greater gifts. Like all forms of pride, however, *playing* God is all the envious can do. Their strategies are all a big charade. The envious cannot give themselves talent or success; they cannot make themselves excellent or give themselves worth. Nor can they make others less than who they are. Even if Salieri could and did cause Mozart's death, removing him from the Vienna music scene and assuring Salieri a place of eminence, Mozart's music still lived on. Years later, the only tune the priest recognizes is Mozart's. Salieri's greatest efforts to destroy Mozart's place of eminence were, in the end, completely unsuccessful.

If envy is a loser's game, it is also a game we are doomed to lose even if we win. For to "win" at envy is to destroy the possibility of love between oneself and others, and oneself and God. To be envious is to be determined to live in a way that precludes gratitude and contentment, love and happiness. Relationships of love are the only thing that will truly make us happy. The envious thus pursue happiness in a way that necessarily undermines their chances of having it.

The only escape from this vice is to find a completely different foundation for our self-worth. Envy depends on a comparative self-value. The worth of the envious—at least from their perspective—is conditional on excelling their competitors. Moving out of envy into love is analogous to making the transition from dating to marriage. The premise of dating includes needing to outdo the competition to win your lover's affection and secure the relationship, while the premise of marriage is that one is working from an already secure relationship into greater and greater love.

What would it be like to have a self whose worth and value were unconditional and noncomparative? As a spiritual problem, envy requires a spiritual solution. To overcome envy, we need to work from a new, unconditionally loved vision of who we are. God tells us in Isaiah 43:1–4, "But now thus says the Lord, he who created you, O Jacob, he who formed you, O Israel: Do not fear, for I have redeemed you; I have called you by name; you are mine. . . . You are precious in my sight, and honored, and I love you." We are loved already and unconditionally—not because of our moral worthiness, our attractiveness, our worldly achievements—but simply because we are God's own children. "A woman has two smiles that an angel might envy," wrote Thomas Haliburton, "the smile that accepts a lover before words are uttered, and the smile that lights on the first born baby, and assures it of a mother's love."[24] We all need that kind of love. And that is exactly how God loves us.

Jesus in the Gospels—especially in Luke's account—makes a point of affirming and lifting up those who lack status or worth, those who count low or not at all in the social rankings of the day, those who are the littlest and least. His love of them is not based on performance or special qualities. It is a gift. It is undeserved. It is given to them just as they are. In offering love, acceptance, and value especially to these

people, Jesus seems to be deliberately defying envy's competitive view
of love and worth. God's love is noncomparative and unconditionally
bestowed. No effort we can make could earn it—or manufacture a
satisfying substitute for it.

Robert Roberts explains how this love is the antithesis of envy:

> The Christian's self-understanding is that she is precious before God—
> however much a sinner, however much a failure (or success) she may
> be by the standards of worldly comparisons—and that every other
> person she meets has the same status . . . This vision is not only one
> that levels every distinction by which egos seek . . . glory . . . This vision,
> when appropriated, is also the ultimate ground of self-confidence. For
> the message is that God loves me for myself—not for anything I have
> achieved, not for my beauty or intelligence or righteousness or for
> any other "qualification," but simply in the way that a good mother
> loves the fruit of her womb. If I can get that into my head—or better,
> into my heart—then I won't be grasping desperately for self-esteem at
> the expense of others, and cutting myself off from my proper destiny,
> which is spiritual fellowship with them.[25]

A self secure in its unconditional worth, a worth based on God's
love, is a self free to affirm others' gifts without feeling threatened or
thereby made inferior. It is a self free to love without anxiety that its
own contributions will be compared to another's and found wanting.
It is a self able to take joy in its own good *and* in the good of others.
The key, as W. H. Auden wrote, "since all self-knowledge tempts man
into envy," is to "love without desiring all that you are not."[26]

The Evil Eye

Envy's deep link to love and acceptance is important for understanding
its importance, its rank among the capital vices, and its cure. Aquinas
says that sloth undermines our love for God (the first and greatest
commandment) and envy undermines our love for our neighbor, who
is to be loved as ourselves (the second commandment, which is really
another expression of the first, since we love neighbor and self well
when we love them as God loves us). Being overcome by envy involves
serious damage, because love is so central to being human. Overcoming envy likewise requires acknowledging a deeply human need for
unconditional love and acknowledging the source of this love.

Because this vice's distorting power shows itself at the most basic level, namely, at the sources of value and self-worth, perhaps the most difficult question to answer is how envy is to be remedied. Envy had been called "the evil eye." Thus it requires for its remedy a regimen that will reframe our vision of the world, ourselves, and other people. But reframing what we see begins with a change of heart. How do we learn to understand and receive unconditional love? How do we exchange gratitude and contentment for fear and resentment?

Because the envious essentially see the world as a great competition, a world of winners and losers with nothing in between, part of unlearning envy (or better still, preventing it) must involve investing ourselves deliberately and deeply in activities with shared or common goods. Common goods are such that one person's increase in having them does not diminish anyone else's share. For example, enjoying music is such a good, as is taking in a beautiful piece of art or hiking to find a breathtaking view. The benefit of investing ourselves in activities which can involve others without the threat of one person losing and the other winning is that we learn to appreciate goods outside a competitive frame of mind. If successful, it can also teach us how it feels to rejoice in something good and to rejoice in that good *as shared* with others. In ideal circumstances, tasting and sharing in the pleasure of this experience will provide the envier with some incentive to resist its opposite, namely, displeasure over the good because someone else has it and a desire to take it away from them.

Envy is closely related to the vice of vainglory. Aquinas and Gregory believe that envy often arises from vainglory, a vice defined by its excessive love of praise and approval of others. When afflicted by vainglory, we seek the spotlight to win acclaim from others. As in the case of envy, the vainglorious person has a fragile self-worth which rests conditionally on others' approval. An envious person need not seek public acknowledgment, but it is easy to see how envy could be intensified if our inferiority is exposed to the public eye. Both the envious and vainglorious have a self-worth dependent on outdoing and outshining others, even if envy can be private in a way that vainglory can never be (except perhaps in fantasy). If our unfavorable comparison with a rival is something others can notice and judge and reinforce—as it was in Salieri's case, first by the Vienna court, and later by the priest hearing his confession—envy and vainglory can feed off each other.

If the tradition is right in making this link between vices, a remedy for vainglory may help diminish envy as well. In this case, the envious can

practice doing acts of love for others, countering the malicious inclinations of the envious, in ways that no one else notices. The hiddenness
of an act of love helps eliminate any competitiveness or temptation to
have others corroborate our measurement of self-worth by comparing
our benevolent efforts to our rival's. The focus of this discipline remains
on doing little things for those with little status that would likely not
catch others' attention. Why? Because the envier needs to learn what
it feels like to do something good for another, without her usual frame
of reference in which these acts will be noted, tallied up, and made the
basis of comparisons between persons. It also develops a habit of acting for others' sake that is not instrumental to engineering superiority
or status for oneself. Mother Teresa famously said, "If we could only
remember that God loves [us], and [we] have an opportunity to love
others as he loves [us], not in big things, but in small things with great
love."[27] This seems like as good a description as any for actions designed
to counter envy's roots in vainglory. I personally learned to recognize and
receive this kind of love from my children when they were very small.
They simply take you as you are, not having yet learned the calculating
acceptance that comes from having experienced rejection or felt a need
to perform or outperform another in order to earn affirmation. Again,
the experience of such love and its rewards is perhaps one small way to
build a beachhead in the soul against the power of envy to perceive all
goods possessed by others and all relationships to others as threatening
one's own worth.

We might worry that this acceptance of ourselves as unconditionally loved will make us complacent. The key is to see that, like Eric
Liddell's love of running, it actually frees us to stretch ourselves and
take risks. Aquinas distinguishes envy from something he calls "zeal."
Zeal is like envy in that it requires acknowledging one's own lack or
inferiority with respect to attaining some good. A zealous person
can see clearly that another excels her. Because the zealous person
is already secure in God's love for her, however, a love which is not
conditional upon her performance, she is free to look at herself with
honest humility and desire to be better. She acts from the conviction
that the church is a body, not of competitors for God's esteem and
favor (since his love and fellowship are common goods), but of saints
who can encourage each other along the way. To have zeal is to see in
our superiors and those we admire a model to imitate. Envy seeks to
bring another down; zeal seeks to be lifted up and made better. As
always, seeking improvement in virtue is grace-empowered effort: it

is an earnest desire to be all that God wants us to be, not a self-help program driven by willpower and a self-made conception of a new and improved self. Whereas envy isolates us, zeal brings us into mentoring relationships within the communion of saints—those who can help us get started, push us when our enthusiasm flags, rejoice with us when we make strides, and lift us up when we fall.

Our zealous strivings to be better are grounded in the security of knowing we are loved, rather than in a fear that we will not be loved unless we meet a certain measure or excel one another. The saints and those we admire as excellent are not rivals that threaten, but inspirations to become all that we can be—perhaps beyond anything we would have imagined for ourselves. Buechner writes, "The Holy Spirit has been called, 'the Lord, the giver of life,' and drawing their power from that source, saints are essentially life-givers. To be with them is to become more alive."[28] From a secure sense of God's love and life-giving power, untainted by the envier's conditional and comparative lens, we can see the right way to follow Paul's admonition to "in humility regard others as better than yourselves" (Phil. 2:3). Only a nonenvious love, which first of all presumes gratitude and contentment, can ground the zeal George Herbert describes below as "jealousie." With it, we can freely imitate others who are our betters, appreciating but also striving to better ourselves.

> Envie not greatnesse: for thou mak'st thereby
> Thy self the worse, and so the distance greater.
> Be not thine own worm: yet such jealousie,
> As hurts not others, but may make thee better,
> Is a good spurre. Correct thy passions' spite;
> Then may the beasts draw thee to happy light.[29]

3

VAINGLORY

IMAGE IS EVERYTHING

I lust after recognition, I am desperate to win all the little merit badges and trinkets of my profession, and I am of less real use in this world than any good cleaning lady.—Garrison Keillor, quoted by David Heim in *Christian Century*

Aptly enough, the vice of vainglory enjoys a good reputation in contemporary culture. The supermarket checkout is lined with magazines dedicated to the cult of "beautiful people" whom Americans celebrate, worship, and strive to emulate. For some of them, and some of us, maintaining an image with the right approval ratings is a way of life, even a respectable profession. Even in church, we can find ourselves wanting to be (or to be seen to be) what R.E.M. once called "Shiny Happy People."

When I ask the high school students at my church to name a celebrity, they can instantly rattle off a list of twenty. When I ask them to say who their heroes are, their response is usually quiet silence with furrowed brows. After they think about it awhile, however, a few name their grandparents as the people they most admire. Their heroes are people whose names aren't even known in the next town, much less nationwide. When we compare what the celebrities are well known for and what our heroes are admired for, we find a chasm between people whose glory far outstrips the value of the goods for which they receive it, and people whose worth far outstrips any glory they will ever receive. We don't have to be famous, however, to embrace the goal of being well known and well liked, publicly approved of and applauded. To wrestle with the vice of vainglory therefore requires reflection on how much the desire for attention and acclaim can dominate our lives.

Vainglory by Any Other Name . . .

Most of us know this vice well, even if we have never heard this name for it before. Vainglory is the excessive and disordered desire for recognition and approval from others. Whether we are successful in gaining this approval or not, we all know what it is like to desire public acknowledgment and approval of our own person or our accomplishments. There is a deep part of us that longs to be known and approved of, and to have this acknowledged. Take, for example, a stay-at-home mother's work. Most of her labor is invisible to others. Sometimes it doesn't even get counted as work— "Do you work or do you just stay home with the kids?" She knows in her heart that her investment in her children's upbringing is worthwhile, but she often feels like she may be the only one who believes and acknowledges that. The fact that this is painful to her is testimony to the human need for recognition and approval. Aquinas concurs: "It seems to belong to a natural appetite that one wish one's goodness to become known," and "we can rightly . . . desire to please other human beings."[1] But this desire so easily goes askew. The flattery of others, writes William Ian Miller, is "narcotic and addicting. It preys on two desperate and inescapable desires: to be thought well of by others and to think well of ourselves . . . We desire and need approbation so badly that we seem more than willing to accept counterfeit coinage as real."[2]

When caught in the vice of vainglory, we want acclaim too much, so much, in fact, that we will accept it whether it is deserved or not. At home, at school, on the athletic field, or in the workplace—there is no shortage of places with abundant temptations to vainglory. On the other hand, as the early church fathers pointed out, even—or perhaps especially—when we *have* virtue and good character, we are vulnerable to vainglory, for it haunts us most when our virtue goes incognito, or when we deserve honor that is not actually accorded us.

In the *Confessions*, Augustine tells a famous story about his teenage years. One night he and some friends were hanging out with not enough to do. They decided to steal pears from a neighboring farmer. However, they neither needed nor even wanted the pears—they ended up throwing them to the pigs. They took the pears just for the fun of stealing. In his reflection on his crime, Augustine ponders what fueled his desire to sin. In a crucial part of his confession, he notes that he would not have done it alone. He wanted to impress his friends. "As soon as the words are spoken, 'Let's go and do it,'" he confesses, "one is ashamed not to be shameless."[3] The same desire for approval and his fear of shame drove Augustine to excel in school and become an accomplished rhetorician. Even then, however, he was more concerned that his speeches in the law courts had the proper style and erudition to win him applause than that they conveyed truth, even when human lives hung in the balance.[4]

Vainglory has similar forms today.[5] For example, it is difficult to find someone who has never exaggerated something she has done or made up something about herself to impress those listening. Or perhaps we might say something bad or false about another person to get our friends to think we are funny or entertaining. Or we do something good with (or perhaps only because of) the expectation that others will notice it. Or again, we do something good that others did *not* notice, and feel disappointed by that. We may even do something wrong, illegal, or foolish because we want attention from a certain group of people. Many of us lie to seem better than we are, out of an excessive desire for approval. Others of us worry about a performance or task because we are overly concerned about gaining the approval of those judging it. We invest ourselves in building a reputation that is based on shallow, trivial things. Or we do something good, get attention for it, and then take all the credit for our goodness for ourselves, without the slightest nod to the giver of all good and perfect gifts. We may not know these things under the name "vainglory," but the definition fits them to a T.

Vainglory and Its Vicious Cousins

As familiar as these examples of vainglory may be, we can't properly diagnose our struggle with vainglory unless we understand how it

names a reality distinct from a host of other related vices. So first, a
bit of sorting.

Vainglory is easily confused with pride, the root of all other vices.
This is true especially because the two often compete for a single place
on the list of the seven deadly sins and are conflated as a result. Both
pride and vainglory were considered major vices by Evagrius and Cassian, who used lists of eight or nine vices. Later on, Gregory the Great
and Thomas Aquinas included vainglory in their canonical lists of
seven but rooted those seven branches in pride as the ultimate source of
them all. Contemporary lists typically include pride as one of the seven
and fail to mention vainglory at all. Some recent lists—for example,
one used in a recent *20/20* series on the seven deadly sins—mention
pride as a member but define it as "vanity," confusing the desire for
preeminence with the desire to have that preeminence displayed to
others. Still others—including a "Seven Deadly Sins" board game—
names "vanity" as a member of the list, but confusingly associates
it with both the recent cosmetic surgery boom (which fits vainglory)
and the color purple (which is traditionally reserved only for pride).[6]
We will follow the early Christian tradition and leave vainglory on the
list, because it seems right to include the human desire for honor and
glory, recognition and approval, among the great temptations.

Vainglory and pride are also easily confused because they are both
"spiritual" vices—vices that have a spiritual, rather than a bodily,
good as the object of their disordered love. Their objects of love also
indicate their close connection. Pride excessively concerns excellence
itself (excelling others); vainglory, by contrast, concerns primarily the
display or manifestation of excellence.[7]

In short, what makes vainglory distinct from pride is love of "the
show." Prideful people want more than anything else to be "number
one"—they seek greatness and superiority, even in ways that appropriately belong only to God. The vainglorious, on the other hand,
do not aspire to something because it is excellent. Rather, they seek
whatever will bring in the most public applause, whether deserving
or not. Pride is a desire for genuine status; vainglory, a desire for recognition and acclaim. If we had a chance to have some outstanding
quality, which would, however, remain hidden, the prideful would be
tempted, but the glory-lovers would walk away. The whole point for
the vainglorious is that others take notice. When we are plagued by
this vice, we need people to nod and smile approvingly when we walk
by. Vainglory disposes us to be more concerned with our reputation

(what others think about us) than with what we really are. For the vainglorious, image is everything.

On Aquinas's account, vainglory is also different from ambition (used in the pejorative sense), another related vice.[8] Ambition is the vice of excessively seeking the honor and respect that a good quality or accomplishment deserves. The prideful person's excessive desire for excellence and the ambitious person's excessive desire for honor or respect can initially be difficult to distinguish from the vainglorious person's excessive desire for glory, because of our common usage of the terms. Aquinas explains that excellence (having some good quality) makes one worthy of and apt to receive honor (the esteem one receives from others *for* the good you have) and the natural result of being honored is glory, "for the reason a person loves to be honored and praised is that he thinks thereby to acquire a certain renown in the knowledge of others."[9] Unlike the vainglorious, however, the ambitious seek honor not from just *anyone*, but rather from those with the requisite taste or expertise. In pride, we desire to be genuinely superior; in ambition, we want to be respected by "the right people." As a vice, ambition inclines us to choose to seek our own honor over other, more deserving goods. But like the prideful, who often have a good eye for genuine excellence, the ambitious have better taste in friends than those with vainglory—for they excessively desire to be honored by those who are *good* judges of what is worthy of honor. The good student wants to rank high in the esteem of the members of the Honor Society, not that of the dropouts. Her mistake is to make that honor more important than the value of the education for which she earned it, and to seek high marks for the sake of increasing her own honor.[10] Vainglory, by contrast, merely inclines us to seek a big round of applause. The proud person wants be the director of the best show ever produced, the ambitious person wants rave reviews crediting her work as director from a certain circle of critics, but the glory-seeker will happily sink to new depths of shallow sensationalism as long as ratings will be high.

Rather than wanting to be excellent—like the prideful—or to be honored for our worthiness—like the ambitious—in vainglory we seek only the "*manifestation* of excellence," that is, we want more than anything to be well known and widely known. That the name of this vice includes the term "glory" is apt, for that is the end those with this vice seek excessively.[11] The vainglorious primarily desire attention, approval, and applause—preferably (but not necessarily) heard far and wide. The attention is necessary, and the approval is necessary, but they are both for the sake of generating the public acknowledgment—the applause.

A Quick Look in the Mirror

Vainglory is not just any glory-seeking, of course, but rather the *inordinate* seeking of glory. Glory-seeking can be disordered in many ways, but the mode targeted in its name is the "vain" or "empty" seeking of glory. Celebrities are good examples of this. They seek and receive glory not (or at least not only) for genuine talent but also, for instance, for wearing the dress with the least surface area to the award ceremonies. Closer to home, people glory in more mundane matters: the greenest lawn, the flattering cut of a new dress or suit, the cleanliness of the kitchen, a successful diet, the ability to name-drop impressively at social gatherings, the right car corresponding to our desired social status, the appearance of worldly success. We could ask ourselves whether our wardrobe is chosen for comfort and function or for styles that will impress—often even at the cost of comfort and function. Worse yet, we are sometimes even willing to fake it to make it. Even if we are not celebrities, we might have a house we cannot afford, an embellished résumé, and the hair color of people half our age.

Swept away by a desire to be thought well of, the vainglorious neglect questions like this: How much do these things really matter? To what lengths should we go to impress? Whose approval should we desire most, and why?

The cosmetic and fashion industries make billions every year capitalizing on human weakness in this area. But vainglory is not just a female vice. What is behind the tendency to define ourselves by the cars we drive, and the swaggering locker room talk that echoes St. Augustine's confession: "I was ashamed not to be shameless"? Why does the typical description of our past athletic exploits smack more of fiction than fact? When vainglory is truly vain or empty, we are glorying in something with no more substance than the latest fleeting fad. Good looks and athleticism fade quickly with age, the fashions of the day have an arbitrariness that defies reason, career titles are pretentiously euphemistic (from "sanitation engineer" to "customer service representative"), and a perfectly decorated house does not make a home. And yet the vainglorious pursue these things as if their personal worth depends on them. Saturated with savvy marketing, the present advertising culture is fueled by vainglory, and it encourages us to run on its fumes. If we step back for a moment, it is disconcerting to think how much of our lives are spent keeping up appearances to impress lots of other people on the basis of qualities that we don't have or that don't really matter.

What Is Worthy of Glory?

Aquinas opposes vainglory to the virtue of magnanimity—a virtue, interestingly enough, that is completely unknown to most contemporary people.[12] Magnanimous people concern themselves with achieving great and hard-won acts of virtue as something to which God has called them. Their achievements are genuinely worthy of honor. They are things that turn our thoughts to the glory of God because they obviously aren't something anyone could have done without grace. Magnanimous people radiate God's beauty and goodness in the world, drawing others to that glory, a glory that transcends the person and his or her act. When others witness these acts, their attention is elevated above the one acting and is ushered, momentarily, into the cathedral of God's presence in human action. Acts of magnanimity, whether public or private, large or small, inspire not empty glory but genuine awe. A magnanimous action may be something great in the world's eyes or something not easily recognized by the paparazzi (Mary's quiet fiat at the annunciation is a prime example; see Luke 1:26–38). The point is that it is something that stretches human power to its limits. It is a "city on a hill" sort of moment that gives us a glimpse of graced obedience and shalom shining in the darkness. The vainglorious, by comparison, are working for the artificial illumination of the limelight and the canned applause from a sitcom audience. They achieve only the shallow veneer of magnanimity's true substance. Vainglory gives one a quick and fleeting high instead of the substantial and lasting reward of virtue.

Soli Deo Gloria

The contrast with magnanimity makes clearer the fact that what's wrong with vainglory is not the goodness of glory itself—any more than excellence and honor are necessarily bad in themselves. Every year at our college's graduation ceremony, after the last student sits down with diploma in hand, the president invites the audience to applaud. It is a thunderously joyful and celebratory moment. The graduates have worked hard to achieve excellence, they have received high marks and earned respect from the faculty, and at the end of their four years, the faculty and family who love them and encouraged them along the way take delight in publically recognizing their accomplishments with great fanfare, much clapping and cheering, and even tears. Pride and ambition are named vices because they are the *disordered* and *excessive* pursuits of good things. Likewise, what's wrong with vainglory is not the human need for recognition and approval itself, but for the excessive and empty ways we seek to satisfy this desire. The glory itself isn't the main problem, therefore. It's the vanity of how we seek it and what we seek to find it in.

As with the other vices, this vice's problem consists either in desiring the wrong thing or in desiring the right thing in the wrong way. To use the case of wrath, for example, we can be angry over something we shouldn't be (for example, when we want more than our share and can't get it), or we can be too angry, even at a legitimate offense. In a similar way, we can break the forms of vainglory down into two main types—cases in which we desire to be admired for the wrong things, and cases in which we desire to be admired in the wrong way, that is, too much. In the first category of cases—trying to be admired for inappropriate things—we find instances of seeking glory in what is literally vain or empty of glory. In these cases, the vainglorious seek recognition and approval either for ephemeral or superficial goods— things that aren't really worth the acclaim garnered by them—or for qualities they do not actually have. (This last case must be the emptiest sort of glory-seeking possible, for it is glorying in literally nothing but the appearance or outward pretense of goodness.) Our glory-seeking leads us to pursue "worthless goods" and "faked goods," respectively.[13]

In the second category of cases—trying to be admired in inappropriate ways—the desire for glory is excessive because we want approval and applause so badly that we will do whatever it takes to get it, even if that means misusing otherwise good things and misleading others, for example, a case of "stealing" glory through illicit means or for an illicit deed. Whether or not that for which we seek glory is worth the glory we receive for it, the manner of our pursuit or desire for it is excessive and disordered. This sort of glory seeker may be an employee who blames his boss for his own incompetence in order to gain acceptance with his coworkers. It could be a student who plagiarizes a paper to get a better grade and win the approval of her parents or teachers.

The worst sort of vainglory, however, according to Thomas Aquinas, occurs when we fail to give due glory to God as the source of our good.[14] Glory seekers of this type fail to note that they are stewards, not the ultimate source, of the "borrowed" goods they have. Therefore, the glory they receive is not exclusively their own but must be directed beyond themselves to God.

It is worth further exploring this last form of vainglory, since in these cases vainglorious people glory in things that genuinely deserve glory and still get it wrong. Moreover, this form of vainglory is the most morally serious kind, according to the tradition. When they receive renown and praise from others for some good gift from God, the vainglorious either glory in the gift while ignoring its source or glory in the approval and applause of others over (or against) God's approval. This is part of what bothers Augustine about his success in school and in his career.[15] His intellectual acumen and rhetorical skills were truly impressive, but the way he used these talents betrayed his desire to win the approval of his friends and colleagues at the expense of God's approval. Like Augustine, our desire to boost our worldly approval ratings can drive our choices and actions to the point of ignoring the gift-giver who makes their use possible. Later in his life, while writing *The City of God*, Augustine uses vainglory to name the ultimate disorder behind even the greatest virtuous acts of the Romans. "Glory they most ardently loved: for it they wished to live, for it they did not hesitate to die," he writes.[16] His analysis of the problem is simply this: even the Romans' pursuit of *virtue* was ultimately meant to serve the greatness of their own reputations. It was directed to their own glory, rather than to God's glory.[17] In the Romans' case, vainglory drove people to strive for greater virtue; in Augustine's own theft of the pears, recounted in the *Confessions*, it drove him to steal (and, in different circumstances, to feign having performed other sinful acts). Whether we ignore God and take his glory for ourselves, or whether we seek human over divine approval, both cases share a disordered dedication to seeking glory for ourselves, rather than for God.

Implicit in all expressions of vainglory, therefore, is the desire for our *own* glory, however we can get it. Not ultimately referring glory to God for the true goods he has given us is thus not one more type of vainglory, but the disorder behind *all* forms of vainglory. This problem shows us to be both unjust and ungrateful, because we are so busy seeking to manifest our own goodness that we fail to manifest its ultimate cause and source. Praise for the gift should redound to the glory of the Giver. Augustine says,

> Accordingly, two cities have been formed by two loves: the earthly by the love of self, even to the contempt of God; the heavenly by the love of God, even to the contempt of self. The former, in a word, glories in itself, the latter in the Lord. For the one seeks glory from [human beings]; but the greatest glory of the other is God, the witness of conscience. The one lifts up its head in its own glory; the other says to its God, 'Thou art my glory, and the lifter up of mine head' [Ps. 3:3]."[18]

To give up vainglory thus requires us to relinquish our place at the center of attention—to admit that from beginning to end, "it's not about me." Johann Sebastian Bach is remembered not only for writing beautiful cantatas and organ music, but also for writing on every manuscript "*soli deo gloria.*" Using our gifts well, appreciating genuine goodness wherever one finds it, and recognizing beauty and magnificence, whether large or small—these ways of celebrating goods with genuine value are all ultimately meant to point us back to God.

When I think back on the birth of our children—the greatest blessings my husband and I have been given—I think our delivery-room reaction was probably right on target. In the moments after birth, we were simply awash in waves of profoundest gratitude and overwhelmed by the wonder of the tiny bundle that lay in our arms. For that moment, at least, we breathed our glorias in hushed tones. That frame of mind contrasts sharply with the parade of family portraits and congratulations at the typical high school reunion, where vainglory whispers suggestions in our ears about who has the nicest-looking children—as if that would be to our credit anyway. The amazing goodness of a child points one to the giver of all perfect gifts in the first case, while in the second the gift is used merely to put oneself in the spotlight. This example reveals how vainglory centers our attention on ourselves and gives us a myopic vision of goodness, rather than allowing created goodness to be fully appreciated for itself and to point us to its Creator.

Hypocrisy and Onions

Jesus directly confronts vainglory in his Sermon on the Mount. Interestingly, he warns especially against the *religious* form of vainglory. Aquinas quotes John Chrysostom as saying that "while other vices find their abode even in the servants of the devil, vainglory finds a place even in the servants of Christ."[19] Is it not tempting to try to *look* like a better Christian than one *really* is in order to win approval and acclaim from others? Christ's sermon targets the cherished fantasies of the vainglorious: "Beware of practicing your piety before others in order to be seen by them . . . so that [you] may be praised by others . . . so that [you] may be seen by others . . . [by] heap[ing] up empty phrases . . . [to] be heard because of [your] many words . . ." (Matt. 6:1–8).

As he makes clear in that passage, the applause of others is all the reward this religious show will ever earn. A life spent craving human awards of glory and praise, full of empty-hearted acts for the sake of appearances and audiences, will bring only the fleeting applause the world can give. The desert father Evagrius makes the point this way:

> Do not sell your labours for people's esteem, nor hand over the future glory for the sake of paltry fame, for human esteem settles in the dust (cf. Ps. 7:6) and its reputation is extinguished on earth, but the glory of virtue abides for eternity.[20]

Especially in the area of religious practice and devotion, hypocrisy—traditionally marked as a vice that springs from vainglory—trades truth for a false front or respectable reputation, all in God's name. Jesus reserves some of his harshest words for the Pharisees, because they were more concerned about the appearance and outward observances of piety than a heart truly dedicated to worshipping God:

> Woe to you, scribes and Pharisees, hypocrites! For you are like whitewashed tombs, which on the outside look beautiful, but inside they are full of the bones of the dead and of all kinds of filth. So you also on the outside look righteous to others, but inside you are full of hypocrisy and lawlessness. (Matt. 23:27–28)

Hypocrisy is the natural result of a heart sold out to vainglory. Imagine Jesus updating his warning this way: "Everything you do is done for others to see: You come each week in Sunday clothes clean and pressed, on time for church, with your tasteful gold cross around your neck, your check visibly placed in the offering plate, and your well-worn Bible tucked under your arm. You love to be introduced as an influential board member of the most recognizable and respectable charities. You secretly cherish your reputation as a devoted Christian pastor of a well-attended church or as the one people laud as a 'woman of prayer.' " Whether our reputation is measured by worldly or religious standards, if our own reputation is the ultimate motivation for action, vainglory is a real and present danger.

Evagrius describes the just punishment for the monk who, after attaining some small moral gain, "acquires the horse of vainglory and rushes into the cities, getting its fill of the lavish praise accorded to its repute": it is to be humiliated by falling into some previously vanquished and shameful sin for all to see. The lesson, says this desert father, is that the monk should not presume to show off his virtue until he has learned real humility of spirit and has entirely thrown off concern for the opinions of others.[21]

Besides hypocrisy, the tradition also names boastfulness and the "love of novelties" as offspring vices of vainglory, mostly because they are typical means to getting favorable attention. Boastfulness is a direct way of attracting attention and approval to one's good qualities. Talking big manifests our excellence to others, and showing off does in action what big talk does in words. YouTube and other Internet sites like it are just the newest venues for displaying this ancient vice and creating publicity for one's achievements. We are a culture that loves to watch itself.

The name of the second offspring vice, "love of novelties," is just an archaic medieval expression for a phenomenon that is also still very much with us. It means having or doing the latest, greatest thing to win recognition and applause. This can include getting to perform a "stupid human trick" on *David Letterman*, the stunts of Evel Knievel, and everything ever documented in *Ripley's Believe It or Not!* Or perhaps it takes the form of being the kid on the bus with the newest electronic gadget or toy based on the latest hit movie, the first one in the office to have the newest, coolest features on one's cell phone, or the first one to wear the newest fashions or vacation in the latest exotic location. In all these forms and more, this driving desire to use novelty and newness to become the center of attention is the same tired old vainglory game that Gregory the

Great identified more than a millennium ago. In fact, it is a testimony to our love of novelties that it's hard to find current examples of this phenomenon that won't already be out-of-date by the time this book is published. The attention and approval based on them are just as fleeting.

Vainglory, according to Cassian and other early teachers in the church, is a problem especially for Christians who are making progress in the spiritual life—that is, especially for the virtuous and holy. For the more progress we make, and the more virtue we attain, the more we have for others to notice and admire. And if we lack an audience, we are often happy to supply the part ourselves. Cassian tells an entertaining story of two monks, both living in solitude in the desert. One monk went to visit the other and heard him speaking aloud in his cell. He listened in for a moment, wondering which psalm his brother was reciting with such passion. It turned out, however, that the monk was in the middle of a vainglorious fantasy, playing the part of a great preacher, exhorting his imaginary congregation to virtue with great flourish, relishing their attention and admiration. The visiting monk knocked on the door, and when the "great preacher" answered it, he sheepishly asked how long ago his visitor had arrived. "The old man replied in a pleasantly amused manner: . . . 'when you were announcing the dismissal of the catechumens.' "[22] Evagrius likewise warns against vainglorious self-congratulation in our daydreams about our great virtues:

> One gets a fantasy of the priesthood and then spends the entire day thinking through the things that that involves; or as if the charism of healing were about to be granted, one sees in advance the miracles that happen and fantasizes about the people who will be healed, the honors coming from the brothers, and the gifts brought by outsiders, all those that come from Egypt and also from abroad, drawn by our renown.[23]

Vainglory does not attack only when our virtues are mere fantasies. It is also a struggle when the gains in virtue are real. Vainglory is like an onion, says Cassian. You peel away one layer of vainglory, only to find that that very achievement is more fodder for a further temptation to the same vice.[24] "It is difficult to escape vainglory," says Evagrius, "for what you do to rid yourself of it becomes for you a new source of vainglory."[25]

A Living Doxology

The apostle Paul quotes Jeremiah saying, " 'Let the one who boasts, boast in the Lord.' For it is not those who commend themselves that are approved, but those whom the Lord commends" (2 Cor. 10:17–18). Real disciples bear fruit, says Jesus, fruit that bears witness to God's glory (John 15:8). What would it look like to seek God's approval and praise first and foremost, instead of human glory? This may be more complicated than it first appears.

In his Sermon on the Mount, Jesus calls his followers to be witnesses for him, saying, "You are the light of the world. A city built on a hill cannot be hid. No one after lighting a lamp puts it under the bushel basket, but on the lampstand, and it gives light to all in the house. In the same way, let your light shine before others, so that they may see your good works and give glory to your Father in heaven" (Matt. 5:14–16). But only a few verses later, he cautions, "Beware of practicing your piety before others in order to be seen by them; for then you have no reward from your Father in heaven. So whenever you give alms, do not sound a trumpet before you, as the hypocrites do in the synagogues and in the streets, so that they may be praised by others. Truly I tell you, they have received their reward. But when you give alms, do not let your left hand know what your right hand is doing, so that your alms may be done in secret; and your Father who sees in secret will reward you" (Matt. 6:1–4). As in Augustine's discussion of the virtues of the Romans, the point is that any acclaim for a virtuous act must be ultimately directed beyond ourselves, whether implicitly or explicitly. When we are a "light" to the world, we are not shining a spotlight on ourselves but illuminating the Source of our goodness for others to see.

Why do we prefer to garner glory for ourselves, rather than letting God's glory shine through us? Maybe vainglory is the vice for those convinced deep down they will never really be good enough to shine without artificial lighting and a little extra polish. Maybe we are faking it because we fear we will never make it. Vainglory may have a fearful form. In Miller's words, we live in "a world of posing and shams, anxieties of exposure, and a fear that the genuine may be just another sham whose cover is too tough to be blown."[26] But even our fears can lead us to clutch at more control than we ought. Vainglory also has an arrogant form. We might realize that being virtuous often requires us to make real sacrifices for others' sakes,

to die to our selfishness, and to give up on what the world calls success and happiness to achieve real peace. Vainglory, in its religious or
nonreligious forms, can be for those who prefer to take a shortcut to
these real goods. Why work at really being pious, face difficulty and
the possibility of failure, if we can pull off the mere reputation more
easily? Or perhaps reputation building does take significant effort,
but not effort that is painful, because at least that way we can stay
masters of our lives, comfortably surrounded by self-manufactured
affirmation. Devoting oneself to a life that "glorifies God and enjoys
him forever,"[27] and receiving our own good and others' good as a gift,
takes humility and the yielding of control. As in the fantasies exposed
by the desert fathers, we would rather manufacture our own image
than try to live up to being image bearers of God—never a project
known for its popularity. It is not so surprising, then, that pride—that
desire to have control over our own happiness, whether out of fear
or overconfidence—is the root of vainglory after all. In fact, Gregory
calls it pride's "immediate offspring."[28]

Tragically, vainglory wins applause and approval at the price of distancing us from others. Relationships cannot flourish when we dupe or
use others—as sources of flattery, as a dull background against which
we can shine, or as tools in our reputation-building program. Human
as well as divine relationships flourish in the context of sincerity and
truthfulness. The publican, not the hypocritical Pharisee, receives forgiveness, because he exposes what he truly is to God. So too the deepest
love flourishes in the openness of marriage, not the best-face-forward
games of dating. Communion with others is among vainglory's greatest casualties. Like other sins, this vice isolates us, rather than bringing
us into loving fellowship with other people and with God. Vainglory's
antidotes are sincerity, humility, truthfulness, and gratitude. The reward
of giving up mere reputation-seeking and pursuing these virtues instead
is to have a chance be truly known and loved.

It's ironic that the art of impressing others and gaining applause
involves carefully hiding ourselves just as much as it involves showing
ourselves off to advantage. To be lauded by others, there are things we
cannot let them see. Winning their approval and praise requires not
only that we put forward a false facade, but also the flip side of the
coin: that we carefully conceal the ugly truth about ourselves. The sort
of acceptance and approval this strategy wins us rightly feels fragile
and hollow. It leaves the deep human need for full and unconditional
welcome unfulfilled and unsatisfied.

The great vices all make the list of seven because they are perversions of the deepest and most significant of human desires. Vainglory is a cheap substitute for true fulfillment of the human desire to be profoundly known by another person—to be known by name, for who one truly is—and to be loved just that way. Scripture itself acknowledges this need. Isaiah 43:1 says, "But now thus says the LORD, he who created you, O Jacob, he who formed you, O Israel: Do not fear, for I have redeemed you; I have called you by name, you are mine." Psalm 139 says "O LORD, you have searched me and known me . . . For it was you who formed my inward parts; you knit me together in my mother's womb" (vv. 1, 13). God promises to fulfill the deep desire to be known, to be acknowledged, and to be accepted with unconditional love. Before we make any effort to bolster approval ratings for ourselves, God has already freely given us what we need. From where, then, does the inclination come to resist that gift? From the knowledge that to receive that gift is to live by God's standards of honor and glory, and to relinquish our own? Because what comes by gift is not under our own control? Because we want the power to create ourselves in our own image?

Augustine's *Confessions* makes a further claim. Not only are we made to be known and loved, but we are made for praising our Creator—for knowing and loving him. A life spent praising ourselves, or seeking our own praise, will thereby stunt our growth and flourishing as human beings. To know God is to understand that he deserves our praise and worship. To love him is to want to give him glory. Augustine says,

> "You are great, Lord, and highly to be praised (Ps. 47:2); great is your power and your wisdom is unmeasurable" (Ps. 146:5). Man, a little piece of your creation, desires to praise you, a human being "bearing his mortality with him" (2 Cor. 4:10), carrying with him the witness of his sin and the witness that you "resist the proud" (1 Peter 5:5). Nevertheless, to praise you is the desire of man, a little piece of your creation. You stir man to take pleasure in praising you, because you have made us for yourself, and our heart is restless until it rests in you.[29]

An honest, clear-eyed look at ourselves—we who are creatures, created by the living God, "a little piece of [God's] creation"—takes all the attention away from our worldly reputations and directs it back on God, who has made us what we are.

From "Spin" to Silence

It may be very difficult to imagine living a life in which we care more about what God thinks of us than what others think. Vainglory may have more power in human life than we often recognize. What practices reveal and counter its power?

Two spiritual disciplines in particular pull some weight against vainglory—silence and solitude. Richard Foster suggests letting our lives and actions speak for themselves by silencing away all our self-made "spin."[30] Instead of elbowing into the conversation to justify ourselves or reframing the situation to make ourselves look better, he advises, be still. In silence we can recognize this anxious seeking for others' approval for what it is, acknowledge our need to constantly put ourselves in the best light and create an approving audience for ourselves, and meditate instead on God's love to quell our desire for recognition and acclamation when it goes awry. The discipline of silence gives us a break from the voices of the world, including our own. Likewise, "Solitude . . . frees us from the panicked need for acclaim and approval," writes Foster.[31] The discipline of solitude removes our audience. It is designed to turn off the voices that constantly push us to seek recognition in ways that distract us from seeing the Lord and hearing his voice. Foster writes, "I am free from desiring public gaze when I need hiddenness."[32] The need for hiddenness and rest from "spin" is often drowned out by the constant voice-overs of vainglory. Listening in prayer for God's voice of love, without filling the time with our own image-building plans, brings relief from the incessant work of propping up our self-image and feeding our vainglorious desires for attention and approval.

We can start small, trying to take the spotlight off ourselves. Would it be difficult, for a single day, to let our actions speak for themselves, without defending ourselves when we suspect others are being critical? How hard would it be not to look in the mirror at all, or store windows, or reflections, and to refrain from asking others about our appearance? Could we listen to others, while refraining from conversation about ourselves—without telling stories about ourselves, recounting our own version of events, or offering an account of our own feelings? Reflecting when the day is over can reveal how much mental effort and conversation and activity we devote daily to enhancing our image in the eyes of others or calling attention to ourselves to make others approve of us. Are we engaging in activities from a desire to win recognition and renown or because we think they are genuinely important and worthwhile in themselves?

Living with excessive desires for the approval of others can be crippling. Anne Lamott recounts the ritual with which she begins her writing—a rather unconventional and slightly irreverent take, perhaps, on the disciplines of silence and solitude. She imagines all the voices in her head—both positive and negative, constantly reciting their high expectations and devastating criticisms of her writing—as little mice. She drops them one by one by their tails in a big glass jar and screws the lid on tight. She can see the mice pawing at the sides and squeaking away furiously, but she cannot hear them. She sets the jar off to one side. Only when the voices are stilled and moved out of sight can she find the freedom to focus on hearing the characters she is writing about.[33] What would it be like for each of us to work, with voices silenced, before an audience of One? In our work and elsewhere, we can choose to serve others in anonymous ways, and refrain from talking about these acts of service to others. As the desert fathers warn, however, we should be aware of the lingering temptation to create an imaginary internal "audience" for our good deeds in our fantasies, long after we have withdrawn from public view and the outer voices are stilled.

Another practice to counter the influence of vainglory is "fasting" from advertisements and shopping malls and TV commercials and mail-order catalogs for a period of time—another form of silencing the voices around and within us instructing us how to craft our image for successful worldly consumption. Often, with enough time off, our thirst to be well known for certain superficial qualities dies down or fades away, we discover how easily and happily we can enjoy life without constantly thinking about refashioning our image, and it becomes easier to recognize the emptiness and superficiality of most of the goods vainglory inclines us to pursue.

Ultimately, however, vainglory needs to be pulled out at the root, which means cutting it off from pride, which feeds and nourishes it. Cassian notes that "we wrong . . . God by preferring to do for the sake of human beings what we should have done for his sake, [and are] convicted by him who knows what is hidden of having preferred human beings to God and the glory of the world to the glory of God."[34] Both pride and vainglory involve privileging our own conception of happiness and our own power to achieve it. Both pride and vainglory seek to make us the center of the universe. With vainglory, our best energy goes into enhancing and controlling our image, appearance, and reputation. In the end, however, trying to manage our own reputation and manufacture approval for ourselves yields a life of isolation, falsity and shallowness, and self-preoccupation. What a contrast with a life rooted in God's unconditional approval, a life in which we "lay down the crushing burden of the opinions of others" and "give up on all the little human systems of self-aggrandizement" and self-promotion that lead to exhaustion and emptiness.[35] Like Garrison Keillor's cleaning lady, perhaps that life—whether it earns worldly attention and applause or not—will be of some real use to the world.

To give up on a life devoted to self-glorification is really to take up a life of freedom, a life free of vainglory's empty grasping, a life founded upon the recognition and acceptance human beings most deeply need. Such a life can provide the security and satisfaction of being known and loved by the One whose approval we cannot live without, with eyes not so blinded by flash and dazzle that they fail to see the Light of the World.

4

SLOTH

Resistance to the Demands of Love

The secret is that God loves us *exactly* the way we are . . . *and* that he loves us too much to let us stay like this. —Anne Lamott, *Traveling Mercies*

Grace is costly because it compels a person to submit to the yoke of Christ and follow him; it is grace because Jesus says: "My yoke is easy and my burden is light." —Dietrich Bonhoeffer, *The Cost of Discipleship*

Laziness and Diligence

Picture a hairy, long-toed sloth hanging from a branch, with headphones on, listening to "sloth motivational tapes": "Relax, take your

Material in this chapter draws from research presented in "Resistance to the Demands of Love: Aquinas on the Vice of Acedia" (*Thomist* 68:2), and sections of it were previously published as "Resistance to the Demands of Love: A reflection on the vice of sloth" (*Calvin Spark*, Spring 2005) and "The Vice of Sloth: Some Historical Reflections on Laziness, Effort, and Resistance to the Demands of Love," *Other Journal* 10 (Fall 2007).

time, what's the hurry? Life goes on whether you're asleep or not."
So one of my favorite cartoons of sloth depicts this supposed vice.[1]
"Supposed," because on first glance hardly anyone would think of
sloth as a serious, much less deadly, sin!

Why is this? It's mostly because, like the cartoonist, we typically
think of sloth as laziness. Does laziness really rank with sins like envy
and lust in its evil and destructive power? Since when was sitting on
the couch watching reruns of *The Office* and munching on a bag of
chips a moral and spiritual failure of the first order?

Our first reaction might be to say that sloth *doesn't* belong on the
list of the great seven vices. If putting it on the list in the first place
wasn't an outright mistake, keeping it there now is certainly outmoded.
One author describes the contemporary view of sloth this way:

> ["Sloth"] is a mildly facetious variant of "indolence," and indolence,
> surely, so far from being a deadly sin, is one of the world's most ami-
> able of weaknesses. Most of the world's troubles seem to come from
> people who are too busy. If only politicians and scientists were lazier,
> how much happier we should all be. The lazy [person] is preserved
> from the commission of almost all the nastier crimes.[2]

Likewise, Wendy Wasserstein's recent book on sloth uses a conception
of sloth as laziness and sheer inertia to construct a delightful parody
of self-help literature. From the book's jacket:

> With tongue in cheek, *Sloth* guides readers step-by-step toward a life
> of non-committal inertia. "You have the right to be lazy," writes Was-
> serstein. "You can choose not to respond. You can choose not to move."
> Readers will find out the importance of Lethargiosis—the process of
> eliminating energy and drive, the vital first step in becoming a sloth.
> To help you attain the perfect state of indolent bliss, the book offers
> a wealth of self-help aids. Readers will find the sloth songbook, sloth
> breakfast bars (packed with sugar, additives, and a delicious touch of
> Ambien), sloth documentaries (such as the author's 12-hour epic on
> Thomas Aquinas), and the sloth network, channel 823, programming
> designed not to stimulate or challenge in any way.[3]

In *Harper's* 1987 spoof of the deadly sins, the caption of the ad for sloth
read, "If sloth had been the original sin, we'd all still be in paradise."
From scholarly to popular accounts of the vice, then, contemporary culture seems often to equate sloth with laziness, inactivity, and inertia.

On the other hand, we *could* accept the same description of sloth and conclude that it *does* deserve to be called a sin—even a serious one. There is both a sacred and a secular version of this answer.

The sacred version goes like this. Sloth is opposed to the great Christian virtue of diligence—that powerful sense of responsibility, dedication to hard work, and conscientious completion of one's duties. And what is hard work and dedication at its best, after all, but an expression of love and devotion? The telltale root of our word *diligence* is the Latin *diligere*, which means "to love." Sloth, on this view, is apathy—comfortable indifference to duty and neglect of other human beings' needs. If you won't work hard, you don't care enough. Sloth becomes a sin not merely because it makes us lazy, but because of the lack of love that lies behind that laziness.

Communities that value diligence in this way point to proverbial warnings to "go to the ant, you lazybones" (Prov. 6:6) and the apostle Paul's admonition to do useful work with one's hands (1 Thess. 4:11–12), echoed a few centuries later by John Cassian's call to manual labor in the monastery as a remedy for sloth (or *acedia,* as Cassian and other early Christians called it).[4] Especially if our work is a divinely appointed vocation, as Reformed theology likes to emphasize, sitting around isn't just useless; it's thumbing our noses at God's call. Hence the (in)famous Protestant work ethic. Notably, those who hold this view are not nearly as concerned about the dangers of workaholism, often excusing or praising it under the euphemism "sacrificing for the sake of the kingdom."

Even outside religious circles, however, the virtue of diligence is glorified, and slothful "slacking off" is frowned upon. In the stirring words of Henry Ford, "Work is our sanity, our self-respect, our salvation. Through work and work alone may health, wealth, and happiness be secured."[5] Likewise, the *Chronicle of Higher Education* put "discipline"—that is, how diligently we work—at the top of their list of the five top virtues necessary for success in graduate school.[6] "In popular thought the 'capital sin' of sloth revolves around the proverb 'An idle mind is the Devil's workshop,'" writes Josef Pieper.

> According to this concept, sloth is the opposite of diligence and industry; it is almost regarded as a synonym for laziness and idleness. Consequently, *acedia* has become, to all practical purposes, a concept of the middle class work ethic. The fact that it is numbered among the seven "capital sins" seems, as it were, to confer the sanction and approval of religion on the absence of leisure in the capitalistic industrial order.[7]

Since the modern, industrial era, diligence or "industriousness" has become a pragmatic virtue aimed at profitability and professional success. When careers replace religion as a source of meaning, worth, and identity, laziness still carries significant weight. Our society measures personal worth in terms of productivity, efficiency, and the maximization of our potential. So we'd better get busy, or we'll be good for nothing.

Love and the "Long Course of a Lifetime"

I should confess that when I started studying sloth, I was fairly confident that this would be the *one* vice about which I would never have to worry. If anything, I reasoned, I'm too busy, hardworking to the point of a fault, and something of a perfectionist besides. Carelessness, apathy, laziness, and lack of effort would definitely *not* be my problem! My fragile bubble of self-righteousness quickly burst, however, when I read a little book that argued that busyness and workaholism were not virtuous, but rather sloth's classic symptoms. According to its author, "Not only can *acedia* and ordinary diligence exist very well together; it is even true that the senselessly exaggerated workaholism of our age is directly traceable to *acedia*."[8] It turned out that the apathetic inertia of the lazy person *and* the perpetual motion of the busy person could both reveal a heart afflicted by this vice, according to the traditional conception. How could this be?

If sloth were simply laziness—a vice opposed to the virtue of diligence—that question would be impossible to answer. The full explanation requires turning back to the original definition of sloth found among the desert fathers of the fourth century AD and developed by the Christian medieval theologians who followed in their footsteps. Looking back through sloth's long history in the Christian tradition of spiritual and moral formation, it is striking how far the contemporary conception departs from sloth's original spiritual roots. Retrieving the traditional definition of sloth will help us see how we now tend to mistake sloth's symptoms for ostensible virtues, and how sloth has more to do with being lazy about love than lazy about our work.

For these early Christians, sloth commanded much attention in the spiritual life. Sloth was always categorized as a spiritual vice, as opposed to one with a "carnal" object, like lustful physical pleasures. Sloth could drive one to abandon one's religious commitments altogether.[9] Hence, Evagrius of Pontus's colorful fourth-century description of the vice:

> The demon of acedia, also called the noonday demon (cf. Ps. 90:6), is the most oppressive of all the demons. He attacks the monk about the fourth hour [viz. 10 a.m.] and besieges his soul until the eighth hour [2 p.m.]. First of all, he makes it appear that the sun moves slowly or not at all, and that the day seems to be fifty hours long. Then he compels the monk to look constantly towards the windows, to jump out of the cell, to watch the sun to see how far it is from the ninth hour [3 p.m.], to look this way and that . . . And further, he instills in him a dislike for the place and for his state of life itself, for manual labour, and also the idea that love has disappeared from among the brothers and there is no one to console him. And should there be someone during those days who has offended the monk, this too the demon uses to add further to his dislike (of the place). He leads him on to a desire for other places where he can easily find the wherewithal to meet his needs and pursue a trade that is easier and more productive; he adds that pleasing the Lord is not a question of being in a particular place: for scripture says that the divinity can be worshipped everywhere (cf. John 4:21–4). He joins to these suggestions the memory of his close relations and of his former life; he depicts for him the long course of his lifetime, while bringing the burdens of asceticism before his eyes; and, as the saying has it, he deploys every device in order to have the monk leave his cell and flee the stadium. No other demon follows immediately after this one: a state of peace and ineffable joy ensues in the soul after this struggle.[10]

What the desert fathers meant by acedia *does* imply a failure of effort, a failure linked to a lack of love—the Greek word they use (*a-kedeia*) literally means "lack of care." For them, this vice was primarily a grave spiritual malady, expressed in dejection or a feeling of oppressiveness or even disgust. A lack of physical effort was, if anything, a symptom of a deeper problem.

Throughout Evagrius's account (only briefly represented here), two things are evident: first, sloth is an extremely powerful and serious vice; and secondly, it is a vice that threatens one's fundamental commitment to one's religious identity and vocation. It is a serious vice because the entire commitment of one's life to God is at stake. It is a spiritual vice, for Evagrius, because it involves inner resistance and coldness toward one's spiritual calling or identity and its attendant practices. He describes it as distaste, disgust, sorrow, oppressiveness, and restlessness, because the slothful feel that it is an intolerable burden to stay true to one's commitment to God with all its daily drudgery and discipline—they would much prefer to escape and run away and be free of their wearisome vocation. This is why, in Evagrius's and Cassian's work, sloth was on the spiritual end of the chain of vices.

In the writings of Evagrius's disciple, John Cassian, we see a shift in emphasis toward the external manifestation of the inner resistance characteristic of sloth. Cassian transplanted desert asceticism into the Latin West, establishing communal forms of monasticism more familiar to us today. Each monk was expected to contribute to the spiritual and physical well-being of the community. Although the desert fathers also emphasized the spiritual importance of manual labor, they did not associate it primarily with sloth, as Cassian did. Cassian explicitly and extensively discusses the importance of manual labor as a remedy for this vice. Early on in its history, then, sloth picked up its association with physical inactivity and shirking manual labor. Cassian uses language like "laziness," "sluggishness," "sleepiness," "inertia," and "lack of effort" in his descriptions of *acedia*, such as this one:

> [Monks] overcome by slumbering idleness and acedia . . . [have] chosen to be clothed not by the effort of [their] own toil but in the rags of laziness . . . [and] have grown remiss as a result of sluggishness and . . . are unwilling to support themselves by manual labor.[11]

Even for Cassian, however, idleness is clearly intended to be symptomatic of the inner condition of one besieged by sloth. In this he echoes Evagrius's description of the vice:

> Once [*acedia*] has seized possession of a wretched mind, it makes a person horrified at where he is, disgusted with his cell . . . Likewise it renders him slothful and immobile in the face of all the work to be done within the walls of his dwelling.[12]

On Cassian's account, physical inactivity or lack of effort is *an effect or expression* of one's inner condition. "The work to be done within the walls of his dwelling" includes both spiritual practices and physical duties done on behalf of the religious community. Shirking this "work" in any form signals a distancing of oneself from one's identity and investment as a member of a spiritual community bound by its love for God. Mere (physical) laziness is not necessarily slothful. Rather, shirking one's spiritual duty—whether this involves devotional practices or manual labor on behalf of one's brothers in the monastery—is slothful only if it is linked to inner discontent and resistance to the monk's religious identity as a member of the monastic community.

Both inner and outer manifestations of sloth are thus linked to one's religious commitment and one's attitude toward the demands of the spiritual life. Like Evagrius, Cassian thinks sloth is a serious vice because it threatens to undermine one's fundamental identity as one devoted to developing a lifelong relationship with God and it erodes one's commitment to the religious community formed by that identity.[13] Psalm 119 highlights the contrast between devotedness and *acedia*. In verse 28, the psalmist—defined as one devoted to God's Word—finds himself overcome with weariness and feels this oppression interfering with his ordinary daily meditation on God's law, which is an expression of his love and devotion to God.

The Now and the Not Yet

The medieval theologian Thomas Aquinas gives an account of sloth that stands at the crossroads between this ancient ascetic tradition and modern conceptions of sloth as laziness. Aquinas explains why sloth makes the traditional list of great vices. He also explains how sloth reflects a lack of love that can be expressed both as laziness and as restless busyness. His definition needs some unpacking, though. He begins with the cryptic statement that sloth is "aversion to the divine good in us." Huh?

An analogy will help us get a handle on what Aquinas is talking about. Imagine a typical husband and wife. In general, they have a relationship of genuine love and friendship. One evening, they quarrel at dinnertime and head off to opposite corners of the house for the rest of the night. They find it much easier to maintain that miserable distance and alienation from each other than to do the work of apologizing, forgiving, and reconciling. Learning to live together and love each other well after a rift requires giving up their anger, their desire to have their own way, their insistence on seeing the world only from his or her own perspective. Saying "I'm sorry" takes effort, but it is not *simply* the physical work of walking across the house and saying the words that each resists. It might be that this is another wearying version of the same fight they've been fighting for years, and it doesn't feel like they are getting any nearer to resolving it. What's the point of going through the motions of apologizing one more time?

Do they want the relationship? Yes, they do—neither would renege on their commitment to each other. But do they want to do what it takes to be in that relationship—do they want to honor its claims on them? Do they want to learn genuine unselfishness in the ordinary daily task of living together? Well, maybe tomorrow. For now at least, each spouse wants the night off to wallow in his or her own selfish loneliness. This is true especially when love takes effort, or feels like a formality or an empty ritual.

Why do marriages and friendships make good pictures of what goes wrong in the vice of sloth? For all its joys, any intense friendship or marriage has aspects that can seem burdensome. There is not only an investment of time, but an investment of self that is required for a relationship to exist and grow and flourish. Even more difficult than the physical accommodations are the accommodations of identity: from the perspective of individual "freedom," to be in a relationship of love will change us and cost us. It will require us to restructure our priorities. It may compromise our plans. It will demand sacrifice. It will alter the pattern of our thoughts and desires and may transform our vision of the world. It's not just "your life" or "my life" anymore—it's "ours." Seen in this light, it can seem that staying at arm's length and not engaging or investing would be easier and safer—even if ultimately unhappier—than risking openness to love's transforming power and answering its claims on us.

Sometimes marriage or other friendships feel euphoric and energizing; other times, they are tedious, empty, wearying routines, or just plain work. The point is that being committed to any love relationship takes daily nurturing, daily effort, and daily practices that build it up. Neglecting these will slowly break the relationship down. Nurturing grudges or selfish claims instead will erode it and make us resentful of a relationship that now feels like a suffocating trap. Kathleen Norris once said that married love is "eternal, but it's also daily, about as daily and unromantic as housekeeping."[14] It is through daily practices and disciplines, whether we feel like doing them or not, that the decision to love is renewed and refreshed, and the commitment of love is kept alive. The slothful person, in this sense, is one who resists the effort of doing day after day after day whatever it takes to keep the bonds of love strong and living and healthy, whether he or she feels particularly inspired about doing it or not.

If we think of our relationship to God like that, we'll be well on our way toward grasping Aquinas's definition of sloth. We know there must be something awry if sloth shrinks back and recoils from something good and divine, instead of taking delight in it. What that good is, however, requires a little more explanation.

"The divine good in us" is just Aquinas's medieval-ish way of talking about the indwelling of the Holy Spirit in our hearts—God's life in us. Paul puts it this way: "I have been crucified with Christ; and it is no longer I who live, but it is Christ who lives in me" (Gal. 2:19–20). When God lives in us, our whole being is transformed: the old has gone, the new has come. By the power of the Spirit, we are to "clothe [our]selves with the new self, created according to the likeness of God in true righteousness and holiness" (Eph. 4:24; see also Col. 3:10). Aquinas calls this grace "a beginning of glory in us."[15] The gift of the Holy Spirit and our new identity in Christ—this is the target of sloth's resistance.

For Christians, God is present in our hearts by his Holy Spirit, empowering us to become new people. The key, however, is that our new identity in Christ is both "now" and "not yet," a promise and a present reality. For now, that presence is a promise and a beginning, a new self born but not yet perfected. Why not yet? Because the Holy Spirit doesn't jump in and create a new self in us overnight or wave a magic wand to conjure up perfection. The project of growing into our new identity takes a lifetime, and a lifetime of cooperation on our part. It's called sanctification. In one sense, we *are* Christians, and in another sense, we are still *becoming* Christians. God is both "already" and "not yet fully" present in us. Our love for him has the character both of longing *and* of the restfulness of delight. Thus, it makes sense for Paul to encourage Christians to grow in faith and become more and more like Christ. We can't just say, "I'm saved! Praise the Lord!" and then sit back and assume God is done with us.

It's important to remember that the process of sanctification is the fruit of grace. Becoming Christlike isn't about us working like crazy to improve ourselves and merit a place in God's favor. Sanctification is about effort—but not earning. Second Peter 1:3–7 clears up any misunderstanding here:

> [God's] *divine power has given us everything needed for life and godliness,* through the knowledge of him who called us by his own glory

and goodness. Thus he has given us, through these things, his precious and very great promises, so that through them you may escape from the corruption that is in the world because of lust, and may become participants of the divine nature. For this very reason, *you must make every effort* to support your faith with goodness, and goodness with knowledge, and knowledge with self-control, and self-control with endurance, and endurance with godliness, and godliness with mutual affection, and mutual affection with love [emphasis added].

According to this picture of the Christian life, being a Christian is like being married: both involve accepting a new identity that needs to be lived out, day by day, for the rest of your life. A man and a woman take their vows on their wedding day, and from that moment on they *are* married. Yet *being* married, living out those vows and making them a living reality, will take all of their efforts for a lifetime. Their love and identity have a now and not-yet character. It is both a gift and a life-transforming task. It is this transformation of our identity by God's love that the slothful person resists.

That transformation takes time. This is why the tradition consistently opposes sloth to perseverance and commitment. Aquinas once argued that the demons can't have sloth. On the "sloth-as-laziness" interpretation, we might think it's because the demons are spiritual creatures who can't be physically weary or sick of making physical effort. It's rather because their wills were wholly conformed either to love of or rejection of God in a single choice in a single moment, while the human will is sanctified through many choices and actions over a lifetime. Our love for God, our choice to be like him, must be lived out over and over, day after day. The need to persevere in one's commitment over time is what yields an opportunity for sloth.

In a nutshell, to be slothful is to be opposed to the joy we should have over being united with God and committed to him in love. Instead of rejoicing at God's presence in us, the slothful chafe at it and resent the claims that God's love makes on them. Rather than being willing to dedicate themselves to developing and deepening the relationship, they resist its demands. Although sloth can appear symptomatically similar to chronic depression, it is not a matter of brain chemistry, but rather a habit of the heart. Sloth is not primarily a feeling: it is well-entrenched and willful resistance, even as love is fundamentally a choice.

Aquinas's take on sloth explains why it is a really serious vice. In sloth, we resist our identity in Christ and his presence in our hearts. We balk at God's invitation to "be imitators of God" (Eph. 5:1) and to be transformed by him over the rest of our lives. If that's not a description of a significant vice, it's hard to see what else might count.

The War Within

At the same time, this very explanation raises a hard question. How could we possibly feel put out by God's presence in our heart? What could make us *un*happy about the gift of love that is the secret to our own happiness? God's love and grace is the greatest gift that we could ever possess! Why would anyone who received it want to keep it at arm's length?

Aquinas answers with the apostle Paul's words in Galatians 5:17: Sloth is caused by the opposition of the spirit to the flesh.[16] Initially, this may seem confusing. Does his answer mean that sloth makes us prefer to be a lump of flesh on the couch than to pursue our spiritual duties? It sounds like he is saying that sloth strikes when spirituality takes a backseat to bodily comfort. Is sloth laziness after all?

Aquinas and Paul both say no. In the early as well at the later Christian tradition, sloth is always a spiritual vice. That means it is *not* primarily focused on bodily goods like comfort and ease and pleasure, as lust and gluttony are. Instead, when Paul makes the "spirit–flesh" distinction, as Aquinas notes, he is contrasting the old sinful nature with our new redeemed nature in Christ. The battle here is not between body and soul, between the physical and the spiritual. Rather, sloth is the old sinful self resisting transformation into the new self in Christ.

Spiritual battles take place on many fronts. Sometimes bodily pleasures or bodily weariness do make us more susceptible to sin. But in the case of this vice, the battle is first and foremost waged within our hearts. In sloth, we are literally divided against ourselves. We were made for relationship with God. If we are slothful, we have chosen to reject that relationship as the way to find fulfillment and chosen to try to make something else do its work instead.[17] We are trying to make ourselves content with being less than we really are.

Think back to the marriage example with which we began—the way loving another person requires a thousand little deaths of our old individual selfish nature. *This* is the "work" the slothful one resists. This work may or may not include bodily effort (on some occasions our resistance to it may be prompted by the physical effort required), but the two should not simply be equated. In fact, sloth *cannot* be defined as laziness, since slothful people often pour great physical effort and emotional energy into the difficult task of distracting themselves from the unhappiness of their real condition. As we will see in the next section, slothful people can be very busy. On the other hand, we should also not automatically equate overwhelming physical weariness with sloth: think of parents caring for a newborn infant. Their weariness results from their love and devotedness. The need or desire for rest is not itself a vice.

Lazy about Love

In the film *Groundhog Day*, weatherman Phil Connors gives us an example—at least by analogy—of sloth's resistance to the daily transformation required by real love.[18] Through an inexplicable turn of events, Phil finds himself waking up each morning, day after day, on February 2—Groundhog Day—having to relive the same day over and over again in Punxsutawney, Pennsylvania. A shallow and self-centered Phil first amuses himself with various hedonistic pleasures, since what he does each day apparently has no consequences. "Don't you worry about cholesterol?" his coworker asks as he scarfs down a table-full of doughnuts. "I don't worry about anything anymore," replies Phil with a smug chuckle. Soon, however, he settles on the project of getting his producer, Rita, into bed with him. He now spends a long succession of days making a great effort to seduce her. While he finds her attractive, he does not really love her—at least, not yet. Rather than change himself, he painstakingly figures out by trial and error what she likes and finds appealing. Then he puts up a false front designed to get her to fall for him—he memorizes lines of French poetry and pretends to share her interests in world peace and her taste in ice cream. His elaborate scheme is meant to manipulate her into giving him what he wants. Although she is initially taken in, Rita eventually sees through his strategy and rejects his advances. "I can't believe I fell for this!" she cries at him in anger. "You don't love me! I could never love someone like you, Phil, because you could never love anyone but yourself!"

Phil falls into despair. He sits on the couch all day, eating popcorn and drinking whiskey, apathetically watching the same episode of *Jeopardy!* for the hundredth time. He can't get what he wants the way he is, but he also refuses to change. And so he is at an impasse.

After a few unsuccessful suicide attempts, Phil finally tries a new tactic. He begins, little by little, to genuinely *become* the sort of person who could win Rita's love. Like his earlier seduction project, this takes regular and consistent effort on his part—day after day, he studies for a medical degree, he takes piano lessons, he reads French poetry, he extends a helping hand to the young and old. But these efforts, in contrast to his previous stratagems, change his heart. Unlike the old Phil, he is no longer bored and restless, filling time with self-centered diversions and empty pleasures. For he no longer pretends to be but really becomes—through consistent habit and daily discipline—not just a poet, pianist, and philanthropist, but a person capable of unselfish love. Phil is no longer solely motivated by the desire to produce sexual results in his relationship with Rita. Instead, his help for others shows that he has learned to genuinely care about what is right and good—for its own sake. In the end, his changed character attracts the affection not only of all the townspeople, but also the love of Rita herself.

What Phil's example shows is that the slothful person can be either a couch potato or a person who is very busy and active—very busy, that is, trying to get what *he* wants *without* having to change or give of himself. Love transforms us. The real work Phil resists, then, is not the physical effort itself (of seducing Rita or of helping the townspeople), but the commitment to love that effort represents.

In a sense, then, it's true that slothful people want the easy life. They find detachment from the old selfish nature too difficult, painful, and burdensome, so they neglect to perform the actions that would maintain and deepen relationships of love. They harden their hearts toward any change that requires sacrifice or surrender on their part. Wanting love to come easily and comfortably is like preferring the sentiment of pop songs and Hollywood romances. It feels wonderful for a little while, but these feelings and momentary "highs" cannot sustain a relationship. They come cheap but don't last. The talk about "forever" has to be sustained by commitments that require daily decisions to keep on loving, even when it's hard or unexciting or doesn't yield a big emotional payoff. Likewise, sloth is the vice of those who want the security of having God's love without the real sacrifice and ongoing struggle to be made anew.

So sloth or *acedia* has turned out to be a spiritual vice after all, a vice marked by resistance to the transforming demands of God's love.[19] Why does the slothful one resist love? Because a love relationship marks an identity change and a corresponding commitment to daily transformation. Novelist Anne Lamott recounts the words of a wise old woman at her church who once told her that "the secret is that God loves us *exactly* the way we are . . . *and* that he loves us too much to let us stay like this."[20] Those with sloth object to not being able to stay the way they are.[21] Something must die for the new self to be born, and, as in Phil Connor's case, it might be an old self to which we are very attached.

Here we can finally sort out our initial thoughts on sloth. We are right to think of sloth as resistance to effort—but not only, or even primarily, in the sense of being physically lazy or lazy about our work. Rather, it is resistance to the discipline and transformation demanded by our new identity as God's beloved children, created and redeemed to be like him. The slothful like the comforting thought of being saved by love, of being God's own, but balk at facing the discomfort of transformation—the slow putting to death of the old sinful nature—and the discipline it takes to sustain that transforming relationship of love over the long haul.

Slothful people are like the couple in our earlier analogy, who want the dream of being unconditionally loved without having to condition their own selfish desires in return, or who want a perpetual honeymoon, not fifty years of married faithfulness. The slothful are like Evagrius's monk, wanting to live for God in desert contemplation, but finding their zeal flagging in the heat of the day and pining instead for the comfort and worldly happiness of the life they left behind. Traditionally, Lot's wife was taken to be a picture of sloth, because even while being rescued, she is unwilling to fully turn her back on the only home and life and friends she had ever known (Genesis 19). How many of us have felt like we need two angels to drag us out of Sodom, while we look back over our shoulders, wistfully wishing for what we must leave behind? Are we like the people of Israel, poised to enter their homeland and promised rest in Canaan after years of restless wandering, who would rather retreat to the drearily familiar desert than have to fight giants (Numbers 13–14; Deuteronomy 1)? Pieper writes that the slothful person "will not [fully] accept supernatural goods because they are, by their very nature, linked to a claim on [the one] who receives them."[22] As one U2 song put it, "Love is not an easy thing; the only baggage you can bring . . . is all that you can't leave behind."[23] Their advice in the song is just what the desert fathers would have recommended and what Lot's wife and the nation of Israel should have done: "You've got to leave it behind. *Walk on.*"

Because it's ultimately about love—accepting God's love for us and the cost of loving him back—sloth earns its place among the top seven vices. Human beings are made for love. To resist it is to deny who we are. In her reluctance to die to her old self, the person with sloth chooses slow spiritual suffocation to the birth pains of new life and spiritual growth. She can't fully accept the only thing that would ultimately bring her joy. She refuses the thing she most desires, and she turns away in revulsion or bored distaste from the only thing that can bring her life. In the perversity of her sin, she prefers sorrow to joy, emptiness to fullness, restlessness to rest.

When describing sloth, it can be difficult to find the right balance between grace and discipline. Christian living should not become another long, legalistic list of demands that we have to meet on pain of not really counting as committed children of God. There is no litmus test of required work here. Love relationships have their fallow seasons, their drier times. On the other hand, we also shouldn't carelessly assume that God will happily leave us where we are and never make any demands on our time or effort, or never need to wean us painfully away from old attachments and desires. Love will require us to learn submission to God's will. Sometimes love is work—difficult, daily work. The key difference between sheer meaningless drudgery, on the one hand, and perseverance through times when our energy and fervor are low, on the other, is that in the latter case we are still fueling a relationship of love and investing ourselves for the long haul in something that ultimately brings rest and joy.

Restlessness and False Rest

Sloth sabotages sanctification—the transforming power of God's love in us. By sapping our willingness to lay down our old loves for the sake of love of God, it saps our energy for good altogether, since God is the source of that strength. As a result, sloth has a twofold effect. First, it makes us want to avoid activities and people that bring us face-to-face with our identity in Christ—most obviously, things like prayer, worship, scripture, and the sacraments. Secondly, however, this vice builds a cold wall between us and the demands of love for others. This explains sloth's association with indifference and apathy—what

Aquinas calls "sluggishness" when it comes to heeding the demands of justice. Love for neighbor flows from accepting God's love.[24] The commandment tells us to love our neighbors *as ourselves*. In refusing to accept God's love for himself, with the commitments that brings, the slothful one also forfeits love for his neighbors and his commitment to them. When Rita accusingly says, "You could never love anyone but yourself!" Phil replies honestly, "That's not true: I don't even like myself."

Rooted in resistance to love's demands, slothful apathy and avoidance typically manifest themselves, according to the tradition, in despairing resignation (apathy) or desperate escapism (avoidance). Cassian mentions both effects: "And so the true athlete of Christ, who wishes to engage lawfully in the struggle for perfection, must . . . contend on both sides against this most wicked spirit of acedia in such a way as neither to be *cut down by the sword of sleep and collapse* nor to be driven out from the bulwark of the monastery and *depart in flight*, even for a seemingly pious reason."[25]

Despairing resignation is the form sloth takes if we can't get escape, either in reality or in fantasy, from the thing that makes us sad. When we acknowledge this predicament, we tend to sink under oppressive hopelessness and despair. Phil's drinking and suicide attempts after Rita's rejection show him in this state. Phil realizes that his selfish nature cannot give him what he really needs, but he can't stand the thought of facing life without it, either. There is no way out of his predicament, even through death. Hence, the inner tension and "trapped" feeling that often characterize this vice. We can't escape the truth about who we are called to be, and yet we refuse to face it. Reality is oppressive, unbearable, and distasteful. The slothful person tends to cope by mentally and emotionally "checking out." This sort of resignation is "not to be confused with laziness," according to Buechner.

> Lazy people, people who sit around and watch the grass grow, may be people at peace. Their sun-drenched, bumblebee dreaming may be the prelude to action or itself an act well worth the acting . . . Like somebody with a bad head cold, [slothful people] have mostly lost their sense of taste and smell. They know something's wrong with them, but not wrong enough to want to do something about it. Other people come and go, but through glazed eyes they hardly notice them. They are letting things run their course. They are getting through their lives.[26]

The slothful are inwardly unwilling to be moved; they are stuck between a self they cannot bear and a self they can't bear to become. Their outward behavior—sluggishness and inertia—reflects the state of their heart.

On the other hand, if we think we *can* escape from sorrow, we will pour all our energy into any form of flight that shows promise, no matter how desperate. Phil's life of shallow pleasure-seeking and seduction early in the film is his attempt to escape love's demands. Life becomes one long project of distracting ourselves from the truth about our predicament. Augustine famously said that we would be "restless" until we find our "rest in [God]."[27] Blaise Pascal agreed; he predicted that the best way to make people truly miserable would be to take away all their diversions, whether at work or through recreation: "Without [diversions] we should be in a state of weariness, and this weariness would spur us to seek a more solid means of escaping from it. But diversion amuses us, and leads us unconsciously to death."[28] Victor Frankl paints a similar portrait of the workaholic's "Sunday neurosis"—the vacuum of meaning she feels on the day when her work does not fulfill its distracting function every waking hour.[29] Sadly, this escapist strategy can take even ostensibly pious forms: we can spend our whole lives avoiding the demands of true discipleship, love, commitment, and change, even if we constantly and busily engage in lots of religious activities. Like the aptly named Sebastian "Flyte" in *Brideshead Revisited*, the restlessness that characterizes our escapist strategies betrays a heart not at peace with who we really are and makes us flee whatever a commitment to love would require of us. This is why the vice of sloth was traditionally opposed to the commandment to rest on the Sabbath, which Aquinas says requires that "the soul take rest in God alone."[30]

Sloth can thus show itself in the total inertia of the couch potato or the restless distractions of endless activity. Somewhere in between these two symptoms of vice is a holy Sabbath rest for the heart that has given itself utterly to God, a heart overjoyed, not oppressed, by the thought that "love so amazing, so divine, demands my self, my life, my all."[31]

The slothful person ultimately insists on his own way, his own will, his own self-made pseudo-rest. His lack of commitment speaks of an unwillingness to surrender himself to God. It is this resistance that roots the vice of sloth in pride. Unlike other forms of sorrow, grief, or even depression, all of which can be mistaken for sloth, this capital vice results from a choice not to commit oneself, a refusal to give oneself wholly to God and then stay the course. It is the antithesis of Mary's "yes" at the annunciation, a "yes" that finds her faithful to the end, standing at the foot of the cross. The slothful person tries to find happiness while evading the daily demands of self-giving love. He prefers his own diligent efforts to make himself happy with shortcuts and quick fixes. He chooses to avoid the onerousness of love's demands by putting them off and trying to find fulfillment some easier way. By doing so, however, he cuts himself off from the possibility of fulfillment and happiness. And so, says Gregory, sloth eventually brings one to despair.

It is not to those who take up their crosses who find them an unbearable weight, but those who resist the demands of love—those who suffer from the self-imposed burden of *acedia*—that Jesus gives the invitation, "Come to me, all you that are weary and carrying heavy burdens, and I will give you rest. Take my yoke upon you, and learn from me; for I am gentle and humble in heart, and you will find rest for your souls. For my yoke is easy, and my burden is light" (Matt. 11:28–30).

Stabilitas Loci

Sloth is a vice for which it is difficult to find a remedy. Like envy, it has a self-perpetuating dynamic, refusing the very thing required to cure it. The ancient strategy against sloth therefore seems counterintuitive: rather than seeking some new way to infuse life and breath into one's relationship with God, the desert fathers recommended *stabilitas loci*—stability of place. Evagrius writes,

> You must not abandon the cell in the time of temptations, fashioning excuses seemingly reasonable. Rather, you must remain seated inside, exercise perseverance . . . Fleeing and circumventing such struggles teaches the mind to be unskilled, cowardly, and evasive.[32]

In this discipline, the soul should mirror the body: "The spirit of acedia drives the monk out of his cell, but the monk who possesses perseverance will ever cultivate stillness."[33]

In a nutshell, this discipline is about not running away from what you're called to be and do—whether through busyness at work or through imaginative diversions—but rather accepting and staying committed to your true spiritual vocation and identity and whatever it requires. The monk's commitment to the religious life was embodied in his willingness to stay in his cell, rather than flee to the city. To leave the cell was equivalent to abandoning his spiritual purpose and vocation. To stay put physically was also to stay put spiritually, even when one was not spiritually engaged or enthusiastic—in cases of *acedia*, quite the opposite.

Why did Evagrius and Cassian describe the relevant remedial virtues as courageous endurance, long-suffering, and perseverance? How is staying the course supposed to help? The idea is that enthusiasm and energy will wax and wane, and periods of felt alienation from God or spiritual burnout will threaten. Given the human condition and our sinful nature (both our physical frailty and fickleness of will), what we need most against the daily weariness of *acedia* is steady commitment and daily discipline, even when we don't feel like it. A friend once described worship as like a military drill.[34] It is not meant first of all to be personally uplifting in each and every instance, but rather to discipline us and equip us so we can respond immediately and appropriately in battle or a crisis. Our daily training carries us through those times. Analogously, marriage counselors often recommend continuing to act like we love our spouse in times of emotional dryness (for example, kissing him or her every time we leave and return home whether we feel like it or not), because merely persevering in the patterns of loving action is enough to keep us on track and to prepare our hearts for the appropriate feelings to return.

Perhaps in our age we are more prone than ever to expect too much of love as a feeling, and too little of love as an ongoing choice and commitment. In our worship services and our marriages, we expect emotional highs that will carry us through life's difficult times, when we would better expect engagement in daily disciplines to sustain us in our commitments. *Acedia*'s greatest temptations are escapism and despair—when we don't feel like being godly or loving anymore, to abandon ship and give up, to drift away inwardly or outwardly toward something more comfortable or immediately comforting. "A light breeze bends a feeble plant; a fantasy about a trip away drags off a person overcome with acedia," write the desert fathers.[35] Thus, its greatest remedy is to resist the urge to get out or give up, and instead to stay the course, stick to one's commitments, and persevere.

Applying the wisdom of the desert today, we can see why our culture of busy escapism is spiritually dangerous: it too easily and quickly gives us a way out of this daily, disciplined effort of learning to love. Overcoming slothful tendencies requires us to face up to the sources of our own resistance to the demands of our relationship with God, rather than grasping at a way out or a ready diversion any time we start to feel stretched or uncomfortable or just plain sick and tired of it all. Love flourishes in a context of daily action and lasting commitment (spiritual *stabilitas*), and sloth flourishes in a context of conveniently easy escape. As one prayerful petitioner put it, "Forgive me for letting love die when it demands action in order to live."[36] As the desert fathers knew, the remedy for sloth is staying the course, resisting the temptation to flee—in mind or in body. Likewise for any human friendship or relationship of love—there is a certain stability and endurance that sustains it, a commitment that comes with demands on us. Sloth prefers the easy way out.

5

AVARICE

I Want It All

For what good would their prosperity do them if it did not provide them with the opportunity for good works? —Aristotle, *Nichomachean Ethics*

In the previously mentioned *Harper's* magazine spoof of the seven deadly sins, the ad for avarice featured a picture of Santa Claus, with the headline, "The world's foremost authority speaks out on the subject of greed." The letters piled in front of him all begin, "Dear Santa, I *want* . . ." Santa looks up over his glasses and comments, "Do you remember all of the things you told me you wanted as a child? Well, your list may have changed, but I bet it hasn't gotten any shorter." As in Gordon Gecko's famous "Greed is good" speech in the film *Wall Street*, greed is such a commonplace part of everyday life that it is hardly counted as a sin anymore.[1] The idea that greed is the necessary psychological fuel for a capitalist and consumer economy is only the most recent way to justify it. Two millennia ago, in his *Republic*, Plato felt compelled to respond to opponents who argued that the self-aggrandizing desire for more and more without limit (*pleonexia*) was the driving force behind human nature.

Scripture also takes a hard line against greed: there are many more references to money than to sex in the Bible, indicating the frequency and seriousness of human sinfulness in this area. The most famous is Jesus's warning, "It is easier for a camel to go through the eye of a needle than for someone who is rich to enter the kingdom of God" (Matt. 19:24; Mark 10:25; Luke 18:25). But, we wonder, why can't we be rich in material wealth *and* rich in love for God? Abraham, that great hero of the faith, was a wealthy man, after all. The apostle Paul labels the love of money as "a root of all kinds of evil" (1 Tim. 6:10), a text that raised questions about whether avarice, instead of pride ("the beginning of all sin," according to Ecclesiasticus 10:13), deserved the distinction of being the "root" of the tree of vices. In addition to all these puzzles, there is long-standing controversy in the Christian tradition over whether owning possessions is good or bad, whether the desire to possess is natural or unnatural to human beings, and whether the Christian life demands moderation in acquiring wealth along with charitable giving, or poverty (living on bare necessities), or total abandonment of possessions.

What Is Avarice?

Before we tackle these larger issues, we need a definition of the vice itself. In common parlance, avarice or greed can be identified in a variety of ways—by intentions and inner qualities, acquisitions, and spending habits. In this chapter, we will define avarice primarily by what it looks like on the "inside," since vices are habits of the soul. The inner condition of the heart is what gives rise to greed's outer manifestations, which are typically categorized as excessive acquisition and excessive retaining of money or possessions. Aquinas's definition bears this out: greed is an excessive love of or desire for money or any possession money can buy.[2] The greedy person's attachment to wealth can wear many faces—an overflowing shopping cart or a single purchase, a stock portfolio that is aggressive or conservative, a wallet full of credit cards or a safety deposit box with a few carefully guarded treasures, a garage full of expensive cars or a closet jammed full of "great deals." It can affect the young, the old, and everyone in between. In all of its varied expressions, however, greed is a perverted love. Its profile has disordered desire written all over it.

As much as greed is an internal attachment problem, we shouldn't underestimate the connection between external actions and the formation of inner thoughts and desires—between the "outside" and the "inside" of greed. As with any habit, this vice depends on actions wearing a groove or pattern in the longings of our heart. In both our giving and our getting, greed corrodes the virtue of generosity and leads us to ignore the claims of justice. Contrasting avarice with these two virtues will help us see both greed's internal character and its outward expression, and the way they feed off each other. Moreover, in our exploration of this vice, we will see that our greedy tendencies to trust in money for happiness and security undercut our trust in God. Like the other vices rooted in pride, greed expresses the do-it-yourself method of finding happiness, instead of the contentedness of receiving the good that God has to give and depending on his provision.

Aquinas sets greed up as the opposite of generosity, except that he uses this virtue's Latin name—liberality. *Liberality* comes from the same Latin root as our word *liberty*. The linguistic connection gives us a hint: this virtue is about *freedom*—in this case, freedom from attachment to money and whatever money can buy. The liberal person's free and open attitude contrasts with the greedy person's tightfisted grip on money as *mine*.

In Genesis 13:1–13, Abram and Lot illustrate the opposition between this virtue and vice. Abram gives Lot first choice of the land for his flocks. Like a grabby child, Lot chooses the best for himself without a moment's hesitation, leaving Abram the desert (which Abram takes without complaint). Lot's choice of the fertile valley, however, lands him in the city of Sodom. There he grows so attached to the good life that angels later have to drag him and his family away, even though Lot knows they face mortal danger if they stay. Lot's greed holds him so fast in its grip that he even resists God's drastic plan to rescue him, because it means leaving all his treasure—and the life built upon it—behind. Abram, on the other hand, trusts in God's provision, even when the present reality doesn't seem to match the promises.

Avarice is being too attached to money and possessions—*caring too much* about them, as its own Latin root reveals (*aveo, avere*: to crave). Liberality is also opposed, however, to *carelessness* about the real value of things and our responsibility for them, which is the vice of prodigality. The most dramatic example of the latter vice is found in Luke 15, the parable of the prodigal son. The prodigal's use of money shows him too eager to acquire wealth (he wants his inheritance before his father has died) and then too eager to spend it unwisely on things of ephemeral value. The prodigal is wasteful with money, for he does not care enough about it or value it enough. (Is it merely coincidental that the money he is careless with was not earned by him?) In contrast to these two vices, then, the virtue of liberality stands on the fine line between excess (too much attachment to money) and deficiency (too little attachment).

As a depressing side note, Aquinas mentions that it is possible for a single person to have *both* vices opposed to liberality—both avarice *and* prodigality. If we are entrenched in a lifestyle of excessive and careless spending, we are likely to be regularly in dire need of getting more. It is too easy, once we are out of cash, to rationalize unjust acquisition and spend too much time longing to have more. So, in our dealings with money there is the possibility of a (literally) vicious circle. (Perhaps there is a consumerist version of this cycle too: first we overacquire—avarice—and then we overtrash—prodigality.) Nevertheless, the inner attitude behind prodigality is much closer to the virtue of liberality. For both prodigality and liberality are characterized by the practice of parting with money, of giving things away. Avarice stands apart, holding on to its possessions with an unyielding grip.

Liberal or generous people are defined primarily in terms of their inner *de*tachment from material wealth and goods. They may care about their possessions, but they do not have an "immoderate love of possessing" them.[3] There is a rule, or limit, to what they want to acquire and what they need to retain for themselves. The generous, according to Aquinas, are thus "ready to give with pleasure . . . when and where they ought."[4] Generosity's loose grip makes it easy to give things away. A mark of having a virtue is the way it becomes a natural part of who we are, so that giving is delightful, not an onerous duty or a dull chore. The test of liberality is whether giving things away is easy and enjoyable.[5]

The Heart of the Giver

This condition of the heart is the key to generosity. Generosity's measure is not *how much* is given away, in terms of the flat amount, but rather the *way* it is given: the manner of giving reveals the inner desires and attachments of the giver. In Luke's Gospel the widow gives away her last two copper coins out of devotion to the Lord, and Jesus commends her (Luke 21:1–4). Her coins couldn't buy a single church bulletin, but even in her poverty, her love and devotion made her willing to give. Likewise, the gospels recount the costly gift of a newly cut tomb for Jesus's body, given by a rich man, Joseph of Arimathea (Matt. 27:57–60). The mark of generosity is not the size of the gift, or the wealth of the giver, but the readiness to give what one does have to God. Aquinas quotes both the Greek philosopher Aristotle and Bishop Ambrose of Milan to reinforce this point: "The Philosopher says (*NE* iv.1): 'Liberality is proportionate to a person's . . . means, for it consists, not in the quantity given, but in the habit of the giver'; and Ambrose says (*De Offic.* I) that 'it is the heart that makes the gift rich or poor, and gives things their value.' "[6]

Unfortunately, this can also make for easy excuses to justify greed. If we are used to having too much, even giving up luxuries feels like a sacrifice. Like a Lenten fast in which we deem it adequate to give up a luxury (chocolate), instead of the main course (meat), does what we give away consist merely of the leftovers we would have garage-saled anyway? Compare this measure of generosity to the counsel of Aquinas: "It is enough for people to have only a few things, so liberal people are commendable because in general they give away more than they keep."[7] As if it were obvious, he explains that God gives some people excess riches "so that they might have the merit of good stewardship."[8] Aquinas assumes that most of one's income and possessions are not to be spent on upgrading one's own lifestyle, but to be given away. To contemporary Christians, this isn't obvious at all. It is a daunting challenge.

What makes it so hard to give things away? What drives acquisition and possession of material goods? Aquinas names two hindrances to generosity that make it hard for us to detach. First, having sweated for it. It is harder to give away what we have earned ourselves. Children find it enjoyable to put Mom and Dad's money in the offering plate in worship or shop with a parent's paycheck for food-pantry items. But when it is their own tithe of their own meager, hard-earned income, suddenly they feel much less eager to give. It is easy to rationalize that the little we give, from the little we earn, will make no difference anyway, or that we should first make sure we have enough to spend, and then give. Of course, these rationalizations miss the point of the offering as a remedy for the inner attachment of avarice—the point is not just to succor the needy, nor does God require imprudence when giving: rather, our acts of giving are meant to be part of a practice of habitual detachment that inscribes dependence on God in our hearts.

In the case of the first hindrance, what makes giving painful is the feeling that the money is our own. In Aquinas's words, "The avaricious person takes pleasure in the consideration of him or herself as a possessor of riches."[9] It's much easier to be generous with other people's money, since it's always easier to judge in their case that they don't need it for themselves. Similarly, it's easier to swallow our anger when the belongings that get wrecked or misused or neglected are someone else's ("It's just a rental"), because what we earn and buy and make our own feel like a part of ourselves.[10] Avarice is not just about having *more*; it's about what is *mine*. Do we possess our possessions, or are we possessed by them?

Along with the attachments that come with having earned it ourselves, the experience of poverty can also shape our internal detachment and our patterns of saving and spending. This is the second hindrance Aquinas mentions. Knowing want can also shape the habits of the heart. Many members of the generation that lived through the hard years of the Great Depression lived in the shadow of this experience of need for the rest of their lives. The fear of want dies hard.

Part of being generous now is adequately trusting God for the future. My grandfather taught me this—not by words, but by example. His family was too poor to pay for his tuition at the local Christian high school. In a moment of boldness, he went to the principal and told him he wanted to attend school but couldn't afford it. The principal promptly admitted him, on the condition that "you remember us someday." The principal's generosity was an act of trust, an investment in an uncertain future, and likely done on an already tight budget. His trust was rewarded. My grandfather was still writing checks to that school until his death.

It's true that our giving always needs to leave adequate provision for ourselves and those under our care. Aquinas and others are insistent upon this point, with respect to both spiritual and temporal goods.[11] It is a matter of the virtue of practical wisdom and part of avoiding prodigality. The difficulty comes with trying to discern what counts as adequate provision and what counts as excess. The Christian ascetics of the fourth century maintained a solitary existence in the deserts of Egypt, broken only by trips to the market to sell the baskets they made in order to buy a bit of bread. The spiritual directors of that community counseled selling below the market price, and giving alms with any money left over after buying bread. Bringing a profit home would only tempt them to regard their store of coins as security for the future, instead of learning daily reliance on God. The question is, can we translate desert asceticism into daily practices now? How much is enough for us? Cassian teaches monks that total renunciation of possessions must include renunciation of the heart,

> Just as the words of the Gospel declare that even those who are not soiled in body have committed adultery in their heart, it is also possible for those who are not weighed down by money to be condemned along with the avaricious for their disposition and attitude. For it was the opportunity to possess that they lacked, not the desire, and it is the latter, rather than [poverty itself], that God is always wont to crown.[12]

Avarice in Action

Greed's internal attachment is revealed in both getting and giving. The most familiar image of avarice is the miser, such as Ebenezer Scrooge, whose greed is expressed in the excessive hoarding of possessions he already has. But greediness is also evident in excessive acquisition, a tendency not always as easily detected. James Twitchell defines a luxury as "something we absolutely do not need."[13] How much stuff *is* enough?

When my husband and I were first married, we lived in a small apartment. It was old and quite run-down, but to us, its most noteworthy disadvantage was the size of the closets. They were barely deep enough for a single pair of shoes and about an eighth of the size of any closet in any place we had lived previously. Our workout clothes alone filled one of them. "What did the people who built that house ever do with all their clothes?" we wondered. Then I recalled my mother telling me that when she grew up, she had two dresses to her name—one for school and one for church on Sunday. That would have fit in our closet with room to spare! While our current house doesn't have a walk-in closet, it does have double closets in every room and a cedar closet in the hallway. They are all full.

A professor once devoted a course to the topic of Christian discipleship. He challenged his students to consider Jesus's example of voluntary poverty, a lifestyle the professor himself had adopted and lived out for many years. Two of his students were so inspired by the course that they gave away all their clothes except two shirts and two pairs of pants, resolving to live according to their needs instead of according to the standards of endless acquisition and consumerist excess. Their commitment was praiseworthy, to be sure—it even made the campus newspaper. But it bears mentioning that what they defined as voluntary poverty entailed living at or above the level of many people for most of human history. Not to mention that their parents were still footing the bill for their college tuition, to the tune of a hundred thousand dollars or more. Yet when I ask my students how hard it would be for them to give up all but two outfits, they regularly reply, "Nearly impossible."

When Aquinas and Augustine discuss "the needs of this life," whether in the context of food or money, they emphasize not just what is necessary for bare subsistence, but also what is necessary for living a life "becoming" or appropriate to human beings. The point is not to live on crusts of bread with bare walls and threadbare clothes. The point is that a fully human life is lived in a way free from being enslaved to our stuff. Our possessions are meant to serve our needs and our humanness, rather than our lives being centered around service to our possessions and our desires for them. What is "needful," even in this more expansive sense, is meant to be a limiting rule, so that our acquisitiveness does not expand without any bounds.

Even if we aren't all called to a life of voluntary poverty, however, we also needn't be misers or "shopaholics" to think twice about our buying and spending habits and what they reveal about the desires and attachments of our hearts. What would the following thought experiment reveal? Imagine that others had access to all of our financial records and spending habits (investment portfolios, savings, checkbook registers, tax returns, cash flow), but knew nothing else about us. What sort of judgments could they make about our character, our loves, our excesses and deficiencies? Greed is an internal problem, but it does not necessarily stay hidden inside. Patterns of getting and giving can reveal our hearts' deepest priorities and attachments. Another exercise in self-examination would be to calculate how many hours a week we spend thinking about buying or acquiring things—either by going to the mall, browsing through catalogs, working longer hours or overtime, or watching home improvement shows on TV. Are our feelings of frustration or depression temporarily alleviated by buying something for ourselves? Does earning more money or acquiring more things create a renewed sense of power over our lives? These exercises in self-examination may take us beyond the stereotypical pictures of avarice we clearly avoid to confession of our own avaricious tendencies to seek *more* things we can call "*mine.*"

Seeking Justice, Loving Mercy

Greed's inner clutch on the heart can corrode the virtue of generosity and dampen our enthusiasm and eagerness to give freely. At its worst, however, greed also incites us to the obstinate refusal to meet even the demands of basic justice, as we opt instead to keep more than our share. The greedy are excessive in acquiring and keeping possessions even to the point of depriving others of what they deserve or need. Greed causes callousness toward those in want. In this case, justice— giving others their due—is the virtue avarice attacks.

Sometimes the greedy hoard more than their share out of malice; other times, out of sheer thoughtlessness. The Greek philosopher Plato thought that the supreme virtue was justice (*dikaiosunê*). Justice is about giving others what is due to them. Its opposite is the vice of *pleonexia*—always grasping for more, and more than our share, with no regard for anyone but ourselves. Despite the divide of two millennia between Plato and the present day, contemporary people seem instantly to understand what *pleonexia* is. Avarice can lead us to trample justice when we want what rightfully belongs to another, to the point of doing anything to get it, even when we don't need it. Some cases—like elbowing out a sibling for the last piece of pizza— may seem benign, but avarice can also turn murderous, as the story of Naboth's vineyard illustrates (1 Kings 21). The biblical prophets have plenty to say about how the lifestyles of the wealthy and "religious" cause oppression of and callousness toward the poor, a critique that could just as easily be applied to twenty-first-century first world nations as to ancient Israel. "In this way avarice is a sin directly against one's neighbor, since one person cannot overabound in external riches without another person lacking them, for temporal goods cannot be possessed by many at the same time."[14]

We have already seen that avarice has many symptoms, revealing itself in the time we spend planning what to buy and how to acquire things, and the belief that we will be happy and content if only we can purchase some new thing. It is expressed in the anxious restlessness we feel until we can acquire something, and the consumerist conviction that acquisition will quiet that feeling. Avarice does not just feed our wants, however; it tramples others' needs. It is also behind the fantasies and desires that move us to rationalize lifestyles in which we regularly and programmatically take more than we need, or more than our share, regardless of injury to others.

Basil, in a sermon on the parable of the rich man who builds bigger barns, comes down hard on the avaricious for their injustice. In cases in which your acquisition or keeping deprives another person of what they need, he says, "It is the hungry one's bread that you hoard, the naked one's cloak that you retain, the needy one's money that you withhold. Wherefore as many as you have wronged, you might have succored."[15] Or, as a contemporary paraphrase might put the point: "Your second doughnut this morning belonged to the child who came to school with no breakfast, the new winter coat hanging in your closet next to four other coats (now out of style) belongs to the homeless person you passed on your way downtown last weekend, and the money you have saved for retirement is the difference between subsistence and starvation for the sweatshop workers who made your favorite hiking boots (worn only twice). Wherefore as many as you have wronged, you might have aided."

Like a child listening impatiently to his mother plead the case of starving children in Africa over a dinner he won't eat, perhaps it is easy not to care if our spending and acquiring deprive someone else, especially if that someone else is safely out of sight. Not a surprising result, given that the tradition identifies one of greed's offspring vices as "insensibility to mercy"—hard-heartedness.[16] The trouble with apathy is that it is only one step short of being willing to injure outright. From Cassian to Gregory to Aquinas, Christian thinkers taught that avarice's bitter fruits included being willing to deceive, to lie outright or under oath, to steal, to injure, and to betray others for the sake of money. That is to say, when avarice gets one in its grip, the excessive desire to possess trumps even the most fundamental demands of justice.

What's the Use?

As with all the vices, greed is an attachment to a good thing gone wrong. Money and possessions are not themselves evil; in fact, they are useful goods. Even luxury has its place in human life: fasting does not preclude feasting. Neither should simplicity and stewardship imply that living on bare necessity is the only way to avoid avarice. Several years ago, my high school students cited their vast collections of music on compact disc as an example of luxury spending. But if all CDs were indeed luxuries, was it wrong or greedy to own any? When I was in graduate school (a state of relative poverty!), a fellow student with a particularly generous nature, and much less money than I had, overheard me raving about a new recording of my favorite piano concerto. He gave me the CD as a gift, likely using some of his own grocery money to do so. Listening to that music was a great consolation to me later, however, in a time of grief. His act of extravagance, and my ownership of a luxury item, contributed to a friendship, my spiritual well-being, and a more fully human life. The fact that a single concert Steinway piano costs enough to feed everyone in a small African town for a month is not enough, all by itself, to stop buying Steinways. However, what *this* view of luxuries sees that greed does not see is that the value of possessions can reach beyond their monetary value.

The hallmark of well-entrenched greed, then, is a willingness to use people to serve our love for money, rather than the use of money to serve our love for people. Even King Midas was stopped short when his lust for gold cost him his daughter—for unlike his gold, she represented a value beyond all measure. Because he loved her, he was unhappy to see her used to satisfy his greedy desires. It was a sign of the depths of his avarice that it took a human sacrifice to shake him out of his lust for more.

In the film *Ocean's Eleven*, Danny Ocean and Tony Benedict are both greedy for gain. But in a telling scene near the end of the story, Danny's former wife, Tess, who is now with Tony, secretly watches an exchange between the two men via security cameras. Danny asks Tony whether he would give Tess up if Danny could tell him who had just robbed his casino and get his money back. Coldly and without any hesitation, Tony says "Yes." The difference between the two men suddenly becomes crystal clear, for Danny would—just as unhesitatingly—leave all his illicit gains to have Tess back.

Aquinas describes greed's object as money, or whatever money can buy, *considered as useful or profitable.*[17] Lust and gluttony, on the other hand, desire things insofar as they give us physical *pleasure*. It is worth pondering how much of our struggle with avarice is linked to a tendency to value things solely in terms of their usefulness. When the older generation laments that they are only a burden to society, since they are no longer capable of useful work or productive labor, and their medical care is a constant drain on others' resources, have they internalized a system of value that measures people's true worth in terms of a cost–benefit analysis? Time spent with children also becomes "unprofitable" in more than one sense, for we have precious little in the way of tangible payoff to show for such investments. The very use of metaphors of financial transactions to describe personal care for other human beings points to a conceptual framework tilted toward the distortions of avarice. The salary charts for the helping professions, especially compared to the salaries of those who work in financial fields managing investments, also point not so subtly to implicit assumptions of what is truly of value and worth. We are measured by our usefulness, and our usefulness is measured by the production of things and the possession of money. Greed now invades human life and its value in this subtler way as well.

Pope John Paul II argued that avarice's pernicious tendency to measure all else in terms of monetary value had successfully infiltrated contemporary society. He criticized contemporary culture on the grounds that it valued *having things* over *being human persons*—with all the moral and religious significance personhood includes. The darkest form of avarice, according to his view, has as its "only goal . . . the pursuit of one's own material well-being. The so-called 'quality of life' [of human beings] is interpreted primarily or exclusively in terms of economic efficiency . . . functionality, and usefulness."[18] If the ultimate measure by which society judges everything is its monetary or material value, then people who are no longer economically valuable are too easily seen as no longer valuable, period. Even ending life becomes an attractive alternative, John Paul II argues, when "justified by the utilitarian motive of avoiding costs which bring no return and which weigh heavily on society." The weak, the young, the disabled, and the elderly are most vulnerable in a society that makes money the measure of all things. But then, isn't every human being in one of those categories sooner or later? Making money the measure of all things, John Paul II continues, is really a cover for making *human beings*—the makers and controllers of money—the measure of all things, including the value of other human beings. This instrumentalization and commodification of human beings by others reveals a deeper connection between avarice and injustice than one individual's impulse to steal or hoard. Cassian likewise analyzes Judas's betrayal of Christ as motivated by avarice: "He no longer

secretly stole from the purse but sought to sell the Lord himself."[19]
In the same stealthy way, avarice moves us to betray one another's
humanness. In so doing, we betray our own humanity as well. One
of the more striking illustrations of this phenomenon in scripture is
Ahab and Jezebel's murder of Naboth to acquire his vineyard. The
story concludes with this telling line: "Indeed, there was no one like
Ahab, who *sold himself* to do what was evil in the sight of the Lord,
urged on by his wife Jezebel" (1 Kings 21:25; emphasis added).

A "Capital" Vice

"The love of money is a root of all kinds of evil," says the apostle
Paul (1 Tim. 6:10). Why is that? Because money is so attractive that
we will commit many sins in order to acquire it? Or because money
gives us the power to satisfy any sinful desire—and then get away
with sin by buying influence or immunity?

Even more, perhaps, loving money is the root of evil when having
money itself becomes the goal. Aquinas argues that human beings
are tempted to seek material wealth because it gives us the illusion
of self-sufficiency—and therefore serves as a powerful incentive to
deny our need for God.[20] Who among us would want to give up the
power to make ourselves comfortable and secure in this world? The
possession of money represents this self-sufficiency and the power to
secure it, and is a convenient and much less demanding replacement
for God. As Frederick Buechner once put it,

> The trouble with being rich is that since you can solve with your check-
> book virtually all practical problems that bedevil ordinary people, you
> are left in your leisure with nothing but the great human problems to
> contend with: how to be happy, how to love and be loved, how to find
> meaning and purpose in your life. In desperation the rich are continu-
> ally temped to believe that they can solve these problems too with their
> checkbooks, which is presumably what led Jesus to remark one day
> that for a rich man to get to Heaven is about as easy as for a Cadillac
> to get through a revolving door.[21]

Greed is the root of all kinds of evil, because it is itself rooted in
pride.

This last explanation cuts deeper than we might first think. Having
the means to provide for ourselves is much easier than trusting God

to provide. Greed, like all the deadly sins, is anchored in pride and nourished by it. Prideful greed is the desire to take over God's role and make sure we get enough for ourselves—or better yet, to make sure we get what we want. It is the desire to be able to provide fully for ourselves, and therefore not to have to depend on God. Aquinas explains avarice's link to pride by pointing out the way in which it counts as a spiritual vice. Although avarice is ostensibly about money and possessions (which would make it a carnal vice), he argues for a more fundamental dimension of disorder that makes it a spiritual vice beyond the mere love of money: "Avaricious people take pleasure in the consideration of *themselves as the possessor of riches*,"[22] where *riches* denotes "possessions of which we are the absolute masters."[23]

The trouble with prideful possession is that when greed takes over, we find that we don't know what *enough* means anymore, and that greed undercuts our ability to see the true value of things. As Boethius pointed out centuries ago, after he lost all his earthly possessions, the more money and stuff we possess, the more money, time, and energy we need to protect and care for it all.[24] Rather than securing freedom from anxiety and ample provision to satisfy our desires, wealth actually increases our worry, insecurity, and desire for more. Evagrius of Pontus, one of the desert fathers, concurs: "A monk with many possessions is like a heavily laden boat that easily sinks in a sea storm. Just as a very leaky ship is submerged by each wave, so the person with many possessions is awash with his concerns."[25]

Augustine explains the insatiability of desire for temporal goods like this: we will never be able to satisfy our deep, human need for an eternal, perfect good with any amount of temporal, imperfect goods.[26] So greedy people's desires for more keep extending without limit, dooming them to a life of frustration and dissatisfaction, rather than contentment. Evagrius observes, "The sea is never filled up even though it takes in a multitude of rivers (cf. Eccles. 1:7); the desire of the avaricious person cannot get its fill of riches. He doubled his wealth and wants to double it again, and he does not stop doubling it until death puts a stop to his endless zeal."[27] Aquinas makes this point in terms of the distinction between natural wealth and artificial wealth. Natural wealth is what we need to satisfy our natural desires for genuine human goods. Artificial wealth is what we need to satisfy desires that are artificially created and inflated. (It's hard to imagine a more prophetic word about the effects of the advertising industry.) Possession of these desired things, he notes, just makes us "despise them and seek others," because once we possess them, we "realize their insufficiency."[28] Jesus's Sermon on the Mount makes the same point, linking contentment and freedom from anxiety to where we place the source of ultimate value and seek lasting satisfaction, emphasizing the ephemeral nature of earthly goods, which can always be lost (Matt. 6:19–34). They can never make us fully secure from want.

Getting Free from the Grip of Greed

Avarice has unquestionably got many of us in its grip. The question is, how can we struggle free? By knowing our own weakness, first of all. Try documenting all expenditures for a month and list them in categories (savings, food, entertainment, repairs, car expenses, etc.). If we then take a highlighter and mark the items we could have done without, how many of those purchases (or the amount of money spent on them) would we discover to be superfluous? To avoid the temptation to constantly upgrade whether we need to or not, Richard Foster, in *The Freedom of Simplicity*, recommends resolving to live for the next year at whatever our current level of spending is, even if our income increases. If we have extra, that's more we can give away.

Even further, others suggest taking a Sabbath rest from consumerism—for at least one month, refrain from going to the mall, or looking at catalogs and magazines, and limit exposure to advertising as much as possible, even if this means giving up television. We may well be shocked at how jaded we have become to the daily assault of marketing designed to inflame the desire to possess beyond all reasonable measure. In an article called, "Why the Devil Takes VISA: A Christian Response to the Triumph of Consumerism," Rodney Clapp quotes one retail analyst from the 1950s: "Our enormously productive economy . . . demands that we make consumption our way of life, that we convert the buying and use of goods into rituals, that we seek our spiritual satisfaction, our ego satisfaction, in consumption."[29] Taking a break from constant exposure to this relentless assault on our desire to acquire and possess may feel like a welcome relief, rather than a burden. It may be the most countercultural thing we ever do.

Perhaps the best advice, however, is the oldest: tithe. Total renunciation of possessions is an option for some, but material goods are something no one can live entirely without.[30] So for most who struggle with the excessive desire for money, there is often no give-it-all-up, cold-turkey cure. Tithing, like fasting, is the habitual practice of limiting our use of a good thing to regularly and continually loosen our attachment to it, an attachment that builds and tightens before we are even aware of it. Doing without realigns our appreciation of the value of things, an appreciation which makes us content with less and free from slavishness. Tithing is, in an extended sense, a "Sabbath" from our natural tendencies to replace God with money or stuff. Like a Sabbath rest from working, and like feasting after fasting, the habit of tithing, and the generosity for which it frees us, is meant to be a part of the constant rhythm of life, not a one-time obligation.

A remedy for avarice is therefore to give money away every week, and to give our best. To spend on ourselves first and then to give away what remains, either to God or to others, is to remain in the mindset that our possessions are really our own to dispense as we see fit and that we are the ultimate providers for ourselves. Tithing first, and spending on ourselves later, is a discipline that teaches God's ownership of all good things and trust in his provision, as well as a stewardship of goods that does not put ourselves first. Elijah asked the widow of Zarephath to give up her last bit of bread (1 Kings 17) and to trust God to provide for the future. Tithing may be just the sort of practice that over time prepares us for an act of trust and generosity like hers.

The point of tithing is not to rigidly conform to a code of behavior, but to re-form our hearts so that we learn to give, not because we ought, but from gratitude and joy and love. Although many disciplines feel burdensome and difficult at the outset, what we realize over time is that we are traveling lighter and breathing more easily, relieved from the anxiety of always having to manage future acquisitions. Tithing in particular, and simplicity more broadly, is not defined by percentages given, but by its yield in freedom, lightness, and joy: "With every gift show a cheerful face, and dedicate your tithe with gladness" (Ecclesiasticus 35:11).

In God We Trust

Perhaps our daily or weekly tithing will prepare us for holy extravagance in our giving to God. Recall the Gospel story of the woman who poured a bottle of expensive perfume on Jesus's feet. Judas's reaction (and doesn't it sound stewardly? prudential? charitable?

fiscally responsible?) was that it could have been sold and the profits given to the poor (John 12:5). It's true that Judas was hoping to skim a little off the top. But his basic reaction—"What a waste!"—also resonates. Can it be that what looks like waste is really good stewardship, if only we could see the world without greed's insistence to measure the worth of every thing and every act and every person by its utility and material profitability? How do we acquire that vision?

Centuries ago, the Greek philosopher Aristotle ruled out money as the definition of what made human life happy. His reason? Money is only an instrumental good—it is only valuable for the sake of other things that one can acquire with it. The greedy mistakenly make money, or perhaps more accurately, the possession of money and stuff, an end in itself—*their* ultimate end. Why do they make this mistake? The wealth in their hands represents security and freedom from fear and want, and these are deep human needs indeed. Thus, the tendency to substitute money's promise of self-sufficiency for God's promise to be our all in all is a temptation that easily takes hold of human hearts. Could we imagine a life free from worry over what we will eat or drink or wear (Matt. 6:25–34), a life in which we do not store up for ourselves treasures on earth (Matt. 6:19)?

It is no coincidence that scripture recurrently mentions fear in connection with avoiding avarice: "Do not be afraid, little flock, for it is your Father's good pleasure to give you the kingdom. Sell your possessions, and give alms. Make purses for yourselves that do not wear out, an unfailing treasure in heaven, where no thief comes near and no moth destroys. For where your treasure is, there your heart will be also" (Luke 12:32–34). The writer of Hebrews likewise counsels: "Keep your lives free from the love of money, and be content with what you have; for [Jesus] has said, 'I will never leave you or forsake you.' So we can say with confidence, 'The Lord is my helper; I will not be afraid. What can anyone do to me?' " (Heb. 13:5–6). We can try to assuage our fears by accumulating stuff that won't last and isn't secure, or we can invest our trust in God, who alone can promise and deliver real security. The refrain from the Taizé community reflects this biblical connection between lack of fear, security in God's provision, gratitude rather than grasping: "In the Lord I'll be ever thankful / In the Lord I will rejoice / Look to God / Do not be afraid / Lift up your voices / The Lord is near / Lift up your voices / The Lord is near."[31]

Avarice is the temptation to try to create this security for ourselves by procuring and providing for ourselves, rather than trusting God for what we need. As Augustine writes, "Avarice wishes to have large possessions; you [God] possess everything." This makes our avaricious grasping for more but a "dim resemblance to [God's] omnipotence."[32]

Avarice is dangerous because when we are in its grip we believe that the things we own are ours and that we have control over them and, therefore, control over our lives. As C. S. Lewis's fictional devil Screwtape says,

> The sense of ownership [in human beings] is always to be encouraged. The humans are always putting up claims to ownership that sound equally funny in Heaven and in Hell and we must keep them doing so . . . [They act as if they were] a royal child whom his father has placed, for love's sake, in titular command of some great province, under the real rule of wise counselors, [who comes] to fancy that he really owns the cities, the forests, and the corn, in the way he owns the [building blocks] on the nursery floor.
>
> We [the demons] produce this sense of ownership not only by pride but by confusion. We teach them not to notice the different senses of the possessive pronoun—the finely graded differences that run from "my boots" through "my dog," "my servant," "my wife," "my father," "my master" and "my country," to "my God." They can be taught to reduce all these senses to that of "my boots," the "my" of ownership . . .
>
> And all the time the joke is that the word "Mine" in its fully possessive sense cannot be uttered by a human being about anything. In the long run either Our Father [i.e., Satan] or the Enemy [i.e., God] will say "Mine" of each thing that exists, and specially of each [person]. They will find out in the end, never fear, to whom their time, their souls, and their bodies really belong—certainly not to them, whatever happens. At present the Enemy says "Mine" of everything on the pedantic, legalistic ground that He made it: Our Father hopes in the end to say "Mine" of all things on the more realistic and dynamic ground of conquest.[33]

The freedom to give generously and to live free from anxiety, by contrast, is founded on the conviction that not just our things, but our very selves, belong to God. To claim all that is ours as "the gifts of God for the people of God" is to relearn and rediscover a creation to be gratefully celebrated, rather than consumed by greed.

6

ANGER

HOLY EMOTION OR HELLISH PASSION?

[Wrath] is the love of justice perverted into the desire for revenge and for the injury of someone else; justice is the proclaimed motive for every manifestation of Wrath.—Henry Fairlie, *The Seven Deadly Sins Today*

Not forgiving is like drinking rat poison and then waiting for the rat to die.—Anne Lamott, *Traveling Mercies*

The power of anger is actually the power of resistance in the soul.—Josef Pieper, *The Four Cardinal Virtues*

To Be Angry or Not To Be Angry? That is the Question.

Is it bad to be angry? When we picture anger, it can be ugly and violent, or invigorating and alive with passion. There is something inspiring about Martin Luther King Jr. denouncing injustice from the pulpit. If he had not been angry at racial injustice, his words would have

117

lacked the right force. As one author said of Jesus, "I am unable to commit to any messiah who doesn't knock over tables."[1] But anger can destroy too—we are aghast at the frenzied wrath of an abusive parent lashing out at a child, and dumbstruck at the animosity with which ordinary citizens turn on someone who has done them harm. I will never forget a television interview with the vengeful mother of a child who had been killed by a drunk driver. Fists raised, her face contorted with rage, she denounced the justice system for failing to dole out the death penalty. In her wrath, she demanded nothing less than a life for a life—the *lex talionis* served up with relish.

Anger is a complicated case. The Bible tells us that even God burns with anger. Every mass includes a "*dies irae*"—fear the day of the Lord's wrath! But the apostle Paul's "sin lists" invariably include a warning against fits of anger or wrath (e.g., Gal. 5:20; Col. 3:8). And most of what scripture has to say about anger is negative.

The Christian tradition is divided about anger and has been from the beginning. Anger, for Thomas Aquinas, is a natural expression of human passions, one response among many aroused by threats to ourselves and others. Anger is not inherently bad, although it becomes disordered when it attacks the wrong target or gets out of control. Those who take this view of anger are careful to distinguish anger, the *passion*, a part of normal human emotional makeup, from wrath, the *vice*, which is anger in its sinful, excessive, misdirected form.[2]

Aquinas goes further to claim that anger is a response to injustice: it requires recognition that someone has been wronged, followed by a subsequent desire to set things right. Anger is not simply lashing out at any hurtful thing, but a response that tracks retributive justice. So Aquinas says that anger is the instrument of justice, so long as (quoting Gregory the Great) we never let it "withdraw from following reason like a handmaid ready to render service."[3] The model for rightly expressed and targeted anger is Christ. Aquinas argues that the Gospels describe Jesus as a human being with the full complement of sinless emotions—from sorrow to anger to delight—but whose character was nonetheless defined by the virtue of gentleness.

On the other side of the Christian tradition stand thinkers like John Cassian, who counsel that anger is rarely if ever justified. Like the apostle James, he argues that "[our] anger does not produce God's righteousness" (1:20), and likely not anything righteous at all. Anger can be properly directed only at our own sin, and perhaps the evil demons that incite us to it, never at a human being. Love of neighbor precludes anger targeted at another. Evagrius, likewise, warns of anger's power to perturb prayer:

> Everything you do to avenge yourself against a brother who has wronged you will become a stumbling block for you at the time of prayer . . . When you are praying as you should, such things will come over you that you may think it utterly just to resort to anger, but there is absolutely no such thing as just anger against your neighbor. If you search you will find (cf. Matt. 7:7) that it is possible even without anger for the matter to be settled properly. Therefore, make use of every means to avoid an outburst of anger.[4]

Cassian describes anger in terms of its blinding effect:

> For any reason whatsoever the movement of wrath may boil over and blind the eyes of the heart, obstructing the vision [of another's fault] with the deadly beam of a more vehement illness [our own sin] and not allowing the sun of righteousness [Christ] to be seen. It is irrelevant whether a layer of gold or one of lead or of some other metal is placed over the eyes; the preciousness of the metal [i.e., the righteousness of the motive] does not change the fact of blindness.[5]

Their concern is that anger so disturbs reason that it twists any real concern about sin or injustice into service of the self—protecting our own ego, demanding something from the world we would not reasonably expect for anyone else, feeding our own reputations for righteousness instead of admitting our complicity. True selflessness would eliminate anger. When Cassian comments on Ephesians 4:31—"All anger and indignation and uproar and blasphemy should be removed from you"—he says, "When [the apostle] says, 'All anger should be removed from you,' he makes *no exception at all* for us as to necessity and utility."[6]

While both sides seem to agree that anger must be directed at the sin to be put right, not at the sinner, they seem to disagree about whether anger is something we should strive to moderate or work to eliminate altogether.[7] Perhaps there is wisdom in both positions. In a world full of injustice, it is hard to imagine a right response that doesn't include anger. At the same time, given how much of our anger is selfish, rather than just, practicing the regular purgation of anger would likely be a worthwhile discipline for us.

Target Practice

If anger can be a healthy emotion as well as a hellish habit, if it is something we can use well or badly, then what marks the difference between good anger and the vice of wrath?

On Aquinas's analysis, anger is a type of emotional force of resistance or attack that wells up within us when something blocks our way to something good. It attacks obstacles so that we can successfully reach a good goal. This means it's a complex emotion. It combines open antagonism toward the obstacle (the cause of injustice) with a passionate devotion to the good (reestablishing justice) that lies behind it. Or as Aquinas puts it elsewhere, "Anger regards two objects, viz, the retribution that it seeks, and the person on whom it seeks retribution."[8] When things go well, the retribution or redress of a wrong is sought as a good, and the harm of punishment for the offender (which is an evil) is sought for its sake. Righteous anger therefore expresses the desire to punish injustice, not because we delight in the evil of punishment as evil, but because punishment is required to redress a wrong. The end that moves the rightly angered person is the good of justice, a desire for things to be made right between persons. It is a testimony to the power of the good of justice that the wrongly angered person also perceives his or her end as just, or works hard to rationalize it as such, even when it is not. In both cases, we acknowledge justice—whether real or apparent—to be a great and greatly motivating good, and the banner under which our anger marches. Recall that the capital vices are defined as desires for great goods, which, when pursued wrongly or excessively, tend to produce much other sin. Thus, the excellence and desirability of its self-proclaimed end make wrath a capital vice, as does its "impetuosity," since wrath easily incites us to many other sinful actions by its force. Wrath is also a human sin, for it requires that those who have it be the sorts of creatures with a capacity to recognize and care about justice. Wrath's disorder requires that we have a sense of justice to be perverted.

Anger as a passion is also experienced physically and can thus be difficult to hide—our faces get red, our adrenaline surges, our hearts beat faster, and our blood pressure rises. Even in its effect on our bodies, it makes us alert and ready for action. Anger is the "fighting" half of our "fight or flight" response to danger, evil, and difficulty. As such, it can be our ally in action, by helping us deal with both inner and outer difficulties or threats that would otherwise hold us

back. Someone who would otherwise be too shy may need the push
of anger to stand up and speak out. Someone who would otherwise
feel too weak and afraid may fight beyond the limit of her power if
anger fires her spirit. A complacent congregation may need anger to
lift it out of indifference and mobilize it into action. Aquinas goes
so far as to say that the lack of anger can even be a sin, because it
indicates a "weak movement" or a failure to engage on the part of
our will.[9] His view of human virtue is holistic: given that we are
embodied beings, a wholehearted will for justice should also engage
the passions and the body.

But if anger is in for a fight, then to stay clear of being a vice, it
must fight the good fight. This means fighting for a good cause *and*
fighting well. Anger must serve the cause, not the other way around.
Venting the emotion is not itself the point; in fact, expressing anger
in order to let off steam is often a moral mistake. Aquinas observes
that it is true of all sins against temperance—among which anger,
lust, and gluttony are all numbered—that, like two-year-olds, the
passions get more unruly and hard to control the more we indulge
them.[10] The goal of restraining anger is to keep reason's judgment
clear. The fittingness of anger's expression is measured by whether
it effectively furthers the goal of justice or whether it merely destroys
everything in its path—including the good it was originally fighting
for, or even the angry person herself.

This is usually a pretty tall order. Garret Keizer confesses that he
wrote his book on anger because: "My anger has often seemed out of
proportion—that is, too great or too little, more often too great—for
the occasion that gave rise to it. My anger has more often distressed
those I love than it has afflicted those at whom I was angry. [And] my
anger has not carried me far enough toward changing what legitimately
enrages me."[11] While admitting that anger can be a natural and healthy
God-given emotion, we have to come to grips with the fact that more
often than not, our anger burns out of control.

When it is good, anger is a passion for justice, motivated by love
for others. We get angry when someone we care about is hurt or
threatened. This person may be ourselves or a "neighbor whom we
love as ourselves." This is often most intensely expressed in families,
where ties of love are strongest: novelist Alan Paton described one
mother as "like a tigress for the child."[12] The fiercer the love and the
greater the good at stake, the more intense our capacity for anger.
Great love is the root of great anger. You don't get angry unless you

care. Like all the passions, for Aquinas, anger is rooted ultimately in love. Apathy is the tepid alternative to both love and anger. At its best, and rightly expressed, anger is "the power of resistance in the soul,"[13] a passionate protector and defender of good.

Anger turns vicious, however, when it fights for its own selfish cause, not for justice, and when it fights dirty. That is, anger becomes a vice when there are problems with its target—whatever it is that makes us angry—or with the way we try to hit that target—how we express our anger. Let's look at each of these problems in turn.

First, good anger fights for a good cause. The vice of wrath turns a passion for justice into a passion for self-aggrandizement. I want what I want, and woe to anyone or anything that gets in my way. The cause it promotes is the Me-First Agenda. "[Wrath's] purpose and desire is to eliminate any obstacle to our self-seeking, to retaliate against any threat to our security, to avenge any insult or injury to our person."[14] Anger's fighting power is directed toward protecting me and my interests, to the exclusion of the claims of others. A slight to my honor, damage to my reputation, disrespect to my person—these are frequent anger triggers. "The underlying message of highly angry people," according to the American Psychological Association website, is that " 'things oughta go my way!' Angry people tend to feel that . . . any blocking or changing of their plans is an unbearable indignity and that they should not have to suffer this way. Maybe other people do, but not them!"

It is a common experience to respond more to the apparent insolence of another's action against you than to the gravity of the crime itself. It is the disrespect that rankles and inclines us to avenge without thought and without measure. Do we typically get as angry about an injustice done to others as we do about a cutting personal insult to ourselves? Where does our own honor and status rank among the goods our anger rises to safeguard and avenge? Does our image of a just universe mean that things have to go "our way" and we will personally take it upon ourselves to set them right if they don't? Wrathful people's need to have their own way and their overprotectiveness about their own honor and status are clues to wrath's roots in pride. On the other hand, good anger depends on a rightful sense of what is "due," either to oneself or another, and a sense of what justice requires. Differentiating justice from self-justification is not always easily done. But as the opening quote from Henry Fairlie shows, it is crucial, lest our "love of justice [be] perverted into the desire for revenge and for the injury of someone" since "justice is the proclaimed motive for every manifestation of Wrath."[15]

For all its physical force and fury, anger also has a wily way of duping our reasoning powers to justify itself. And by "justify," I mean to invoke the link to justice mentioned just above. Wrath is self-promoting—but in a dressed-up, self-righteous way. We can invent all sorts of ratio-nalizations in the form of why we *deserve* what we want, why others didn't give us what we were really *owed,* why we *need* to act this way to claim *our rightful share.* With the banner of self-righteousness over us, anger can storm in and take over by force. Aquinas says that anger is an ally of justice and courage, but only if it *follows* a reasonable judgment about what is right. This is a major caveat. Too often, we begin with anger and make our best judgments its puppet.

We have said that anger can go wrong in its target *and* in the manner of its expression. When anger has the wrong object, *what* we are angry about is inappropriate. Perhaps there has been no real injury—only a misunderstanding or an imagined offense, not an actual one. Or the recipient of our anger is the wrong person . . . or the person who happens to be closest, most available, or most readily wounded—the easiest target within range. The waitress bears the wrath directed at the unsatisfactory efforts of the cook, the underpaid customer ser-vice representative bears the frustration directed at the stonewalling health care insurer, and the slight misstep of an older child receives the pent-up explosion of the parent worn down by two hours of deal-ing with an aggravatingly whiny two year old. Have you ever been guilty of lashing out at an intermediary because you could not find or fight the real offender? Perhaps we even lash out at others around us because we feel impotent shaking our fists at God. Often the real culprit in cases of wrath at the wrong object is our excessive expecta-tions of what we deserve or the sort of treatment we are due. In the tradition, one of wrath's offspring vices is to mentally magnify the offense, our woundedness, and our worthiness compared to that of the offender. If we find ourselves habitually wrathful, the first ques-tion to ask is what we are really getting angry about and why. If we are concerned that our anger is missing the right target, sometimes the best thing to do is double-check our perspective and get a second opinion on whether our anger is as justified as it feels, or whether we are rationalizing to cover up something else. We have to broaden our scope of the situation, both to include the rightful claims of others and to put our own claims into perspective.

The second way anger can go wrong is in *how* we express our anger. Anger can make us feel out of control, enraged, furious. In some medieval writings, *ira* (anger) is used to describe righteous anger, the kind that rightly expresses a just judgment, while a different word, *furor* (fury) is used to describe the form that is irrationally expressed or wildly disproportionate.[16] Even if we have a legitimate grievance, we can deal with it in destructive and disastrous ways. A quick scan of a biblical concordance yields a dozen passages, most of them from Proverbs, giving counsel about anger. Interestingly, none of these mentions a single word about the *object* of our anger. The passages on anger's rightful expression can be briefly summarized in the advice, "Cool it."

Aquinas breaks down wrath's disordered expression into three main categories. We can get angry too easily (for example, when we are quick-tempered); we can get angrier than we should (for instance, when our anger is disproportionate to the offense); and we can stay angry too long (that is, when anger smolders into resentment and grudge holding).

The first type often takes the form of irritability. When anger poisons our mood, every little thing sets us off. We feel quarrelsome and contrary. We respond to the slightest provocation with bickering, rudeness, complaint, annoyance, cutting remarks, and profanity.

A prototypical case of the second type is the familiar "blow-up" scene, complete with shouting and door slamming. The blow-up is often ostensibly over some small incident, but the excessiveness of the emotion betrays an accumulation of grievances or a perceived assault on one's ego. The excess of our anger is a symptom that we see some bigger issue here—as when the oldest child's angry outburst is not merely over having to wash the dishes two nights in a row while her younger siblings get off easy. It is about the fairness of her role in the family, the way her parents always single her out for more responsibility, and the injustice of being held to higher standards of behavior than the other siblings are. Her life is just not fair! And given her self-importance, she feels like this sort of injustice must not be tolerated with equanimity. The cumulative effect of her long-nurtured resentments in this area and the demands of the self behind them mean that she is already primed and ready for an excuse to bring it up on even the slightest provocation, and that her reaction will be proportionate to the long years of unjust treatment by her parents, not this single event. There may well be other, more serious occasions in which we have a legitimate grievance, but the way we demand that it be redressed is excessive, due to overblown anger and an overblown sense of what we are owed.

Holding on to our anger too long is the third way our expression of anger becomes vicious. Resentment is often expressed in sullenness, the refusal to forgive or to accept reconciliation, fantasizing about vengeance, or passive-aggressive tactics like spoiling another's pleasure by being uncooperative or disdainful, letting our anger out in relentless pinpricks rather than mighty blows and great shouts. We spend our time plotting revenge and taking consolation in our fantasies of getting back at another person, showing them what they deserve. Grudge holding and nurturing resentment, even for real harm done in the past, also make us more prone to the first two vicious ways of expressing anger. When resentment smolders beneath the surface, we go through the day like a snake poised to strike at the first sign of movement (we become quick-tempered), and our anger at the present moment swells to the size of the whole history of harm done (our anger is disproportionate to the offense). All anger is in danger of rationalization, but resentment more than anything perhaps can distort the truthfulness of our memory. As the saying goes, "The older I get, the more vividly I remember things that never happened."

Worst of all, wrath can go wrong in several of these ways all at once, as when we get excessively angry or stay angry much too long at someone who does not deserve it all. All expressions of wrath move us beyond being upset about an injustice and wanting to set it right to a desire to hurt someone, to make them pay, to inflict punishment on them not as a good, but as an evil. This is what the desert fathers warned about, and what Aquinas says distinguishes cases of wrath from the passion of anger.

In the Christian tradition of the capital vices, wrath's "offspring" vices primarily catalog the manifestations of wrath, both internal and external. Wrath leads us to demean our offender by magnifying our own importance and the gravity of the offense. Today, we might call this the first mental step in rationalizing an excessive response. It also leads us to plot all manner of revenge, whether we intend to carry it out or simply savor it in our fantasies. Our speech and words also express wrath: these sinful habits include angry outbursts, insulting others, and blaspheming God. Finally, wrath can lead us to deeds, especially those that inflict injury and even kill.

Sword in Hand

In my collection of cultural artifacts based on the seven deadly sins, I have a book containing "a lavish collection of wicked home interiors" depicting each one of the seven deadly sins. One of my favorites is a photograph of a large crystal chandelier lying smashed on the floor, with a crystal-handled knife plunged into the middle of the heap of shattered, sparkling rubble. The authors call it an "unsettling still life."[17] Although wrath—along with lust and gluttony—is one of the "warm" sins, and the wrathful are often called "hot-blooded," the effects of wrath are ultimately chilling.

In *The Mission*, a film depicting the eighteenth-century European colonization of South America, we find another set of portraits, this time contrasting wrath at its most murderous with righteous anger at its most loving.[18] In the first scene, Rodrigo (Robert De Niro) is a slave trader returning from a recent foray into the jungle. Looking for the woman he loves, he discovers her in bed with his brother, Felipe. He storms out of the room in furious silence. His brother hastily dresses and rushes after him, begging for understanding. Words clash, and soon swords. The fight ends when Rodrigo stabs his brother and then stands over him and watches him die. Rodrigo's anger expresses itself in vengeful and deadly harm to his own brother, over a woman to whom he claimed exclusive rights, although he had not married her.

Rodrigo is overcome by remorse. Father Gabriel (Jeremy Irons) hears his confession. Rodrigo eventually becomes a priest and follows Father Gabriel to a remote native village above the great waterfall, where the Guarini Indians have become Christians and the Jesuits have established a mission. A short time later, the peaceful village is threatened with extinction when the slave trade is extended above the falls. Rodrigo has renounced the sword and become a Catholic priest—forbidden to take up arms and use violence against another, because he stands *in persona Christi*. How will he and Father Gabriel confront those who come with military might to destroy the village and enslave its people?

In the second scene, Rodrigo enters Father Gabriel's room and declares his intention to renounce his priestly vows, take up the sword again, and fight in the villagers' defense. Father Gabriel, who is usually a gentle, humble, and soft-spoken man, turns on him in anger. "You should never have become a priest!" he tells Rodrigo. The world will always try to solve its problems with violence, death, and the power of the sword, he argues passionately. If you want to help the villagers, "then help them *as a priest!*"

To take up the sword would undercut not only Rodrigo's vows but also all their work with the Guarini. In one last appeal, Father Gabriel vehemently admonishes Rodrigo, "You have given your life to God, and *God is love!*" As we see in a later scene, he has not rejected Rodrigo, despite being grieved to the core at his actions. His vehement words are inspired by equally vehement love and concern for Rodrigo's spiritual well-being and for God's honor. His words are meant to teach and correct Rodrigo, not to wound him. In fact, what he pleads for is not his own way but what he believes *God* is due. Even though he is Rodrigo's superior in the Jesuit order, his words and manner clearly show that it is Rodrigo's disobedience to God that troubles him, not Rodrigo's disobedience to himself. His anger betrays a deep grief and frustration at Rodrigo's choice but does not express antipathy toward the man himself. For the man is still his brother in Christ.[19]

In the end, both Rodrigo and Gabriel die, Rodrigo while fighting valiantly but futilely to defend the villagers with the sword, and Gabriel while solemnly carrying the eucharistic host out of the village church, offering it to the attacking enemy. Rodrigo lived by the sword, and he died by it. Even though he wielded it in the end not for his own selfish interests but for the love of others and what he thought was justice, from a greater perspective, his just cause was still really his desire to make things right himself, in this world, and by his own might.

What is the difference between Rodrigo's anger at his brother and Gabriel's anger at Rodrigo? In the first scene, Rodrigo's wrath is motivated by self-centered love—a woman he presumed to claim as his own. Moreover, his ill will toward his brother culminates in murder—a death that brings grief and harm to himself, his brother, and the woman they both wanted. Gabriel, on the other hand, is motivated by concern for Rodrigo's spiritual good, the spiritual good of the villagers, and the honor God was due. His anger did not have much if anything to do with what he claimed for himself. And it was expressed in a passionate admonition to be faithful to God's way, not harmful blows or words designed to wound. Rodrigo's wrath shows us anger that is both misdirected and disproportionate, aroused by selfish desires and rationalizations to cover them. Gabriel shows us anger in the service of justice and love, anger that seeks to win the offender back, rather than inflicting harm on him for harm's sake or to assuage an offended ego. His anger—in both its object and its manner of expression—respected what was due to God and neighbor; Rodrigo's violated it.

God's Anger

From the stereotypical portrayals of an Old Testament God of wrath to Jonathan Edwards's famous sermon "Sinners in the Hands of an Angry God," our expectations about what scripture actually says about God's anger might be misconceived. What is God angry about, and how does he get angry? In the Old Testament, the majority of passages mentioning God's wrath are found in the Pentateuch and the Prophets. This is worth noting because before we even look them up, we can anticipate the results. The first five books of the Bible deal with the giving of the law to Israel—the terms of the covenant and the Ten Commandments. The prophets in turn deal out warnings aplenty about Israel's breaking of the covenant and the law. The people's sins of idolatry and lack of mercy toward the poor and needy are the focus of the prophets' concern. God's wrath is thus inspired when we are unfaithful to him and when we oppress the powerless—in other words, when we disobey the first and second tables of the law: love God above all and your neighbor as yourself (e.g., Matt. 22:37–39; Mark 12:29–31). Aquinas explains the commandments as moral precepts laying out the demands of basic justice, although these precepts are perfectly fulfilled only by love. When we transgress justice—what is owed to God or our neighbor—we arouse God's anger. When our self-love edges out neighbor-love and love for God—we can expect to find God angry. Why is God angry? Because he is loving and just. What is God angry about? People who fail to offer one another and God what is due. And what is due is love.

Many of us would identify Jesus's clearing of the temple as an act of anger, and a violent one at that, but three gospels describe his action, not his inner state (John quotes scripture to describe him as "consumed" with "zeal"). In a different story, however, Mark explicitly describes Jesus as angry (Mark 3:1–6). Jesus's anger in this New Testament passage parallels the Old Testament portrait above. Despite its brevity, it is a poignant and moving account, worth quoting in full:

Again [Jesus] entered the synagogue, and a man was there who had a withered hand. They watched him to see whether he would cure him on the sabbath, so that they might accuse him. And he said to the man who had the withered hand, "Come forward." Then he said to them, "Is it lawful to do good or to do harm on the sabbath, to save life or to kill?" But they were silent. He looked around at them with anger; he was grieved at their hardness of heart and said to the man, "Stretch out your hand." He stretched it out, and his hand was restored. The Pharisees went out and immediately conspired with the Herodians against him, how to destroy him.

Mark's Gospel is notoriously terse, but he spends a whole verse describing Jesus's feelings in this passage. What angers Jesus? He is grieved at the Pharisees' lack of love for another human being, at the hardness of their hearts toward a man in need. He is angry that they care more about being justified by their own rule-keeping than about the restoration that God's kingdom justice brings, and that they value the maintenance of their own reputation and status more than healing and compassion. Their sense of "due" has everything to do with self-interest and precious little to do with justice toward God or neighbor, despite their ostensible piety. They are cold keepers of the letter of the law, ignoring the justice and love that inspired its commands.

"What is the law really about?" is Jesus's real question to them. Is Sabbath keeping and its strictures about honoring God, or is it about your own honor? The teachers of the law stand before Jesus in stony silence. It is not that they are dumbfounded by his wisdom; rather, they stubbornly refuse to give him the satisfaction of an answer. They will not be moved by love.

Jesus is angry because he loves the man with the shriveled hand, and because he sees that the Pharisees do not. But Jesus is angry because he loves the Pharisees too and is frustrated—in Mark's words, "grieved at their hardness of heart"—because they won't let God's love reach them. The minute Jesus leaves, they turn their thoughts toward killing him. The Pharisees here illustrate Buechner's point about anger:

Of the Seven Deadly Sins, anger is possibly the most fun. To lick your wounds, to smack your lips over grievances long past, to roll over your tongue the prospect of bitter confrontations still to come, to savor to the last toothsome morsel both the pain you are given and the pain

you are giving back—in many ways it is a feast fit for a king. The chief
drawback is that what you are wolfing down is yourself. The skeleton
at the feast is you.[20]

Jesus sees past their desire to wound him to the effect of their
anger on the man with the withered hand and on themselves. As
deeply angry as he is at their stubborn refusal to love, how does he
respond to them? By lashing out with words or whips? Jesus does not
retaliate or do harm. But neither does he back down. He simply heals
the man. He loves; he restores the man to wholeness; he does what is
right—according to God's justice. He does it right in front of them,
on their supposed turf, in violation of their supposedly righteous
Sabbath laws. He counters their stubborn refusal to do justice and
love mercy with a picture of God's love and justice. And in doing so,
he is a picture of self-possession.

Anger, when it is a *holy* emotion, has *justice* as its object and *love*
as its root. Both love and justice are focused on the good of others.
Justice concerns giving to another what that other is due. Good anger
is expressed in passionate efforts to make sure others get the respect
they deserve, to bring about the end of oppression and tyranny, to
give due punishment to those who cause injury and damage, to honor
covenants and promises, to give equal treatment to the marginalized,
and to uphold the law. Motivated by good anger, we hunger and thirst
for righteousness, an appetite that depends on justice for its object, but
on love for its right expression. Anger in these cases adds energy and
passion to the execution of justice. The love that underlies it, however,
keeps it in check, for love does not seek to destroy the other, but to set
things right. In this way, our anger can imitate God's in its object.

Vicious anger, by contrast, is self-regarding and selfish. The wrathful seek revenge, not due punishment; they protect their own honor
and cause at all costs, instead of defending what is truly good or
deserved. Unhinged from justice, bad anger aims at another's injury,
rather than another's good. This is why, in his Sermon on the Mount,
Jesus links wrath and wrathful insults to murder: "You have heard
that it was said to those of ancient times, 'You shall not murder'; and
'whoever murders shall be liable to judgment.' But I say to you that if
you are angry with a brother or sister, you will be liable to judgment;
and if you insult a brother or sister, you will be liable to the council;
and if you say, 'You fool,' you will be liable to the hell of fire" (Matt.
5:21–22). These words are not designed to even the score—they are

designed to harm and destroy.[21] As Martin Luther King Jr. once put it, "Returning violence for violence multiplies violence, adding deeper darkness to a night already devoid of stars . . . Hate cannot drive out hate: only love can do that."[22]

The virtue opposed to wrath in Aquinas's *Summa theologiae* is gentleness, but it is probably better described as "self-possession." People with this virtue keep anger as a finely tuned instrument of their will and do not let it master them. In the tradition there is a master–servant metaphor used to describe anger. Anger is first aroused by reason's recognition of an injury and a desire to set it right. But like a "hasty servant,"[23] the passion then runs off to attack without listening to the rest of reason's command regarding how to go about redressing the wrong. This is why Gregory and Cassian describe anger as "blind": the passion is a force without direction, because it has not been disciplined to listen to reason and follow its direction. When wrath becomes a habit, we learn to see the world through angry eyes: laden with an excessive sense of our own entitlements, we let anger direct reason's vision and judgment, rather than the other way around.

Our anger can align itself with God's anger in choosing justice as its object—justice defined by God's terms, not our own. In addition, we can be like God in *how* we get angry. Here again, we face some common misperceptions of scripture. Is God's usual method of expressing anger to rain down fire and brimstone?

When I teach the vice of anger to my students, I have them look up scripture passages about how God gets angry. The long list of texts stretches through Exodus, Numbers, Nehemiah, Psalms, Jonah . . . and after a few of them, a recurrent theme quickly emerges. A single verse is repeated verbatim time and time again, as if to pound the idea into the reader's heart. "The LORD is merciful and gracious, slow to anger and abounding in steadfast love" (Ps. 103:8).[24] Like a constant refrain in the narrative of Israel's history, this theme resounds. Your God is slow to anger; he abounds in steadfast love.

There are undoubtedly many ways God's anger should be different from ours.[25] He has all of human history in view; our perspective of what is just may perhaps always be too small to adequately honor God's plans and purposes. More importantly, it is simply not our job to secure ultimate justice in the universe as if we were the God in charge. Perhaps this is why Paul warns the Christians in Rome against prideful expressions of anger, "Beloved, never avenge yourselves, but leave room for the wrath of God; for it is written, 'Vengeance is mine, I will repay, says the Lord' " (Rom. 12:19). We should not dole out retribution as if we were gods; our anger must show that we remember we are stewards under a God who remains in providential control. Still, there are ways our anger *should* imitate God's, and scripture's constant refrain seems to offer us the best model of how that should look. Like Jesus in Mark's Gospel, like Jesus on the cross, we can be passionate about God's justice, and yet be slow to anger and abounding in steadfast love. A passion for justice is consistent with self-possession.

We have noted that Proverbs is the book of scripture with the most information about how we should be angry. In Proverbs 14:16–17; 17:27; 22:24–25; 29:1 and 29:22, to sample just a few passages, the writer warns against flying off the handle, becoming quickly and easily enraged, being hotheaded and too quick to anger. This theme about human anger is repeated almost as many times as the refrain about God's anger, balancing point with counterpoint. James's words in the New Testament—"Let everyone be quick to listen, slow to speak, slow to anger; for your anger does not produce God's righteousness" (1:19–20)—furthermore suggest that the "what" and "how" of our anger are connected. When we take for ourselves the responsibility for making everything right, and rely on our own power and plans for effecting justice, our anger becomes excessive, aroused too quickly and too easily and smoldering too long when unassuaged. The problem with human wrath is not merely the damage to others it may or may not inflict, but the heart-problem behind our anger's excess.

Even when we think we have a just cause in view, then, easily triggered and excessively vehement or long-lasting anger is a warning symptom. It is as if we—like Rodrigo and unlike Father Gabriel—do not have enough patience to trust God to ultimately make things right, if not in this world, then in the next. Even when we believe there is a just cause at stake, and rightly so, *how* we get angry and *how* we express our anger can also show us the ways our own agendas and timetables intrude. Wariness over the temptation to wrath should *not* temper our passion for justice now; rather, it *should* keep our anger and its frustration focused on God's agenda. Keeping our anger under control allows us to keep a clear view of the goal—justice, the need of the people for whom we will it, and the humanness of those who currently thwart it. Martin Luther King Jr., for example, was undoubtedly passionate in his pursuit of racial justice, but he was not a person dominated by anger or one who hated his racial oppressors.

His passion for justice was deeply rooted in his desire that all people learn to love one another and see others as God sees them, and his manner of pursuing justice showed that he knew that the matter was not solely in his hands. The righteously angry person can still pray, "Not my will, but yours be done." Moreover, King engaged in his project among a community of believers. He did not attempt to discern God's will all by himself or mete out God's judgment as an individual. The checks and balances of shared power and wisdom are good ways to prevent wrathful rationalizations about the ways our agendas and God's do or do not coincide.

Anger and Control

Why is wrath, or vicious anger, such a temptation for us? Anger is deeply connected to our love of ourselves, especially our fear of exposure and our need for security. We seem to be in the constant business of bolstering our fragile egos, but the results are extremely tenuous and easily threatened. When it comes to injuries and insults to our honor, anger "takes it personally."

When children ignore a parent's order to come in for dinner, it may well be because they are just happily preoccupied with their play. But a parent can read this as a flagrant act of contemptuous disrespect. When a professor criticizes his colleague's ideas publicly in book review, it's not that he thinks of it as anything other than doing a careful analysis of an idea he judges wrongheaded. The colleague, however, easily sees the situation as a deliberate attack of sabotage on his reputation.

In these cases, the tendency to get angry, or overly angry, seems rooted in vulnerability and fear. Is the parent's sense of authority so frail that she can't let a single act of careless disrespect slide off? Is the colleague's professional reputation so tenuous that one public criticism will ruin it? Their angry response shows that they have lost their sense of perspective and misjudged others' malice out of a heightened sense of their own vulnerability to attack. Their view of reality, of others' motives, and even of themselves is warped by anger.

Anger often rains down with a big show of force, but perhaps the force is a big cover-up, an overcompensation for our own perceived weakness and vulnerability. Like a wounded animal backed into a corner, we're on the defensive and lashing out because we feel threatened.

Aren't we overly eager to rise to our own defense especially when we feel afraid of what others might think? It seems that anger's roots may tap into fear as much as in pride. Or better yet, the fear that is born of trusting oneself in pride is opposed to the freedom and peace of trusting God for assurance and love. If we can look only to ourselves for an ally and a source of security when we are threatened, then we would do well to be afraid . . . and angry.

Our bad anger thus shows us to be trying—and failing—to be God. We are wrathful when we can't control things that hurt us and keep them at bay. Our anger is ready to remedy this vulnerability by taking full control of establishing justice in the world and avenging any wrongs against us. Wrath's expression therefore usually involves the assertion of control, even as—ironically enough—we lose control over ourselves when we are angry. The wrathful presume to judge impartially, when really they are blinded by a selfishly one-sided view of the world. They hand down the punishment they think others deserve, when in truth they are cutting down anything in their path with indiscriminate or disproportionate vengeance. The need to have control, the impatience that things be put things right immediately, the obsessive preoccupation with getting one's own way—all indicate the inner view of one dominated by wrath, a wrath anchored in pride.

Wrath can also be a mask for other sorts of distress. For example, it is easier to lash out at others in a purported show of strength than to acknowledge what's really eating us up inside. Even in grief, it is easier to shake your fist at God than to live face to face with sorrow that won't go away. To be angry is to feel in control again, to assert our will against a world not aligned with it. Anger presumes the power to fix things, to change things—this is why it can also be an effective ally of the will in executing justice. The world just seems unfair sometimes, and although we know deep down there's little we can do to change that, anger tempts us to deny and resist that fact. It's much easier to be angry than to be helpless, to be angry than to accept suffering. The presumption of control also means we often prefer to stay angry than to seek reconciliation or forgiveness after a conflict that causes us pain.

Aquinas defines sorrow as feeling oppressed by a real and present evil of which we cannot rid ourselves. Sorrow overcomes us with its weight, while anger moves us to strike out against the evil. Anger trades on the assumption that we can do something to remedy the problem, since its job is to aid the will in executing justice. In this

sense, anger is a more hopeful emotion, because it is willing to try
to conquer the evil or remove the obstacle. But anger has to proceed
with its eyes open, rather than blindly lashing out. The situation has
to hold out a real problem to be conquered—not one imagined or
rationalized into being. And the problem has to be conquerable by
anger's efforts, rather than being amenable to some other solution—
"a gentle answer," for example.

Antidotes for Anger

How do we know if we have a problem with wrath—the hellish habit
rather than the holy emotion? One suggestion for self-examination
is to try keeping a journal for a week. The journal is meant to be a
record of the times we were angry and what we were angry about.
(If we find that we need to write a paragraph to justify what we were
angry about, we might want to take this fact itself as a hint about the
excessive nature of our anger and our need to rationalize it!) Then rate
the intensity of each episode recorded on a scale from one to five. After
the week is over, shut the journal and put it away for another week.
Returning to it later, we will find that the journal's records allow us
to take stock—after we have cooled off and the incidents provoking
anger are over and done—of how angry we have been and why. Look
for patterns that emerge. With evidence in hand, we can ask: Were we
angry too often? Were we often too angry? Frequently, reactions that
seemed perfectly justified and rational look petty and self-serving in
retrospect, and the situations that occasioned our anger seem more
trivial than genuinely offensive. This record is also useful in helping
us see better what sorts of things tend to set us off.

   Upon checking the list again, do we find ourselves still feeling resentful about any of the incidents recorded? Reasonably so? If someone
were watching the videotape of events, rather than our edited version,
would they come to the same conclusion? If we are still resentful, can
we stop playing the tapes over and over in our heads, choosing instead
to play something else whenever the thought comes up? Even further,
can we destroy lingering evidence of the offense so that we aren't
reminding ourselves of it frequently? (The assumption of course, in
these recommendations, is that the list of incidents will indeed be
occasions of excessive or misdirected anger. But even when the anger
was over a legitimate object, we may find that we can endorse the

judgment that we were wronged far more easily than we can endorse the way we expressed that judgment in the situation.)

Strategies like this are a sort of "time out" that creates distance from the intensity of wrathful anger. If we can achieve reflective distance, we may also try for a more long-term solution by investigating exactly what our expectations were in the situations where our anger was disordered and excessive. Were our expectations realistic—about what we deserve, what we need, what others deserve, and what others need? Are we assuming an overinflated sense of our place and status? (Here again, wrath's roots in pride tend to show themselves.) Is our wrath a defensive cover-up for something else? Are we afraid that the truth about ourselves will come to light? When do we feel most threatened and likely to lash out?

Because wrath is so often rooted in unholy expectations—both of what we are due and what others are due—dealing with this vice requires setting realistic expectations and realizing that the claims we make on the world may be overinflated by our fragile or arrogant egos. A sense of humor is the opposite of wrath's reaction, because the one who can laugh at himself has enough distance from what he wants to be able to deflate his own claims and see them as comically excessive. He is not so intensely concerned with pushing his own way that he cannot step back and see himself as others see him. Wrath narrows our vision of the world, even as it slants our sense of justice toward selfishness. When we can joke about a situation, we have to be comfortable enough with who we are to laugh at our claims on the world, rather than being consumed by them.

Anger is also a bodily emotion, however. That means it can arise when our bodies are strained and overstretched, and that also means we have to honor our embodied condition if we are to remain "slow to anger." Bodily unrest, as well as mental weariness, can make us prone to wrath. Listening to calm music, getting enough sleep, taking a warm bath, getting exercise to burn off tension, finding a place to be alone or have enough space, or receiving a comforting touch from another can also help our bodies resist and recover from the injuries, stressors, and attacks that might otherwise be occasions to "fight" against with wrath. Like the mental discipline of clearing the mind and thinking of something else, rather than running replays of the offending situation to stoke your emotions, sometimes we just need to physically remove ourselves from a situation, take a deep breath, and give ourselves the resources to calm down.

As important as they are, the physical strategies for handling anger are strategies for symptom control. They do not get at the source of the problem. And wrath—as a vice—is a heart-and-mind problem. Unlearning the habit of wrath requires a change of heart, a reordering of priorities, a transformation of one's vision. Once we realize that pride is the root of wrath, when we dig deep to discover the causes of our wrath, we must face our assumptions about who we think we really are, how much control over ourselves and our world we desire and assume we have, what makes us feel threatened and what makes us feel secure. Whereas wrath is rooted in pride, the strength of gentleness and the steadfastness of love in the face of adversity are rooted in a deep trust in God to handle things. How would our angry habits change if we focused more on God's justice and his control than our own claims and our ability to secure them against all threats?

If we can get to the bottom of our vicious anger—that desire to avenge ourselves on others rather than to work against the evil that threatens all of us—we may also find ourselves readier to accept the grace to help us master it. Then we can practice the virtue of gentleness and say with Jesus, "I am gentle and humble in heart" (Matt. 11:29). Humility is a virtue that keeps our claims on the world truthful and restrained. Humility and gentleness are twin powers against wrath, and both are rooted in love, a love that "does not insist on its own way" (see 1 Cor. 13:4–7).

Gentleness, a virtue that imitates Christ's own character, does not imply that he or we never get angry. Nor does it imply that we should never press claims of justice against others. It is that anger should not be the primary mark of our character. Jesus might well have been intensely angry when he cleared the temple of the money changers, and he of all human beings must have been acutely aware of the abundance of injustice in the world, but no one would dream of describing him as the wrathful type. Those with the virtue of gentleness have mastered their anger, rather than being mastered by it. When they act with anger, they channel its power rather than being swept away by it. But gentleness as a character trait—a deeply embedded virtue—depends on much more than just the power of self-restraint. Gentleness depends closely on humility in that it does not put what is due oneself at the center of attention. It does not have to hold the reins of the universe. It responds instead from a heart that acknowledges and trusts the mysterious combination of justice and mercy that is God's way of setting things right. Humility counters the prideful impulse to take over full control when things don't go our way, as well as the unyielding assertion of one's own will and the expectation of honor from others that lies behind so many occasions of wrath. Both gentleness and humility get their strength from trusting God's power and will. When we confront and counteract a wrathful view of the world, along with our power and place in it, the occasions for anger will be fewer and easier to handle without excess and injury. With confidence that we do indeed have a role to play in addressing injustice, but acknowledging that our role is not God's role, our anger can find its rightful, effective place—helping rather than hindering our response to a world that persistently yearns for justice and restoration.

Anger, Pieper says, is "the power of resistance in the soul." Making anger a holy passion rather than a hellish habit means resisting anything that threatens our hope and confidence in carrying out God's calling, rather than resisting what God calls us to do (and not to do), when this call interferes with our own vision of the way things should be. In wrath, we ultimately want our own way. In gentle self-mastery, we pray, "Thy will be done."

7

GLUTTONY

Feeding Your Face and Starving Your Heart

A glutton is one who raids the icebox for a cure for spiritual malnutrition.—Frederick Buechner, *Wishful Thinking*

Pounds or Pleasure?

In the supermarket checkout line, the cover of *Family Circle* vividly
displays a chocolate cappuccino pie. The featured articles of the month
are "Trim Your Tummy: 10 Ways to Curb Your Cravings," and just
below it, "Irresistible Chocolate Desserts." If combating gluttony
requires curbing our cravings for the *irresistible*, it looks like the battle
against our "guilty pleasures" is one we're doomed to lose. And with
food-obsessive mixed messages like this everywhere, is it any surprise
that eating disorders are now something every middle-school kid
knows about?

Fast-food diets have sent obesity rates soaring, while the diet industry makes billions of dollars a year. Food chains are being sued

for not warning customers how many transfats are in their entrées. An elementary school's hot-lunch menu includes pizza, an ice cream sandwich, soda, and doughnuts in a single day's offering. Our craving for tasty food begins early and makes its effects felt for a lifetime—on our health, our lifestyles, and our economy.

Perhaps the most shocking thing about the vice of gluttony is that it may not have much directly to do with any of this. Our stereotypical picture of the glutton is the obese man in the cartoon, who looks at his belt after dinner and comments, "One more notch. Room for dessert," or the billboard ad for a weight loss clinic with a little alien on it warning that "when they come, they'll eat the fat ones first." The spoof ad for gluttony in *Harper's* magazine depicts an enormously overweight man leaping into a pool of water, while an audience of SeaWorld–style onlookers watches with mouths agape. The ad's caption: "The Glutton Society: Helping People Make the Most of Themselves for over 100 Years." But what if gluttony isn't first of all about overeating or being overweight, about dieting and doughnuts? What if being fat is not sinful? What if most of the gluttons among us are not those who tip the scales, but the average Christian consumer? Can the health-food eaters and the gourmets be as gluttonous as the junk-food junkies? People who carry too much weight are already the targets of ridicule and relentless castigation. Do they need to be burdened by shouldering the guilt of gluttony too, while the skinny people walk away with a clean conscience? Gluttony, like many of the other vices we are studying, has been both oversimplified and misunderstood.

As a vice, gluttony is something habitual. It is a routine, a pattern, or a groove that gets worn into our character. As a vice, it is a sinful habit. Because we can't see other people's habits, we tend to identify things by their behavioral symptoms. Gluttony's behavioral cues are more complex than we might think, however. We know gluttony must have something to do with eating, and maybe drinking too. Our certainty, however, should end there. How does the mundane act of taking in food impact our spiritual life anyway?

If there's anything simple about gluttony, it is its focus on pleasure. One's own pleasure. Excessive pleasure. Immediate, tangible pleasure.

Gluttony is really not about how much we're eating, but about how our eating reflects how much pleasure we take in eating food and why. Eating is meant to be pleasurable, and so is feeling filled after being hungry. These pleasures, the food itself, and the act of eating are all good, God-given gifts. God commanded us to eat in the garden, and the New Testament tells us that eating even foods formerly unclean is lawful. Gluttony creeps in and corrupts these pleasures when our desires for them run out of control. In 1 Corinthians 6 Paul talks about gluttony and lust in terms of being "mastered" by pleasure, and elsewhere he speaks of making a god of our stomachs (see Phil. 3:17–21). What's vicious about gluttony is that these pleasures dominate everything else that's important. This vice degrades us into being mere pleasure seekers. This is what gluttony is really all about.

The main question we should be asking is not, "How much is too much?" but rather, "How dominated by the desire for this pleasure am I? How difficult would it be to have to give it up or do without it?" The trouble with gluttony is that it reduces eating to an exercise in gratifying my own desires for physical pleasures, consuming whatever I think will make me full and satisfied. Rather than simply enjoying food, we are using it to give ourselves a needed "pleasure fix." Food and pleasure are goods, not gods. As Aquinas puts it, "Gluttony primarily and intrinsically signifies the intemperate desire to consume food, not the intemperate consumption of food." "It is a case of gluttony," he says, "only when we knowingly exceed the measure in eating from a desire for the pleasures of the palate."[1]

Gluttony's excessive pursuit of the pleasures of the table eventually dulls our appreciation for the food we eat, the pleasure we take in eating it, those with whom we eat, and the God who created what we eat and gave us the ability to take pleasure in it. As Augustine put it, "Virtuous people avail themselves of the things of this life with the moderation of a user, not the attachment of a lover."[2] Or, as Jesus Christ put it, we were not meant to live "by bread alone" (Luke 4:4).

We Like It "F.R.E.S.H."

In the Middle Ages, gluttony had its own little commercial ditty: "Too daintily, too sumptuously, too hastily, too greedily, too much." The little verse probably lacked a catchy tune, but it did have the benefit of outlining five forms of gluttony. A contemporary version of the same five uses the acronym "F.R.E.S.H.": eating fastidiously, ravenously, excessively, sumptuously, hastily. Each form of gluttony is a way of being mastered by the pleasure of eating, whether or not that shows up in our table manners or on our bathroom scales.

"Too daintily" or "fastidiously" is the first form. Along with eating "too sumptuously," it is a form of gluttony which primarily regards *what* we eat. The other three regard *how* we eat. In *The Screwtape Letters*, C. S. Lewis offers a memorable example of this form of gluttony. One devil is bragging to another that they have hoodwinked the human race into thinking that gluttony is no longer of moral concern because everyone knows that eating too much is wrong. But the devils have merely switched strategies, now cleverly tempting us into "the gluttony of delicacy" instead of "the gluttony of excess."

Here is his description of a woman with the gluttony of delicacy:

> She is a positive terror to hostesses and servants. She is always turning from what has been offered to her to say with a demure little sigh and a smile "Oh please, please . . . *all* I want is a cup of tea, weak but not too weak, and the teeniest weeniest bit of really crisp toast." You see? Because what she wants is smaller and less costly than what has been set before her, she never recognizes as gluttony her determination to get what she wants, however troublesome it may be to others . . . The real value of the quiet, unobtrusive work which [the devil] has been doing for years on this old woman can be gauged by the way in which her belly now dominates her whole life. The woman is in what may be called the "All-I-want" state of mind.[3]

Have you ever entertained a guest for whom nothing is ever quite right or who makes half a dozen special requests about their meal—"Oh, I don't like that toasted." "Could I get the pasta dish, but without the sauce and without the mushrooms and with the spinach instead?" "No, no, I never eat *such-and-such*." Are you the restaurant patron who regularly sends the plate back to the kitchen . . . twice? Do you insist on wine of a certain quality, declining to drink if you can't have it? A baby-food ad recently promised that *its* bananas had every last string from under the peel carefully stripped before they were pureed, because the strings tasted so terribly *bitter*. The key to understanding fastidious gluttons is that they arrive at the table focused on their expectation of getting a certain pleasure and with an equally focused determination to do whatever it takes to get it. They may use good manners and eat moderate amounts, but the desire behind it all is the drive to get pleasure for themselves.

Remember that we are talking about the glutton as someone with a habit—the person you can count on regularly to have this sort of reaction to their food. Gluttony is about taking excessive pleasure in food. Eating too daintily is eating with full concern for one and only one thing: the glutton's own pleasure in the experience. The test for this form of gluttony is whether the experience is spoiled for you if the food isn't just what you expected or liked or wanted.

Eating "too sumptuously" is similar to the picky eater's problem in its preoccupation with *what* is eaten. But this glutton excessively seeks the pleasures of satiety and fullness, so she eats foods that promise this feeling. The recent low-carb diets work on the same principle, selecting the foods that offer maximal satisfaction. The typical American diet—heavy on the beef, butter, and cream sauces—is built on the same pleasure principle. These foods taste rich and are filling. The excessive desire for sumptuous pleasures was curbed in the traditional Lenten fast, in which Christians abstained from meat and dairy products. They would restrict their menu to bread and vegetables instead. By contrast, our eating habits are formed by the regular expectation of such pleasures.

To understand this form of gluttony, it's important to realize that we eat not just because food tastes good, but because we desire the satisfaction of feeling full. William Ian Miller points out that dieting would be easy if it were enough to taste the food and then spit it out.[4] We want not only to taste what we eat, but also to fill ourselves and be filled by it.

Illustrating both of these forms of gluttony at once—that is, both eating fastidiously and too sumptuously—religious dieting guru Gwen Shamblin, founder of the Weigh Down Workshop, offers the following "Christian dieting" advice on how to enjoy everything from a buffet to a burger:

> After inviting God into this wonderful eating occasion, I survey all the food choices available at the buffet. I carefully make my selections based on what flavors and foods I am craving at the time. I take very small amounts of the items I most want to try, and once I sit down, I begin to rate the items. That means that I taste a tiny bit of each item and decide which are my favorites. Then I take only the best, most sumptuous bites of each item, making sure I am filling up with only the tastiest parts, since I already know it won't take much to fill me up! (No more saving the best for last—you know you will fill up soon, and it is much easier to leave the drier, less attractive bites on the plate!) . . . Sometimes I like to enjoy a good old-fashioned cheeseburger, French fries, and a milk shake from the local fast food restaurant. I make sure

the burger is fixed just the way I like it, and then before I begin, I cut
it in half, or even fourths. This way, I can get to the best, juiciest bites.
I add the perfect amount of salt to my fries, and I pick through them
to find the ones that look best . . . This is just the start of the great
tips you will learn about how to enjoy regular foods when you join a
local Weigh Down class![5]

The last three forms of gluttony are more familiar to us: eating too
hastily, too greedily, and too much. As we might expect, they often
go together. My children use the term "shoveling" for someone who
eats too quickly, too greedily, and too much all at once. The shov-
eler offers us a living picture of the verse, "All human toil is for the
mouth, yet the appetite is not satisfied" (Eccles. 6:7). Hasty eating
can include putting in another bite before the last one is chewed and
swallowed but also pinpoints the sneaky snacker—the one dipping
into the cupboard or the buffet before the appointed hour because
they can't resist or be without for long.

The excessive overeater is one who will eat past the point of fullness
for the sake of indulging her tastes. Even when she knows she will feel
sick or bloated later, she takes another helping, savoring every mouth-
ful. "I'm full, but I can't resist just one more," she thinks. Or, "Wow,
I'm stuffed, but that cheesecake is too wonderful to turn down." Or
more familiarly, "Supersize it!" The brownie mix advertises that it has
"more than two bars of chocolate in every box!" catering to the glutton who can never have enough of a good thing. Although this type
of glutton does not intend harm to her body, she is willing to risk or
overlook the consequences in order to have more pleasure.

The greedy eater often eats quickly to make sure he gets enough
of the pleasurable dish he wants, before anyone else can elbow in
and get to it before him. His greatest fear is the disappointment of
going back for more and finding that someone else beat him to the
last chocolate truffle or that the box of pizza is empty. In fact, the
greedy eater will tend to want to pile his plate high on the first trip
to the buffet, taking two helpings right away to prevent the disappointment of returning later and finding nothing left. Aquinas says
that intemperance is a childish sin, because like children, gluttons
for pleasure are dominated by their appetites, and their behavior is
unabashedly ruled by them.

There is something sad and a little pathetic about these last three
forms of gluttony. It's a bit undignified to find the type of creature

God created as the crown of creation—able to perform piano concertos, invent spacecraft that take us to the moon and back, and have spiritual fellowship with God himself—sitting hunched over a plate of food, mouth overstuffed, shoveling more in as if he can never get enough. But that's the point of reflecting on what sort of creature we are. Because we are human, the pleasure of food can never completely satisfy.

We have said that eating too fastidiously and too sumptuously usually expresses a desire for pleasure that's focused on *what* is being eaten, while eating hastily or too greedily or too much expresses excessive desire for pleasure in *how* we eat. However, what we consume and how we consume it can both reveal *why* we are eating. Note that we can go wrong about what we eat, or we can go wrong in how we eat, or both at once. Just as someone can be angry about the right thing but express it in the wrong way, it is possible to eat healthy and appropriate foods in a manner that betrays desire gone awry. The question is not whether we are fat or thin, polite or impolite, but whether we are eating to satisfy our own wants, in a way that elevates our own satisfaction above other good things.

I once experimented giving up sweets and snacks entirely for a few weeks. What I found, to my chagrin, was that I had unconsciously been scheduling my entire day around food. I was either eating something or anticipating the pleasure of eating most of the time. I looked forward to special events like parties and social events because of the food that would be there, not the people. If the best food was gone before I arrived, my disappointment would color the whole event. At work, I enjoyed breaks not because they gave me a mental reprieve, but because then I had permission to eat something—and eating something *was* my mental reprieve. I couldn't wait to get the kids in bed at night, because then I could sit back and enjoy dessert, my reward for surviving the day. I would even overeat to try to preempt that hungry feeling from arriving before the next meal. I found this discovery about myself rather horrifying. After I stopped snacking for a while, however, I found that it felt good to go into a meal hungry, and to stop eating before I was overfull. Vegetables tasted better if I hadn't munched on sweets all afternoon. I appreciated a simple dinner after foregoing the afternoon snack, and I felt better about myself too. Like C. S. Lewis's old woman, I was relying on the pleasure of food to compensate for the lack of rest, relaxation, and joy in an overstressed life. I was behaving toward food like a starving animal would, because I had starved my life of other things that kept me fully human. Buechner is right, "A glutton is one who raids the icebox for a cure for spiritual malnutrition."[6]

A Taste of the Good Life

Gluttons judge the world from the perspective of satisfying their own desire for pleasure. The pleasure they have in mind, however, is one that we have as material creatures, beings with bodies. Thus, the pleasures that the glutton's life is focused on are material pleasures, pleasures of the body. The effect of this focus is, inevitably, dissatisfaction. Why?

First, bodily cravings never have anything but temporary satisfaction. No matter how lovely the pleasure we take in eating, we will always get hungry again. The pleasure doesn't last. There is a whole book of the Bible devoted to making this point (Ecclesiastes), and we have already noted the result of a life devoted to such pleasure seeking: "the appetite is not satisfied." This is why these desires tend to escalate. We need "more and better" than the physical pleasure we have in hand to fill us up. Gluttony's insatiability is the opposite of godly contentment (1 Tim. 6:8) and gratitude.

Second, as human beings, we are more than just material beings. Satisfying our desire for the pleasure of eating doesn't "fill up" the whole person. Our spiritual desires are left empty. If we leave those desires unfilled long enough, we tend to lose sight of them and become overly preoccupied with only physical desires in an escalating and futile cycle of avoiding spiritual starvation by indulging ourselves physically. When gluttony becomes a habit, we have effectively trained ourselves to appreciate the latter goods to the eclipse of the former. This is why, traditionally, the glutton is portrayed as being more animal-like than human.[7] Animals go straight for food without any thought for manners, conversation, health, or social commerce—that is, without any thought for the symbolic or social aspects of eating that make it fully human. When in the thrall of vice, if gluttons are exposed to spiritual pleasures, they are left cold or fail to notice them. When they feel empty, they turn for comfort and fullness, not to resources that can satisfy them deep down, but to the quick fix of chocolate, alcohol, a nice meal out, the bag of chips close at hand. Because gluttons don't restrain and train their desires for their own physical enjoyment, eventually that is the only kind of pleasure they are able to appreciate, even though it cannot finally satisfy.

Think about the ways we have responded to gluttony's "ramped-up" demands for physical pleasure. Our society invented things like chewing gum, so that we can have the pleasant taste that comes from putting something in our mouths and chewing it and swallowing minty saliva, without actually taking in any food or calories. Diet Coke has a big zero in every single nutrient category on the label, but it is the beverage of choice for millions of Americans, who choose it precisely for its *lack* of nutritional content. Modern appetites also drive inventions like Olestra—a fat-substitute in products like potato chips that enables us to enjoy their great fatty taste, but which is not itself a digestible substance. It sounds pretty perverse when we think about it: we are eating things *without* calories, chewing things not meant to be swallowed, and consuming foods that cannot be digested, so we can have the unrestricted pleasures of eating while carefully bracketing the real nature and function of food itself. Without caloric consequences, we can consume as much as we want, limited only by the amount of pleasure we crave, not by any bodily need or capacity. Sometimes our food consumption looks like the moral equivalent of substance abuse, however legal. We are ingesting substances for the sake of personal gratification, pure and simple.

Getting Beyond Guilty Pleasures

It is easy to take these critiques too far, however, and start to feel guilty about any pleasure we might take in eating, especially if it is intense. Can we really relish a meal or a dessert or a glass of wine without being vicious? Calling gluttony a vice does not imply that food itself, or eating it, or even enjoying it, is sinful. In fact, Aquinas says that the more natural and necessary the activity—and eating, which is necessary for self-preservation, is a case in point—then the more pleasure God designed to accompany the activity.[8] God did make food good. Eating and drinking are meant to give us pleasure. We are created with bodies that both need and enjoy food. That is all right and good. Then how do we distinguish between the right sort of enjoyment and the wrong sort?

As we have seen, the vices are always linked with virtues. In fact, for every moral virtue there are typically two vices. One vice takes a good thing to one extreme, and the other vice takes it to the opposite extreme. For example, the virtue of courage has two opposing vices paired with it—rashness on the one hand, and cowardice on the other. Courage is the virtue of handling fear well; someone with courage fears the right things, in the right way, and at the right time. The courageous person feels fear when and as she should but doesn't let her fear keep her from doing the right thing.

Rashness is a vice opposed to courage because the rash person has a habit of rushing headlong into danger or difficulty without due caution or apprehension. A rash person is often not properly appreciative of the value of her own life, and will risk it unnecessarily or heedlessly. It is one thing to risk your life running into a burning house to save a child; it is another thing to perform a life-threatening stunt to gain celebrity status. The rash person doesn't feel fear in the right way, about the right things, or at the right time. As a rule, she isn't afraid enough of things that could genuinely threaten the good of her own life, and she isn't careful enough about risking things of genuine value. On the other hand, the cowardly person it too afraid—more afraid than she should be, afraid when she shouldn't be and over things that don't deserve it. Fear holds the coward back from doing the right thing. Overcaution is her problem. She is so afraid of what threatens her that she can't properly value other things that are worth risking or sacrificing herself for.

Both vices—rashness and cowardice—feel fear in the wrong way and therefore handle it badly. But they do so in opposite ways: one vice is deficient in fear, and the other, excessive.

The desire for the pleasure of eating follows the same pattern. Desiring and taking pleasure in eating, like the capacity to feel fear, is a natural part of being human. It is the way God created us to be. These reactions are good and useful to us. Our desire for food and the pleasure we take in eating it can get distorted, however. These desires can get out of control, swelling beyond the use for which God designed them and running roughshod over other good desires, sometimes even drowning them out altogether. When they do so, we have the vice of gluttony, a vice of excess. We should mention that there is an opposite vice here too—the lack of appreciation for the pleasure of food and drink, a vice of deficiency. If we condemn natural feelings as evil, or become unable to enjoy the things God meant us to enjoy, then we have become less than we are meant to be. If we reduce our eating to a bread-and-water subsistence regimen, and make eating into a necessary evil merely to be endured, we will have lost something good.

The film *Babette's Feast* illustrates this point well. What Babette shows the sisters for whom she cooks her feast is that they have flattened and beaten down their ability to appreciate the real goodness of creation by insisting on a joyless asceticism about food. To savor a sip of fine wine or to celebrate a Thanksgiving feast is a right expression of the desire for the pleasure of eating and drinking, not a guilty pleasure. Even in the extreme context of early Christian desert asceticism, with its strict regimen of just a little bread and water, the monk fasting in his cell was expected not only to offer guests a meal, but to eat with them, even if it meant temporarily breaking his fast. This was a matter of hospitality and charity toward one's visitor. These hermits regularly joined together on Sunday not only for worship, but also for a shared meal. To have too little desire—the vice of insensitivity—can be just as wrong as having too much desire—the vice of gluttony.

It is likewise sinful to fast excessively, as Aquinas explains:

> Reason does not retrench so much from one's food as to refuse nature its necessary support: thus Jerome says, "It matters not whether you are a long or a short time in destroying yourself, since to afflict the body immoderately, whether by excessive lack of nourishment, or by eating or sleeping too little, is to offer a sacrifice of stolen goods."[9]

He quotes Gregory the Great on the same point:

> Gregory says in his work *Moralia*: "The flesh when restrained more than right is often weakened even for the performance of good deeds, so that while hastening to stifle the forces of sin within, it does not have enough strength to pray or preach. And so while pursing the enemy, we slay the citizen we love."[10]

Because God designed our bodies with sensitive taste buds and strong natural desires to assuage our hunger and thirst, and because we can't give up food altogether, however, most of us struggle more with gluttony than its opposite vice.

Getting our desires in line with what is right and good is difficult, and more so because our judgments of what is good and appropriate are often shaped by our desires, and our desires are shaped by cultural and social forces that may be warped as well. Sometimes we have such a deeply entrenched habit of self-gratification that our judgment about what is "normal" or good is distorted. In the rest of this chapter, we'll look at some ways to realign and double-check our desires for the pleasure of food.

Bread and Water, Bread and Wine

Augustine offers some practical advice on avoiding gluttony. He says that what or how much food we eat makes no difference whatsoever when it comes to virtue, as long as we are eating in a way that is appropriate to our health, the people we live with, and our vocation.[11] That is, as human beings who were made for more than mere physical subsistence, our eating should be regulated not only by what is physically necessary for life and health, but also for what is "becoming" or "befitting" all that God calls us to be and do, and for those with whom we live out that calling. What really matters is that whatever and whenever we eat, we not be so overly attached to the pleasure that we cannot easily and uncomplainingly choose to give it up when duty or necessity requires this.[12] This advice needs a bit of explaining.

First, Augustine tells us that our usual stereotypes about gluttons may not be on target—we can't necessarily pick them out by what they're eating or how much or how often. Someone who is pregnant with twins may eat every two hours, a professional athlete may consume more at each meal than a nonathlete, a diabetic may have to avoid more sugar, while a hypoglycemic may need to increase his sugar intake. There is, therefore, no rigid rule to tell us what or how much to eat. (In fact, Aquinas ascribes judgments about what and how much we ought to eat in order to be healthy to the art of medicine [nowadays, to the nutritionists], not to moral theory.[13]) The first of Augustine's general guidelines to measure our judgments about eating and drinking is this: are we eating in a way that contributes to or at least maintains our overall health and well-being? If our pleasure from certain foods means that we consume them instead of getting the nutrients we really need, this signals a problem. Sensory desire has trumped a judgment about our overall good. We need to eat well enough for our bodies to function well. Mistreatment of the body—by excess or deficiency—belies a flawed sort of self-love. Just as good parents know that a certain amount of discipline is good for the formation of their children's appetites, our love for our bodies precludes unguided self-indulgence.

The second guideline tells us that physical health isn't the only good at stake in eating: so is regard for those with whom we live. Eating is a social act. How and what and why we eat should reflect what is appropriate given the needs of others in our family and our community. If we are willing to flout justice, generosity, or even etiquette just to get our taste buds on some delicious morsel, we are running afoul of this guideline. If we are willing to deprive others to gratify our own desire for pleasure, this may be a symptom of gluttony. The examples of this may vary widely, including wanting seconds before everyone has been served, being greedy at parties because we think no one is watching to see how many times we came back to the serving table, giving unhealthy foods to our children because we cannot restrain our own appetites for them, or even keeping certain foods constantly available in the house when a family member is not allowed to eat them. Is our desire to eat what gives us pleasure taking precedence over the good of others with whom we are eating? Is our own pleasure-seeking getting in the way of enjoying being together with others at the table?

A Nigerian student of mine described his family's custom. The eldest child would be served first and given the largest helping. That child had to eat slowly enough, however, that if a younger child who finished first was still hungry, that younger child would be served seconds off the eldest child's plate. The eldest child's seeking of the pleasure and fullness of eating was thus always disciplined by and responsive to the needs of others eating with him or her.

The third guideline moves us one step further. The first guideline tells us to double-check that our desire for pleasure isn't interfering with our own physical good, the good of health.[14] The second guideline reminds us to double-check that the good of others isn't being compromised by our cravings. The last guideline tells us that we were made for a spiritual purpose. We have gifts and a role to play in the world that God has given us. This vocation may bring extra factors into play in our decisions about how to handle our desires for food. For example, for Christians, fasting may appropriately play a larger and more necessary role in their choices about how often and what to eat. Greater discipline about food may help us focus on spiritual goods in a way that discipleship requires. Our eating should not be ruled by our desire for pleasure; instead, it should be regulated by what befits this higher goal and our flourishing as spiritual beings. Such a restriction of food and pleasure might be inappropriate for a head of state entertaining foreign dignitaries at a formal dinner, or for someone hosting a wedding celebration. The dignity of office and the goods of hospitality and celebration require serving food of a certain quality and quantity in these social contexts. To take another example, perhaps being a parent or a teacher of children means that we have to curb our own desires beyond what we might otherwise choose, in order to set a good example and encourage good habit formation in them. Or an athlete may have to choose foods not just by how good they taste but by the extra nutrients her body needs to perform at its best. Or perhaps we are Christians living in an overconsumptive culture, and we want to combat the pull of assimilation in order to be faithful witnesses to a different way of life. Aquinas claims that those like himself who dedicate their lives to bearing spiritual fruit rather than physical progeny have a vocation that limits their pleasure beyond what is right for most parents. The point is that who we are meant to be and what we are called to do is a consideration that affects what and why and how we eat. We are pursuing our good as whole persons, not just our physical gratification, in our eating. Gluttony, by contrast, would make our own pleasure the only, or the primary, consideration.

Eating is not merely a physical act for us. It is a human act and an identity-forming one—a social and symbolic one. Take the work of a soldier as an analogy. One of my students was a U.S. Marine, and after a mission abroad he once brought me an MRE—short for "Meal Ready to Eat." These meals come in a thick brown vinyl package and include an entrée, crackers with cheese, peanut butter or jelly; a dessert or snack (the pound cake isn't bad), a dry-mix packet of cider, coffee, or hot cocoa; tiny packets of salt, pepper, and Tabasco sauce, plastic silverware, and a flameless ration heater that produces enough heat chemically when combined with water to cook the entrée. The military designs MREs to last for several years unopened, to survive temperatures from -60 to 120 degrees Farenheit, and to withstand a parachute drop from 1,250 feet (or 100 feet, from a helicopter, without a chute). The meals are designed to provide soldiers in the field with the sustenance they need to perform their mission until they can return to base camp. Some marines I knew had eaten meals like this for weeks on end when they were overseas on a mission.

Being a marine, especially in the field of operations, involves personal discipline and teamwork dedicated to achieving a common mission. If a marine did not subordinate his desire for pleasure to the demands of his mission, he could endanger himself and his comrades. He would also jeopardize his effectiveness in carrying out his assignment. The Meals Ready to Eat were created with the purpose of providing maximal mission support. Note that they were not intended to be unappetizing—they include spices and desserts (although I am told that the marines put the Tabasco sauce on *everything*). Eating can still be pleasurable; it's just that self-indulgence has no part in the character of a marine on duty. Their eating habits and daily discipline have social consequences, and the way they eat expresses both their identity and their commitment to their corporate mission.

Extending this analogy to our Christian life, we can ask ourselves whether our eating habits are dedicated to serving our own pleasure or to serving our spiritual mission. Given what God has asked each of us to do and be, is our eating a daily discipline ordered to equipping ourselves to live up to that identity and carry out that mission? Or, in the words of one author in an essay on fasting, have we disciplined our bodies and appetites to be our "willing partners" in a life of discipleship?[15] The glutton eats for himself, and his mission is to gratify his own appetites. His mission is "pleasure first," and he orders the rest of his life around that goal. His god is his belly, and he serves it faithfully.

In the military, those who are asked to serve do not get thrown straight into battle. They are not immediately subjected to the rigors and stress of field operations on the frontlines. They first go through an extensive training program together. What might training look like for Christians heading into a serious mission? Before Jesus began his ministry, he fasted in the desert for forty days. His spiritual mission eventually required the ultimate bodily sacrifice. Was his desert discipline necessary for his readiness? Is something comparable necessary for us? When we think about developing spiritual discipline about the physical pleasures of eating, we might turn back to Augustine's advice again: Are we ready and willing to do without pleasure, if this is asked of us? Are we overattached to our own comforts? What would it take to get ourselves to that point of readiness?

We should note too that our mission and identity as Christians will include feasting as well as fasting. Human beings are made for celebration and delight too. Food is meant to be enjoyed. One marine

I knew was deployed overseas during the official birthday of the Marine Corps. He sent back a picture of himself and his friends next to an enormous birthday cake that had "Happy Birthday, U.S. Marine Corps" written across it in brightly colored frosting. That day was a day of celebrating and feasting, despite 130° temperatures, grueling hours, the dangers of battle, and a spartan life in dusty canvas tents. Effectiveness in his mission required regular reminding of who he was and what he stood for. That reminder came in the form of a celebration—the enjoyment of a specially prepared food.

As Christians, we have a similar identity marker in the form of the eucharistic feast. Notice that Jesus did not institute a meal of bread and water. The wine is a symbol of his blood, to be sure, but it is also a drink appropriate to a feast and celebration. The Lord's Day, Resurrection Sunday, is a day when the reminder of our identity calls for delight and feasting, in honor of his victory over sin and death, and in anticipation of our final liberation from the power of sin in the eschaton (e.g., see Matt. 9:15). His miracle at Cana shows us that a marriage banquet is to be embraced, not only because we want to celebrate the people involved, but because marriage is another place where we are reminded of our spiritual identity as the bride of Christ. This celebration, and the delight and pleasure we take in it, tells us again who we are.

As the analogy of military discipline and identity illustrates, gluttony is about the pleasure of eating food, but because food is not just for self-preservation—it has social and symbolic value as well—keeping our desires for this pleasure in order is necessary for keeping our relationships to God and other people in order. Eating is linked to social bonds, expressions of love for one another, provision and comfort and security and celebration. Life's most important moments are marked with foods—from a nursing mother's bond with her child, to a wedding cake, to the hospitality of a warm supper brought after a funeral. Eating nourishes us not just physically, but also emotionally and spiritually. This point leads us to appreciate the value of getting this area of our moral lives in order, but it also helps us understand better why both fasting and feasting are characteristic parts of the Christian life.

Gluttony's Remedy: Fasting

If we suspect that eating for pleasure is an area of our lives that needs moral scrutiny, one initial exercise in self-examination we might try is to see how hard it is to give something up for, say, a month. My students and I have tried giving up sugary foods, snacking between meals, caffeinated beverages, alcohol, and even lunch. Some of us found it exceedingly difficult to do without, even though none of these foods was even necessary for health. That says something about how attached we are to certain pleasures associated with eating and drinking—how attached we are to having our own comforts and cravings attended to, and immediately so. As Richard Foster remarks, "Fasting reveals the things that control us."[16]

I think it was important that my students and I tried these disciplines together. Like military training, it is an encouragement to undertake rigorous exercises within a community. The church is meant to be a body, and the fasts of the church were traditionally appointed for everyone, not just for the super-saintly few. Moreover, everyone fasted during the same seasons of the year—Advent and Lent, before the great feasts at Christmas and Easter. It is a good reminder that while the mission is for each of us personally, we are all members of a body, a part of a unit. The body needs us to be fit and ready, but a successful mission will also require that we work together with others, rely on them, and encourage them.

Fasting as a spiritual discipline accomplishes at least two things. By giving up certain foods for a time, and by not eating to satiety, we learn anew to appreciate and be content with simple foods. Who will appreciate a simple piece of cheese more—one who eats several Big Macs every day, or one who has just undergone a Lenten fast, abstaining from meat and dairy for several weeks? It is easy to misunderstand fasting as a practice that devalues eating and food or regards it as evil. Nothing could be further from the truth. Only someone who has experienced the gnawing hunger from a grueling hike up a mountain can say, as a friend of mine on.ce did, "There's nothing better than a peanut butter and jelly sandwich at ten thousand feet." Fasting heightens our appreciation for material goods, while also keeping this appreciation in its place, with room for the appreciation of spiritual goods too. As one spiritual writer puts it,

> It would be misleading to speak only of this element of weariness and hunger. Abstinence leads, not merely to this, but also to a sense of lightness, wakefulness, freedom, and joy . . . While involving self-denial, fasting does not seek to do violence to the body but rather to restore it to health and equilibrium. Most of us in the Western world habitually eat more than we need.[17]

Fasting, secondly, increases our appetite for spiritual goods, and makes us keenly aware of our dependence on God, as Kallistos Ware notes:

> The primary aim of fasting is to make us conscious of our dependence on God. If practiced seriously, the Lenten abstinence from food . . . involves a considerable measure of real hunger, and also a feeling of tiredness and physical exhaustion. The purpose of this is to lead us in turn to a sense of inward brokenness and contrition; to bring us, that is, to the point where we appreciate the full force of Christ's statement, "Without Me you can do nothing" (John 15:5).
>
> If we always take our fill of food and drink, we easily grow confident in our own abilities, acquiring a false sense of autonomy and self-sufficiency. The observance of a physical fast undermines this sinful complacency.[18]

Gluttony, like the other capital vices, grows out of pride. How do a spiritual sin like pride and a vice as physical as gluttony go together? So far, we have discussed what gluttony is—the excessive desire for the pleasure of eating. Why is gluttony so appealing to us? When we are gluttonous, our excessive desire is a marker of our need to fill ourselves, to provide for our own happiness and pleasure. Gluttony is not only about pleasure, but also about being able to find our happiness in a pleasure we think we can provide for ourselves. Rather than accepting food as a gift from God, and looking to God to fill our spiritual hungers as well as our bodily ones, we take on God's responsibility for ourselves. Gluttons want to be in charge of defining their own happiness in pleasure, with its attainment firmly under their own control.[19] When the gluttonous feel need or emptiness, they do not want to have to depend on God or wait on God to fill it. The pleasure of food is not only readily available, but something we can use to quell our own feelings of need and longing. With food, we can comfort ourselves, fill ourselves, provide pleasure for ourselves—if only physically, and if only for a short while. The glutton's pursuit of happiness is found in what he can do, not in what God will give him. The addictive quality of the pleasure seeking is seated, often enough, in this need for control over our own ability to be happy and full. This is pride. The fasting of the desert fathers, by contrast, was an attempt not only to pray but also to live the words, "Give us this day our daily bread."

There is, of course, the self-centeredness of gluttony too, in that those suffering from this vice make their own pleasure the most important value. But the way we use food to comfort us, and its symbolic value as a cue for fullness and provision, also indicates that there is more than just this form of self-centeredness at work in gluttony. The gluttonous seem to want to defy the truth of Christ's remark that as human beings, we "[do] not live by bread alone" (Matt. 4:4). They *do* want to live by bread alone, and moreover, bread stripped of its deeper significance—as the eucharistic sacrifice, the Bread of Life. The gluttonous eat with greed, not gratitude. Food is merely something to be used for their own gratification, rather than a good gift to be received and enjoyed.

Ironically, the pursuit of happiness in material goods and the pleasures they afford, as well as the attempt to provide it for ourselves, in the form of pleasure or anything else, is doomed to failure. We are bodily creatures, but we are made for more than that too. No wonder that even the overstuffed glutton remains spiritually empty, always hungry for more.

8

LUST

SMOKE, FIRE, AND ASHES

> Sex is sinful to the degree that, instead of drawing you closer to other human beings in their humanness, it unites bodies but leaves the lives inside them hungrier and more alone than before. —Frederick Buechner, *Wishful Thinking*

Sex: Is it the enemy, the forbidden fruit, the greatest and most shameful of all sins, or is it the key to happiness, the ultimate fulfillment of desire?[1] Is it a picture of our relationship with God, holy and pure, or a matter of casual weekend recreation? If marriage is truly good, why does most Christian radio broadcast only platonic love songs crooned to God, not to flesh-and-blood members of the opposite sex? If spring-break sexual free-for-alls and one-time hook-ups are premised on a notion of sex as just for fun, why do secular rock songs also extol a "hold me in your arms forever" view of sex that is linked to love and promises of lifelong exclusiveness? Does sex mean nothing or everything? Is it sacred or sinful? Is it for procreation, personal intimacy, or physical pleasure? Why is it so taboo we can't talk about it? Why is it so ubiquitous that we see it broadcast everywhere? Needless to say, both the culture and the church are sending

159

mixed messages about sex—as if we needed confusion on top of the difficulty of handling sexual desire itself!

"Lord, give me chastity and continence . . . but not yet," prays Augustine in his *Confessions*.[2] Make me holy, he implores God, but please don't make me give up my unholy sexual gratifications, at least not today. When he finally wanted to give up his lustful ways, however, he found he couldn't. He describes himself as imprisoned by the "overwhelming force of habit."[3] He found lust to be the demon he had no success in exorcising through willpower.

Is lust just "the sexual impulse dialed up," as William Gass puts it? Then what's the harm in it? It merely makes one "alert and on the search, . . . encouragingly alive, paying attention to one's friends and companions because they may relieve the itch." As a further point in its favor, "satisfied lust may mean that two people are happy." The real problem lies with those who would squelch our natural desire for pleasure, argues Gass—the religious prudes, the pleasure haters who taint it with fear and shame and guilty "thou shalt nots."[4] But when Gass describes lust, does he admit any distinction between lust and sexual desire at all? Is there no other way to pervert sexual desire than to make rules that restrict our unadulterated access to pleasure?

Back to the Beginning

Rather than condemning sex and sexual desires as evil in themselves, or condoning them as a necessary evil, we should start by remembering that God created us as sexual beings. The ability to be sexually aroused and desire sexual pleasure is a natural part of God's design for human beings. Our sexuality, our bodies, the sexual act, the tactile desires and pleasures that go with it—these are all good gifts from God. Thomas Aquinas thought that sexual intercourse would have been *more* pleasurable in Eden than after the fall into sin. There is a whole book of the Bible (Song of Songs) dedicated to celebrating sexual love between a man and a woman in its various erotic expressions.

Acknowledging the goodness of sex is the first step, because we can't define lust as damaging or disordered pleasure-seeking unless there is a well-ordered, delightful form to which it fails to measure up. The right view of this great good will avoid two traps. On the one hand, it will avoid degrading sexual pleasure into meaningless triviality or base instinct. On the other hand, it will avoid elevating it into something so spiritual that any ecstasy involved has to be a spiritual experience disconnecting us from the actual flesh involved.

Some of my Christian college students are under the impression that well-ordered sex works like this: before marriage, you can't have any, and you have to squash your sexual urges. After marriage, all the rules fall away and it's a big sexual free-for-all (as long as it's with your spouse, of course). You can gratify your sexual desires whenever and however you want. Chastity is a virtue you need only if you are actually abstaining in the premarital state or if you are crazy enough to choose celibacy—although they usually fail to consider this latter option altogether. (It's unclear whether their failure to consider celibacy should be attributed to youthful hormones or because most Protestant churches don't hold this up as a serious option for Christians anymore.)

My students are right that sexual desire should be expressed in the right context—marriage. Marriage vows and the sexual consummation that signifies and seals them join two persons into one. The union should last as long as the people in it do. But our typical view of the virtue of chastity is still woefully narrow. Does chastity have a purpose in marriage other than just limiting our sexual expression to the person who is our spouse? Who needs chastity and when and why? Is there such a thing as lustfulness in married, otherwise licit sexual activity? It's notable that Thomas Aquinas, who overemphasizes the procreative purpose of sex almost to the point of forgetting about its potential for intimacy, explicitly warns husbands not to use their wives indecently for their own sexual pleasure. This is "counter to the good of marriage," he says—even to the point of being a worse offense than adultery—because it "breaks faith" between husband and wife.[5] How, then, both before and during marriage, does "being chaste" mean more than bodily abstinence from intercourse? How can chastity free us from lust, and how does it protect sexual desire from corruption? If we frame the conversation in terms of the virtues and vices, perhaps we can keep the goodness of sexuality in the forefront of our attention and ask more fruitful questions than, "How far can I go on a date?" or "At what point do I technically lose my virginity?"

"Sex Is like Nitroglycerin"

People both inside and outside the church think Christians make too big a deal of sexual sin. The church is obsessed with sex, they complain, and the word from the pulpit is always a resounding NO. The youth pastor hosts a purity weekend exhorting teens to abstinence, to add their own personal "NO" to the party line. N. T. Wright tells the joke about Moses carrying the commandments down from Mount Sinai. " 'Good news and bad news,' he says. 'The good news is—we've got them down from forty to ten. The bad news is—adultery is still in.' "[6] The sexual deviance of other people and the lustfulness of our culture are constant fodder for Christian condemnation. But what about anger and self-centeredness and racism and materialism, which are also prevalent and very damaging? The Bible itself seems more focused on other sins, like hypocrisy, faithlessness, and greed. Why do Christians focus so much negative attention on sex?

It's true that Christians do seem to treat sex as if it were the culture's main problem, and other sins as if they were less important. And that is worth complaining about. Yet we can also respond to criticism of the church by affirming that there is good reason to get upset about sexual sin. What is sex and what is it for? First, sex is an act designed to bond two people together into a one-flesh union. Second, it's an act designed to create new human beings—babies. What's at stake in sex? Love and life. Human relationships and human existence. It's hard to see how one could overemphasize the importance of something like that. If lust has the power to damage human love-giving and life-giving, then perhaps we cannot make too big a deal of the destructive potential of sexual sin. Buechner notes, "Contrary to Mrs. Grundy, sex is not a sin. Contrary to Hugh Hefner, it's not salvation either. Like nitroglycerin, it can be used either to blow up bridges or heal hearts."[7]

And yet, we should not forget that lust usually begins as a sin of weakness, not a sin of malice, to put it in Aquinas's terms. People get carried away by curiosity or strong desires. They weren't planning to be awful and hurt people and create scars that last a lifetime. They just got caught up in the moment, or got caught in a current of habits that soon swept out of control. Sexual desires are a natural and powerful and beautiful thing, so it's understandable that we underestimate their force and hold on us before we're in the heat of the moment. So while lust *is* a big deal—something with major potential for damage—people who struggle with it also tend to feel regret and shame, to appreciate offers of help to escape from it, and to respond readily to mercy, rather than condemnation. Of course anyone can get hardened over time—this is why we should guard against making lustful desire a *habit*. But for most of us, lust feels like an uninvited demon who has taken over our lives, and once we see if for what it is, we want to escape from it as much as anyone does.

The cultural conversation needs to more honestly acknowledge sex's power. The church's conversation, however, should start with the goodness of sex and virtuous sexual desire—its love- and live-giving power—not just distortions of that power, since vices can only be understood as deviations from the good of virtue. As with all the natural capacities with which God created us, our sexual desires are not meant to be squelched or sublimated, but expressed in a way that respects our full humanness. Proper use and enjoyment of our sexual nature should track the way sexual desire and its fulfillment can enhance our relationships with God and each other. An approach to lust as a *vice* will ask not just what the "thou shalt nots" are, but what having a lustful habit says about who I am as a human being. How do unruly sexual desires deform my character, my perception, my capacity to love? How do my patterns of pleasure-seeking enhance or corrupt my relationship with God? How does thinking about lust as a vice and not just a behavior problem change the way we think about sexual sin? Lust need not be consummated in sex to be lust. Lust is a problem with the heart above your belt before it is a problem with the heat below it.

Defining the Disorder

Sexual desire and pleasure are meant to be a part of good sex. To put it bluntly, sex isn't as good without them. Sexual pleasure is a good designed to accompany sexual activity. The trouble is lust's reductive impulses: to reduce sexual pleasure to one's own individual gratification, apart from a relationship to a person; or to reduce it to the only end we have in view, apart from all its other purposes; or to strip it down to its purely physical dimension, apart from its integration into our full humanity.

Good sex has an interpersonal and social dimension, a dimension that brings us into connection and relationship with others. Lust is deformed sexual desire because it cuts us off from this potential. Sexual desire is meant ultimately to bring us into a union of intimacy with another person. It has the power to bond a man and a woman together in love. The old-fashioned term for sexual intercourse is "the conjugal act"—an act that conjoins people together into one flesh, creating and strengthening and symbolizing a union of lifelong love. It is a symptom of our lustful culture that we shorten "sexual *intercourse*" to just plain "sex." Sex's natural bonding effect is something we have to actively resist if we want to keep things casual, recreational, no strings attached. Many of us know people who are in unhealthy relationships and stay in them far too long, against their better judgment and others' clear advice, because of the power of the sexual bond.

Sex is also interpersonal in the sense that it has the power to procreate a new human person. Sex is designed not just for pleasure making and lovemaking, but for bringing new life into the world. It links us not only to our spouse here and now in this moment, but to a child who could be born—and thus to future generations. When our second child was born, our pastor visited me in the hospital. He picked up the baby, looked at me, and said, "He's forever, Rebecca." It struck me forcefully there for the first time that the natural result of sex was to bind me inextricably to others beyond myself and the limits of my own lifetime. What sex between husband and wife had joined together, no one could ever separate. Sex's natural links both to love and to life reflect its deep other-connectedness and its future- and forever-directedness. With enough cleverness and technical assistance, of course, we can procure sexual pleasure without its love-giving and life-giving potential (albeit with no guarantee of success), but again, we must willfully work against our social and bodily nature to keep sex solitary or sterile.

Lust, by contrast, pretends sex and sexual pleasure are a party for one. Lust makes sexual pleasure all about me. It is a self-gratification project. This feature of lust more than any other puts it in opposition to well-ordered sexual enjoyment. In lust, sexual pleasure is divorced from love and mutual self-giving. And when we lust we certainly want nothing to do with giving life and the future commitments that might bring—if we even register the thought that the organs involved are reproductive by design. I want *my* pleasure, says the lustful one, and I want it now.

This is why it is characteristic of lust to degrade the fullness of sex into a merely physical act. Ricoeur says, "Everything that makes the sexual encounter easy simultaneously speeds its collapse into insignificance."[8] Perhaps the hardest thing to appreciate about sex until one has experienced it is the way sex is more than a physical act. The emotional bond of intimacy and the union of persons is all part of the "one-flesh-ness" of the thing. If we strip off its personal and social meaning, which lust demands that we do, we are left with the version of sex found in *Cosmopolitan* magazine, which offers tips and techniques on how to achieve the greatest orgasm of one's life and make things "hotter" in bed. *Cosmo*, *Maxim*, and the like have nothing to say about what sexual desire and intercourse look like in the context of love. To anyone who has experienced the beauty and warmth of married intercourse, the *Cosmo* sex experience looks cold, clinical, and downright abhorrent. Lustful sex makes the other person instrumental to getting what I want, or a necessary audience for my successful performance. As Pieper puts it, lust wants "it," while proper *eros* desires a beloved person.[9] Lust aims for the antithesis of real intimacy. No wonder it leaves one feeling used and empty.

Lust is a vice, then, because it does not honor the fullness of sex, and it alienates people from each other just when they are supposed to be experiencing intimate union. There's a betrayal of meaning in lust's use of sex for nothing but self-gratification, and it is difficult to be lustful without feeling that loss at some level. If one *is* successful in becoming immune to the goods involved in sex, one has also been successful in becoming less fully human.

Filling and Fulfilling Myself

The dynamics of lust's search for pleasure are like those operating in its close cousin, gluttony. Their excessiveness reduces something designed for more than pleasure to mere pleasure, and reduces even the fullness of that pleasure to mere self-gratification. Buechner also notes the parallel: "At its roots the hunger to know someone sexually is the hunger to know and be known by that person humanly. Food without nourishment doesn't fill the bill for long, and neither does sex without humanness."[10] Both real love and the sexual pleasure that complements it involve giving and receiving. Sexual desire is *for* sexual intercourse, and in sexual intercourse there's meant to be a mutual gift of oneself, more than an exchange of bodily stimulation. It's a relationship of two whole persons, not a contract in which someone is valued only in terms of their potential to arouse us and is disposable when the pleasure fades. Just as the glutton sees in food only a useful means for filling herself with comfort and pleasure, so the lustful one sees in sex and sexual objects only their usefulness in giving pleasure to herself.[11]

That lust imitates gluttony in this respect is not surprising, since they are both vices dealing with physical pleasures. The glutton, as a result of her disordered love for pleasure in eating, becomes unable to appreciate and be satisfied with the pleasure of a simple meal of ordinary quantity and quality. She needs more and better to stimulate and satisfy. And then more and better yet, for habitual indulgence only strengthens the desire and its demands for satisfaction.[12] Her mistake is to try to satisfy an infinite spiritual need by filling her stomach with food; her dissatisfaction is ensured because her desire for eternal and perfect fulfillment cannot be quenched with the temporary pleasure of eating. The Christian view of order and disorder in both of these areas tells us how to celebrate the fullness of the pleasure, rather than dampening it or forbidding it, despite the tradition's reputation to the contrary.[13] As deceptive as their false reputations are, lust, not chastity's restraint, is the real pleasure-killer. Being able to appreciate physical goods requires that we not try to use them to satiate our spiritual needs.

In a nutshell, lust is the excessive desire for my own sexual pleasure. It's defined in terms of *physical* pleasure stemming from *physical* acts. Sexual intercourse requires a body, and so does sexual desire. The key to understanding lust as a vice, however, is seeing that what we do physically is intimately linked to spiritual effects. As Buechner puts it,

> Adultery, promiscuity either heterosexual or homosexual, masturbation—one appealing view is that anything goes as long as no one gets hurt. The trouble is that human beings are so hopelessly psychosomatic in composition that whatever happens to the soma [body] happens also to the psyche [soul] and vice versa.[14]

The ancient Greek philosophers taught that if human beings were merely animals, bodily pleasure would be enough to fulfill us. But even they knew that there is more to being human than having a body. Why does lust leave us empty? Because it tries to substitute sensual and selfish pleasure-seeking for fully human love-giving.

That lust—the habitual vice—has an insatiable quality to it is a testimony to this fact about us. As beings with a spiritual as well as a physical dimension, we need something more than bodily satisfac-

tion to fulfill us. We aren't designed to be satisfied by a temporary
physical fix, a fleeting passion.

The Greek philosopher Plato once told a myth about *eros* in the
voice of a comic poet named Aristophanes.[15] According to the whim-
sical story he spins, human beings were originally spherical creatures
with four arms and four legs and two heads. As punishment for trying
to usurp the gods' power, the gods sliced them in half "like a flatfish."
In our current condition, then, each human being is really only half
of the original whole. *Eros,* so says Aristophanes, is our yearning to
be reunited with our other half; it is our desire for completeness. But
even if sexual union is the best way to achieve this reunion or lost
wholeness for now, it is imperfect and temporary.

> No one would think that [what lovers want from each other] is the
> intimacy of sex—that mere sex is the reason each lover takes so great
> and deep a joy in being with the other. It's obvious that the soul of
> every lover longs for something else; his soul cannot say what it is, but
> like an oracle it has a sense of what it wants, and like an oracle it lies
> hidden behind a riddle.[16]

It is true "wholeness" and re-union into oneness that they yearn for,
he argues, and no amount of physical intercourse will fill that need.
Trying to make the physical union of sex alone do all the work of
fulfilling us is a strategy doomed to fail. Trying to get sexual pleasure
to fill our fundamental yearning for human happiness is a recipe for
disappointment.[17] Then why do we keep trying it, deluding ourselves
that it will be enough? Why is the lustful person's strategy so tempting to us?

All the vices are distorted or excessive attachments to good things.
Wrath is ostensibly born of concern for justice and honor, greed regards sufficient possessions, gluttony is about food, vainglory seeks
the approval of others. Vice happens when our pursuit of these good
things gets twisted, that is, when we try to make them fill gaps and
needs in our hearts that only God can fill, and when we define happiness in terms of them, rather than appreciating them as (finite)
blessings from God.

Here lust's connection with pride reveals itself. Lust is the habit of
trying to engineer my own happiness for myself, on my own terms.
In lust, my own pleasure is the goal, and I decide where to get it, and
when, and with whom. My life revolves around my desires, wants, and

"needs." I disown my need for God's love or the love of others. I prefer
to find my own delight, meet my own desire for satisfaction, fill myself.
Unlike one who risks depending on the love of another and who risks
giving himself to another, the lustful one chooses to be autonomous,
providing his good for himself. As with avarice, taking for ourselves
is a safer strategy than giving and being open to receive what we need
as a gift. Both our independence and our need to define and create a
false happiness for ourselves are telltale hallmarks of pride.

Human beings were made to be fulfilled by love—for God and for
one another. Love requires real persons and a real exchange. It requires
the freedom to give oneself to another, and the willingness to graciously
receive another person as a gift. It is true that this involves great risk. To
love is to appreciate and value another person for his or her own sake,
and not just for what that person can do for you. The hallmarks of
love—the freedom of giving of oneself to another—are excluded from
lust's manipulative view. To strip sex of its link to love is to make access
to sexual pleasure safer and easier, perhaps, but the safety we seek in
prideful self-provision also insulates us from what we really need.

The Pleasure Paradox

When we misuse something habitually, we find we lose our ability to
appreciate its true goodness. As with gluttony, the more single-mindedly
we pursue something for the pleasure we can get from it, the *less* likely
we are to find our desire for pleasure satisfied. Sex loses its flavor. What
once was titillating quickly becomes boring. Pornography use is a classic example. Using porn is an activity with an incredible addiction and
escalation rate—habitual viewers not only quickly increase their frequency of use to the point where it dominates their lives, but the level
of perversity and novelty required to pique their interest also quickly
spins beyond the range of what would shock even a more jaded adult.
Normal sex (with consenting adults, with the opposite sex, with living
persons, with persons at all) no longer appeals. In the words of one
blogger, "As a struggling porn addict myself, I know what the producer
[of pornographic films] said about porn getting more and more brutal
on the women is true, and it will only get worse. [There's] something
about human nature that gets desensitized to the ordinary."[18] Why doesn't
indulging in lustful pleasure satisfy us? Why is truly fulfilling pleasure
such an elusive goal for the lustful person?

Pleasure, as the ancient Greeks noted, is easy to confuse with human fulfillment, because it is something sought for its own sake. The paradox of pleasure, however, as they also noted, is that you can't get it by seeking it directly. Aristotle said that pleasure is an effect of certain activities done in a certain way; it is the fruit of activity, but not something that can be produced or achieved without the activity itself. Pleasure is also relative to the activity it accompanies. The pleasure of sitting in the sunshine is not the same thing as the pleasure of reading a good book. The pleasure of reading a gripping drama is not the same as the pleasure of reading an action adventure novel. The pleasure of reading to myself is not the same as the pleasure of reading to my children.

Sexual pleasure is like this too. It explains why the pleasure of the porn user requires rapid escalation of sexual stimulation, while a happily married person can still thoroughly enjoy conventional sex decades into a marriage to the same spouse. Sexual pleasure—both its quality and its ability to satisfy—depends on the activity from which you get it. The lustful one gets the sham, shallow version of sexual pleasure, the physical rush that feels great for a moment but cannot satisfy for more than a moment either. It's not news to anyone that studies consistently show the highest sexual satisfaction among those in faithful, monogamous marriages, not those whose sex lives are promiscuous.[19] Why? Because in these marriages the sexual pleasure is the fruit of love. That sort of pleasure is unavailable to those who are in it only for the pleasure, and only for their own pleasure. In her poem, "To a Long Loved Love," Madeleine L'Engle writes,

> We who have seen the new moon grow old together
> Who have seen winter rime the fields and stones
> As though it would claim earth and water forever
> We who have known the touch of flesh and the shape of bones
> Know the old moon stretching its shadows across a whitened
>   field
> More beautiful than spring with all its spate of blooms
> What passions knowledge of tried flesh still yields,
> What joy and comfort these familiar rooms.
>
> In the moonless, lampless dark now of this bed
> My body knows each line and curve of yours;
> My fingers know the shape of limb and head:
> As pure as mathematics ecstasy endures . . .[20]

In this case, with familiarity comes not contempt and boredom but trust and intimacy and more selfless love—the very context in which sexual pleasure comes into full bloom. "Do not stir up or awaken love until it is ready," counsels the author of Song of Songs (8:4). This is advice from those who want the heights of sexual pleasure to be possible for us—as the rest of this biblical book makes clear—not from those who seek to repress it. The simple truth in these examples is this: fulfilling pleasure without commitment and full human intimacy is lust's perennially empty promise. As with the other vices, lust gives you an imitation of happiness, a substitute for the real thing. True playfulness and lasting pleasure find their home in trustful, intimate intercourse with one who takes delight in us for who we really are.

The positive point here is that our sexual desires and pleasures should be integrated into our personal and social and spiritual lives such that they serve to enhance our full humanness and the possibility of loving each other. Our control over them helps them serve us; our indulgence of them makes them our masters, even as they leave us empty.

Lust's Body Count

One of the most problematic assumptions about lust is that it doesn't hurt anyone. Even Aquinas, in the thirteenth century, considers this "no-injury" objection. Fornication involves two consenting adults. No one is injured; therefore, fornication is not a sin.[21] It's lustful activity that is pleasurable and fun, and what's the harm in that?

In some cases the injuries are obvious. Lust's cost to love and life are painfully evident in the story of David and Bathsheba (2 Sam. 11–12). David's selfishness cost Uriah his life, it cost Bathsheba the death of her husband and child, and it cost David a painful rupture in his relationship with God (Ps. 51) and the loss of a son. But the damage did not just stop with those directly involved. Uriah was betrayed by the king he served faithfully, and David's general Joab became complicit in that betrayal. First David's army and then (after a visit from Nathan the prophet) his palace servants and his people saw their king willing to sacrifice his obedient subjects to his own selfish desires. Trust was broken, loyalties undercut, and relationships at all levels damaged.

Even if we are not directly burned by its fire, however, lust's smoke can cause damage far and wide. A neighborhood feels threatened when a sex offender moves in, billboards and magazines expose children to explicit sexual content, teens having premarital sex early put pressure on their peers and struggle with depression, cohabiting young adults impair their chances of stable marriages later (with all the social difficulties broken marriages often bring), sexual abuse and affairs can rip families, churches, and communities apart. We often live with lust's collateral damage for the long term.

The damage may also be less sensational, and more subtle. Recent statistics show that at least 80 percent of teens age fifteen to seventeen have had multiple exposures to hard-core pornography on the Internet. Even if they stop looking, everyone knows the power of these images to remain imprinted on the mind. What does this experience, and our knowledge of it, do to the atmosphere in a co-ed classroom, on a date, or later in a marriage or a life of singleness? Naomi Wolf describes the way college women think men see them now: "real naked women are just bad porn."[22] Lustful attitudes permeate the way we speak about the opposite sex, what we assume we can expect sexually from other men and women, and the misogyny and sexual violence that we find entertaining.

When national department store chains market "sexy" underwear to six-year-old girls, we should see the handiwork of lust, continually ramping up our sexual demands to the extent that even children are normalized as its targets. The demands of excessive and misdirected sexual desire are in the air we breathe. Lust is not a private, personal problem.

Robert Solomon and William Gass poke fun at the religious prudes who condemn the harmless fun of a "few too many peeks at a naughty *Playboy* pictorial,"[23] but their comments betray an embarrassing (or perhaps willful) ignorance. It's almost impossible not to have read the statistics on pornography use and its addictive power, not to have read a testimony by addicts of their self-loathing and the brokenness they caused in their families,[24] not to mention the gender dynamics of the billion-dollar sex industry.

Alan Paton tells a story about the power of lust in his book, *Too Late the Phalarope*. Pieter van Vlaanderen, a police officer in South Africa, commits adultery with a young woman late at night in a vacant lot outside of town.

And how long he stayed there he could not remember, but at least he rose and came out of the vacant ground. And his body and clothes stank with the smell of the weeds, and the stinking was a symbol of his corruption. . . . And he thought again of his children with special agony, for what kind of man would destroy what he had created, and hurt what he had loved? . . . In those last twelve hours the whole world had changed, because of one insensate act. And what madness makes a man pursue something so unspeakable, deaf to the cries of wife and children and mother and friends and blind to their danger, to grasp one unspeakable pleasure that brought no joy, ten thousand of which pleasures were not worth one of the hairs on his children's heads? Such desire could not surely be a desire of the flesh, but some mad desire of a sick and twisted soul. And why should I have this desire? he asked himself. Where did it come from? And how did one cure it? But he had no answers to these questions. . . .

And his terrible knowledge of himself lay in him darkly and heavily, and took away his laughter, and the laughter of his wife, so that the children were the only creatures that laughed in that house. He went to work darkly and heavily, and came back darkly and heavily, and played with the children because that was his habit, but his wife could hear and see that it was not the same.[25]

As both porn and Paton's story show, lust damages the one who lusts too. One author of a book on teen sex describes this damage as "emotional STD's."[26] Even if you don't get gonorrhea or genital warts, you are likely to come home with depression, loneliness, and self-hatred.

Buechner comments: "Who is to say who gets hurt and who doesn't get hurt, and how? Maybe the injuries are all internal. Maybe it will be years before the X-rays show up anything. Maybe the only person who gets hurt is you."[27]

Lust: Body and Soul

On a first glance, the fathers of the church often seem to write as if the body is a kind of enemy of the spiritual life. It is easy to read their asceticism and celibacy as a rejection of the body: witness their references to "filth" and "shame" in the context of sexual desires.[28] Are sexual desires intrinsically evil and to be shunned? John Cassian recommends that monks trying to avoid lust "flee from women."[29] Evagrius likewise says that "the sight of a woman is a poisoned arrow; it wounds the soul and injects the poison, and for as long a time as it stays there it causes an ever greater festering."[30] It might be tempting to think that they believe women, not men, are the real cause of lust! But this reading of the tradition is often oversimplified and exaggerated. For one thing, these radical directives are intended only for those who have vowed perpetual abstinence and who have withdrawn from worldly affairs into the desert in order to pursue a single-minded devotion to God. Despite the deep differences between their context and our own, however, in many ways these early Christian ascetics took the unity of body and soul more seriously than we do. They appreciated that what we do with our bodies affects our spiritual lives, as the apostle Paul affirms (1 Cor. 6:13b–20). The famous modern philosopher Descartes once said, "I am not my body and I can live without it."[31] By contrast, taking the disordered habit of lust seriously means treating the body as part of ourselves, not as an instrument of pleasure accidentally conjoined to us that doesn't affect our souls.

Cassian describes the virtue of chastity as something to be cultivated on the inside as well as the outside; it is a "chastity of body and soul": "And so, first of all, the hidden places of our heart must be very carefully purified. For what those others wish to acquire in terms of purity of body, we must ourselves possess in the depths of our conscience." In discussing celibacy among the monks, he remarks, "the incorruption of the flesh consists not so much in abstaining from woman as it does in integrity of heart."[32]

Paul makes the same point about the unity of the human person: "Do you not know that whoever is united to a prostitute becomes one body with her? For it is said, 'The two shall be one flesh,'" (1 Cor. 6:16). He argues that we cannot divorce sex from its marital "one flesh" meaning any more than we could dissociate a person's body and what it does from the person herself. Our minds and hearts affect us physically: for example, when we are anxious or grieving, we lose our appetites and we can't sleep. And our bodies affect our hearts and minds: when we don't get enough sleep, we become irritable and easily distracted; after exercise, we feel better about ourselves and have a brighter outlook. Why should it be any different with sex and sexual desire? The tradition's claim is that this body–soul link is a feature present in every human sexual act. That means that respecting yourself requires respecting your body too. And if you are to love your neighbor *as yourself*, that extends to your respect for their body—their person—as well.

John Mayer had a hit song a few years ago called "Your Body Is a Wonderland." The lustful view of the body expressed in the title and lyrics does not convey wonder in the sense of awe. Its view of the other's body is that it is one's own personal amusement park. It's a place to have fun and explore and get excitement, and then at the end of the day, we are free to leave it behind, along with our trash and our sweat on the vinyl seats. How do we think of our bodies and the bodies of others? Paul writes that they are "a temple of the Holy Spirit within you, which you have from God" (1 Cor. 6: 19). Are they sacred spaces or a place for cheap thrills? The lustful person's distorted desire for pleasure leads her to treat both herself and others with less value and respect than she ought. Lust is as irreverent about bodies and sex as it is obsessed with them. The body is a pleasure-delivery device, to be used at will. But the Christian view of the body is that it is a place where God dwells, an image of the living God. To degrade each other sexually is to participate in the "degradation of a king [or queen]."[33]

Mind Games

Because it lives in denial of reality—the reality of what human beings are made for, the depth and value of personhood, and our need for love—lust characteristically trades in fantasy. A poem by Steve Turner vividly makes this point:

> She no longer brought him pleasure
> Like girls in magazines
> Who throbbed with lust and fantasy
> And stayed sweet seventeen.
>
> He never heard those beauties moan
> (Except when in the sack!)
> They knew a woman's place to be
> Undressed and on her back . . .
>
> She no longer brought him pleasure
> Like girls in magazines,
> So they slept in separate beds
> And snuggled up with dreams.
>
> He no longer brought her pleasure
> Like men in Mills and Boon

Who were powerful yet gentle
And impeccably groomed . . .

In grey Mercedes cars they drove.
Their teeth and eyes were bright,
They promised their undying love
In pools of candlelight.

He no longer brought her pleasure
Like men in Mills and Boon
So they slept in separate beds,
Then moved to single rooms.

They no longer found their pleasure
In lives where flesh was real,
So muddled on or called it quits
Or chased a better deal.[34]

Trading lustful fantasies for reality makes this couple unable to love
and appreciate each other anymore. Even real love struggles against
the power of fantasy, as L'Engle describes:

Because you're not what I would have you be
I blind myself to who, in truth, you are
Seeking mirage where desert blooms, I mar
Your *you*. Aaah, I would like to see
Past all delusion to reality:
Then would I see God's image in your face,
His hand in yours, and in your eyes his grace.
Because I'm not what I would have me be,
I idolize Two who are not any place,
Not you, not me, and so we never touch.
Reality would burn. I do not like it much.
And yet in you, in me, I find a trace
Of love which struggles to break through
The hidden lovely truth of me, of you.[35]

Lust is in the eye—and mind—of the beholder. When the entire
advertising industry is built upon the power of images, we ought not
to underestimate their effect on our desires and minds.[36] What sorts
of images, desires, and expectations fill our minds and feed our hearts
every day? Do we get them from soap operas, romance novels, Inter-

net porn, magazine ads and catalogs, shop windows, R-rated films, late-night cable shows, or the music we download? Do these sources speak truth about human sexuality and its goodness, or do they feed our lustful fantasies?

The tradition describes the long-term effects of lust by linking the desires of our hearts to the contents of our mind in a vicious cycle. Aquinas and Gregory call lust's most grave offspring vice "blindness of mind"—the inability to recognize and appreciate goods higher than the pleasure of the flesh or beyond the moment of gratification.[37] Lust's effect is to shrink our world and then to make all our powers of deliberation and imagination serve that narrowly self-serving, flesh-aimed vision of the good. Pieper notes the distorting power of what he calls lust's "self-centered will-to-pleasure" by contrast with love's clear vision: "Only those who look at the world with pure eyes can experience its beauty."[38]

Chastity and Other Impossible Virtues

If what to do about lust is the question, sex education is not the answer. We all know that we can be utterly convinced in principle that lust can ruin love between human beings and still in practice find ourselves struggling mightily to resist it. Similarly, in matters of nutrition, knowledge of how many calories are needful and healthy does not equal the will to resist a second helping of dessert or to forgo the French fries. On a beach full of tanned, glowing skin, the demon of lust is still there with us. When we need a remedy for lust, more preaching and more book chapters do not necessarily make temptation fade.

As a first suggestion, we should broaden the parameters of what counts as lustful, so that we can see better the territory that chastity too will need to cover. Often we think of lust only in terms of engaging in sexual intercourse when we ought not—for example, premarital sex for the unmarried, and adultery for the married. Lust is actually expressed in a much wider range of behaviors, as well as the internal thoughts and desires that give rise to them. Scripture reflects this twofold view of lust's disorder. The scriptures prohibit not just extramarital intercourse, but "sexual immorality" in general, including illicit sexual thoughts, desires, and fantasies and all that we do to indulge them in ourselves and others. Abstinence from intercourse, the protection of one's virginity, may be a convenient litmus test, but Christians are also called to have chaste hearts and minds. How can we cultivate our character, inwardly and outwardly, so that our own sexual desires are not the lens through which we see the world and grasp at it?

Lust thrives in privacy and isolation, and lustful people often feel shame, which also motivates them to keep their struggles hidden from others. But when we hide our sin and deny it, we cannot confess it or deal with it. This means lust's remedy requires community, openness, and accountability. Sheer individual willpower doesn't work. It's a cycle a lot like yo-yo dieting. About 90 percent of all diets fail, with failure defined as having gained back the same pounds lost (and usually more) within a year of starting the diet. Lust's cycle is similar: we keep it private, trying to tackle it alone, making fervent new resolutions, failing to live up to them, despising ourselves afterward, and then falling into despair and letting ourselves get in again, this time even deeper. To get out of the cycle, we would have to open ourselves up to someone else who can keep us honest and accountable. Countering lust's alienating tendencies, chastity requires intentionally being part of a community.

There are a host of small, practical things to do, of course. We can keep computers in public areas, get an Internet filter and accountability software. We can know better what makes us vulnerable and schedule alternate activities or call for help during those times. We can keep our language respectful and our jokes clean. We can much more carefully regulate which movies and television shows we watch and which magazines we read. We can dress modestly. One group of teenage boys started a "first row club" at church. So that they wouldn't be distracted by the revealing way girls at their church were dressed, a group of them agreed to sit together in the front pew each week. They physically situated themselves out of the view of temptation and in view of God's Word. That strategy is worth trying outside of church too. Reading the Bible and reminding ourselves of his love also helps; he wants the most beautiful and best for us, nothing less. Our minds *will* be full of images and ideas—but which ones? We can follow Paul's advice to seek out what is true, honorable, just, pure, excellent, and praiseworthy (Phil. 4:8), rather than letting just anything that comes our way drift in.

The bottom line, however, is that *not* doing things is not the only or the best answer. Chastity is not mere abstinence, just saying no. Let's face it, by the time we're tempted—even if we do say no—it can already be too late to avoid lust. So often we try to have it both ways—filling our senses with lustful stimuli and courting sin without actually consenting to it, and then despairing of our ability to keep our hearts and hands pure in the moment of decision. We tend to try to walk as close to the edge of the cliff as we can, hoping that we can keep our balance and not fall off. Chastity commits us to staying away from the edge altogether. "Flee from sexual immorality!" counsels Paul (1 Cor. 6:18 NIV). Don't court it, flirt with it, consider it, bring it tantalizingly close, and then try to stay strong enough to resist it. Flee early and flee often.

If chastity is not a rulebook of "don'ts," then what is it? It is a "pro-love" lifestyle, and therefore a virtue one needs whether single, married, old or young. Chastity is not something you need only when dating or surfing the Internet; it is a quality of one's character, evident in all areas of life. Chastity is a positive project, a project of becoming a person with an outlook that allows one to selflessly appreciate good and attractive things—most especially bodies and the pleasures they afford—by keeping those goods ordered to the good of the whole person and his or her vocation to love.[39] Chastity's fundamental question is not, "How far should I go on a date without crossing some invisible line of 'sin'"? but rather, "How can my life—my thoughts, my choices, my emotional responses, my conversation, and my behavior—make me a person who is best prepared to give and receive love in relationship with others?" Chastity preserves and protects and paves the way for wholeness in all our relationships, all of the time. To channel and control our sexual desires is to empower ourselves to love.

The best advice, then, for resisting lust is not to get an Internet filter (although you should do that too!), but to have good friends. If we have genuine friendships in which we learn to give and receive love in a healthy and satisfying way, we will be less inclined to wander off looking for sham substitutes and quick fixes. Good friendships teach us how to respect one another, to offer appropriate physical affection, to appreciate and care for others without looking for something in return, to trust one another. Someone who knows what real love looks like, whether in a sexual relationship or not, is a person who is less tempted to find lustful pleasures a tempting option. If your relationships with others and with God adequately feed your need to love and be loved, you will both see through and despise what lust has to offer.

Aquinas describes our relationship to God as "the love of friendship."[40] To overcome lust, we need to be anchored in this love. C. S. Lewis said, "What we call 'being in love' is a glorious state, and, in several ways, good for us. It helps to make us generous and courageous, it opens our eyes not only to the beauty of the beloved but to all beauty, and it subordinates . . . our merely animal sexuality; in that sense, love is the great conqueror of lust."[41] The challenge to live out this kind of love is Jesus's new commandment (John 15:12), a command he gives all who are members of his body. Thus, chastity keeps our identity as members of Christ at the fore of our self-understanding and the way we view others.

Sexual vice illustrates that the greater the power and beauty of the good at stake, the greater the destruction and the potential for ugliness and evil. A short film called *Flame* compares sex to fire. When we respect the power of fire and keep it in its proper place, we can appreciate its beauty and bask in its warmth.[42] At the end of the film, a man douses a pile of timber as tall as a house with gasoline. Then he takes the tiny flame of his lighter and sets it ablaze. The whole night sky is illuminated by the conflagration, flames leaping up to the heavens in the middle of a snowy, barren landscape. Don't settle for less than God's good gift of true sexual pleasure, he says. Instead, by respecting and protecting the real power of love, "discover the *big* flame." Sexual desire that is rightly directed and ruled gives us eyes to see the beauty and goodness of our sexuality, and to experience the full pleasure of its virtuous expression.

L'Engle writes, to her "long-loved love":

> Unclench your fists
> Hold out your hands
> Take mine.
> Let us hold each other.
> Thus is his Glory
>   Manifest.

EPILOGUE

Greed, gluttony, lust, envy, [and] pride are no more than sad efforts to fill the empty place where love belongs, and anger and sloth [are] just two things that may happen when you find that not even all seven of them at their deadliest ever can. —Frederick Buechner, *Whistling in the Dark*

Imagine for a moment that you have died. Your friends and family gather to grieve their loss and to remember you. What conversations would they have about you? What sorts of memories of you would they share with one another? What sort of person would they remember you as when they gave your eulogy at the funeral?

Funerals are one of the few places we still take the time to look over our lives as a whole and try to sum up a person's character. At milestones and celebrations such as retirements and graduations, we typically celebrate a person's specific accomplishments or achievements. But that is different than memorializing a person's character. The real question at a funeral is not, "Has this person been successful at some great task?" or "What recognizable milestones or markers of success has this person reached?" but rather, "Who was this person?" and "How would we characterize his or her life?"

It might be a worthwhile exercise to spend ten minutes trying to write down the speech you think a friend or family member might write about you if you died today. What sorts of character traits would they mention? What traits would they know about but politely *not* mention? Would there be a dominant theme in discussions about what sort of person you were among colleagues, church members, and family? Would they mention qualities like integrity, a good sense of humor, generosity, kindness, or perseverance? Would your irritability or stubbornness or impulsiveness be part of their conversation? What stories from your life would best illustrate those "telling moments" that revealed who you were, at your best and at your worst?

I regularly assign this exercise to my philosophy students. (In fact, I find it helpful to do it myself, year after year.) After they jot down a sketch of the speech, I ask them to write a second speech—the speech they *wish* someone could have given at their funeral, a speech about the person they aspired to be but had not yet become. What ugly qualities of character do you wish you'd overcome or put behind you? What character traits would you want in the epitaph on your gravestone if you had more time or a chance to do it over again?

If you are anything like me, there is a rather unhappy gap in the content of those two speeches—the one that would be given and the one I wish someone could have given. Which is just to say there's a character difference between the person I am and the person I wish to become. But that difference or gap is a place to begin reflecting about ourselves and then working toward real change.

This *memento mori* exercise, designed to look back on the past and honestly assess who we are now and where we have been, is not meant to be an end-point but a starting point. As for the early desert fathers, self-examination prepares us to look ahead to what we can and will become. It is not regretful or narcissistic navel-gazing. It is a first step toward becoming more than we are now.

The premise of this book is that the tree of capital vices, each vice rooted in pride and shooting out branches of further vice and sin, is a helpful tool for engaging in this type of self-assessment. These seven vices name perennial areas of human weakness and typical displays of pride's provide-your-own-happiness program. To study them is thus to study ourselves. When you look closely, what do you see? And what does seeing yourself clearly make you yearn to become?

Examining the vicious malformations of character canvassed in this book is meant to prompt us forward, in a more clear-sighted way, toward being people of better character, people whose lives are well lived. In the Christian tradition, this is not a self-help project but a Spirit-empowered movement. At the same time, however, it is not a license to drift along, but an encouragement to be intentional, reflective, specific, and energetic about moving *with* the Spirit's formative work. Like Augustine, when we look back on the way our lives are disordered by vice, we are moved to pray for the future, "Order me in my love."[1] The vices, their offspring, and the remedies traditionally suggested for them give us the language to identify and track the disordering of our desires we must actively resist. Discipleship takes discipline—the work of straightening what is bent, retraining and strengthening our capacities, working loose the bonds that constrain us.

In this study of the vices, one theme kept rising to the surface, confirming the pastoral instincts and Augustinian theology of Gregory the Great. Pride is the root of the seven capital vices. The reason there is no separate chapter in this book on the vice of pride is that *every* chapter in this book is on pride.

When we had our backyard maple taken down, the tree removal crew started with the upper branches, lopping more and more off until they got to the biggest limbs. Then they took down the main trunk piece by piece. But as anyone who's ever had a tree removed knows, you can chop off as many branches of the tree as you like, but eventually you have to dig it out roots and all, or the stump will relentlessly send out new shoots and grow new branches. The roots buried below the ground keep feeding the tree and giving it life. So pride feeds the other seven capital vices.

The difficulty with pride is that it can show itself in many guises— we have identified only the main seven here. When we carefully examine each of the vices, we eventually unearth the same familiar prideful pattern: a quest to provide happiness for ourselves through whatever god-substitute we choose—pleasure, approval, wealth, power, status. We are not willing to let God be in control, so we refuse to keep these goods in their place and accept them as gifts from his hand.

We most readily recognize pride in its arrogant forms: the person who resists submitting to God because he thinks he can handle things just fine on his own, who snubs advice and counsel because he knows best what is good for himself, and who shuns dependence on anyone else as unnecessary weakness. This form of pride can show itself in vicious responses like an avaricious desire for self-provision and control, or a wrathful desire to avenge ourselves on our own terms.[2] We should also be aware, however, of the way fear can drive us into vice, showing our lack of trust in God's provision and control and tempting us to seek happiness in safer, more secure, and self-sufficient ways. Each vice can therefore also show us compensating for our perceived vulnerabilities with an attempt to take control.

When we are afraid we won't get what we need, or worry that we won't have enough, it makes sense to spend our energy on constant acquisition, pursuing abundance to achieve self-sufficiency—this is the vice of avarice. When we are afraid that justice will not be done or that we won't get our just deserts unless we personally take charge of doling out vengeance in the way *we* see fit—then the vice of wrath takes hold. When we are afraid that we will not be accepted by others, that we won't fit in or live up to others' expectations, and thus do our best to hide behind a falsely inflated reputation—this is vainglory. When we are afraid we are not worth anything unless we are better than others, and we are afraid we can't compete with them, so we engineer their downfall—this is envy. When we are afraid we will always feel empty and needy, so we overfill ourselves with pleasures we can supply for ourselves—this is gluttony. When we are afraid we are unlovable, so we use people to gratify ourselves without ever giving ourselves in return—this is lust. When we are afraid of the effort loving others will cost us, so we hold everyone, even God, at arm's length in indifference—this is sloth.

It is a sad and dark truth about us that the tree of vices, rooted in pride, continues to live and grow and thrive in human nature in all of its malignant forms. The more we understand the dynamics of sin and the deep network of its combined forces in us, however, the more amazing we will find the grace and power promised to us to help us change. The Christian tradition is a centuries-long witness to the hope and promise of our transformation from vice to virtue, and a venerable guide to the ways and means of engaging in this difficult but fruitful process. Although we are separated by many years from the counsels of the desert hermits and the reflection of medieval theologians, we have found much of their witness and their wisdom still compelling today.

We have just looked backward—to imagine our death and the summation of our character that might be offered at our funeral. Now we turn forward—to imagine our re-formation and the road that might lead us into the future. It's a journey for which we have a map, fellow travelers, and well-seasoned guides. "To flee vice is the beginning of virtue." And the ending?

> In flesh's solitude I count it blest
> That only you, my Lord, can see my heart
> With passion's darkness tearing it apart

With storms of self, and tempests of unrest.
But your love breaks through blackness, bursts with light;
We separate ourselves, but you rebind
In Dayspring all our fragments; body, mind,
And spirit join, unite against the night.
Healed by your love, corruption and decay
Are turned, and whole, we greet the light of day.[3]

NOTES

Introduction

1. A version of this story was first published in my article "Aquinas's Virtues of Acknowledged Dependence: A New Measure of Greatness," in *Faith & Philosophy* 21, no. 1 (April 2004), 214–15. I would like to thank my colleagues in the Calvin College Department of Philosophy and participants in a roundtable discussion at the Calvin Institute for Christian Worship for their helpful comments on an earlier draft of the introduction and chapter 1.

2. N. T. Wright notes that the most frequent command God gives in the Bible is, "Do not be afraid." *Following Jesus: Biblical Reflections on Discipleship* (Grand Rapids: Eerdmans, 1994), 66.

3. James Stalker, *The Seven Deadly Sins and the Seven Cardinal Virtues* (Colorado Springs: NavPress, 1998; originally published by the American Tract Society, New York, 1901–2), 81. Stalker thus focuses his chapter on gluttony on the sin of drunkenness instead.

4. Francine Prose, *Gluttony: The Seven Deadly Sins* (New York: New York Public Library/Oxford University Press, 2003), 85–86.

5. Robert Solomon, ed., *Wicked Pleasures: Meditations on the Seven "Deadly" Sins* (Lanham, MD: Rowman and Littlefield, 1999), 2–3.

6. Wendy Wasserstein, *Sloth: The Seven Deadly Sins* (New York: New York Public Library/Oxford University Press, 2005), p. xiii; Michael Eric Dyson, *Pride: The Seven Deadly Sins* (New York: New York Public Library/Oxford University Press, 2006).

7. Simon Blackburn, *Lust: The Seven Deadly Sins* (New York: New York Public Library/Oxford University Press, 2004), 133. The "bad ideology" is a not-so-subtle reference to chapter 5, "The Christian Panic."

8. Solomon Schimmel, *The Seven Deadly Sins: Jewish, Christian, and Classical Reflections on Human Psychology* (New York: Oxford University Press, 1997; originally published by Free Press, New York, 1992), 125–28. In general, Schimmel tries to take the moral tradition seriously. The chapter on lust is a glaring exception.

9. Evelyn Waugh, "Sloth," in *The Seven Deadly Sins* (Pleasantville, NY: Akadine Press, 2002; originally published by Sunday Times Publications, London, 1962), 57.

10. Martin Marty, "Glittering Vices," *Christian Century,* April 5, 2003, 47.

11. "You Can Have It All! Seven Campaigns for Deadly Sin," *Harper's,* November 1987, 43–50.

12. We should be clear that acting on a virtue is not mechanical or unthinking, as in the common sense of the English word *habitual*. Virtues dispose us to perform good human acts—that is, actions that are voluntary and involve the use of the intellect and the will.

13. Aristotle, *Nichomachean Ethics* ii.6 (1106a15–25).

14. Alasdair MacIntyre, *After Virtue* (Notre Dame, IN: University of Notre Dame Press, 1984), chapter 14, "The Nature of the Virtues," 188.

15. To return to the point just made about habituation, if Jane not only consistently heeds her nagging voice of conscience, but also engages in loving and faithful behaviors toward her husband (helped by the good example and encouragement of her friends, and more importantly, by the grace of God), we would expect her to move from her current state of conflicted self-control to a state of virtuous fidelity.

16. Josef Pieper makes the same point in arguing for the importance of the virtues: "Because it *is* not always the same thing when two people *do* the same thing, a moral doctrine which regards only the actions of a man but not his being, is always in danger of seeing only the sameness . . . of the actions, and missing important differences . . . at a greater depth." *The Four Cardinal Virtues* (Notre Dame, IN: University of Notre Dame Press, 1966), 163.

17. *Nichomachean Ethics* ii.4 (1105b5–10).

18. *Nichomachean Ethics* vii.10 (1152a30–35).

19. Howard Fineman, "The Virtuecrats," *Newsweek,* June 13, 1994, 28–40.

20. *Summa theologiae* IIIa, prologue (emphasis added), trans. Fathers of the English Dominican Province (New York: Benziger Bros, 1948; repr., Westminster, MD: Christian Classics, 1981). Hereinafter abbreviated *ST*. The quote (as changed on page 7), is my translation. Other quotes from *ST* are from the English Fathers translation cited here, unless otherwise noted.

21. See 2 Peter 1: 3–11, for example.

22. This is exactly the question that Christian thinkers like Augustine (350–430 AD) and Aquinas (1225–74 AD) had to answer when they appropriated the Greek and Roman ideas about the virtues. For more on this subject, see my "Power Made Perfect in Weakness: Aquinas's Transformation of the Virtue of Courage," *Medieval Philosophy and Theology* 11 (2003), 147–80, and *Aquinas's Ethics* (Notre Dame, IN: University of Notre Dame Press, 2009), chapters 7–9.

23. In Aquinas, there is a cardinal virtue assigned to perfect every power of the human soul: practical wisdom perfects the intellect, justice perfects the will, courage perfects the part of the soul that deals with emotions like fear and hope, and temperance perfects the part of the soul that deals with feelings of desire and pleasure. Likewise, the theological virtue of faith elevates the intellect to divine things, while the virtues of hope and charity direct the will beyond human good to God. Because the intellect and will comprise our rational nature, all aspects of a human being's rationality are perfected by these virtues.

24. For example, the desert father Evagrius of Pontus also cites Ephesians 4:22–24 in *Thoughts* 3 and 39, in *Evagrius of Pontus: The Greek Ascetic Corpus,* trans. and ed. Richard E. Sinkewicz (Oxford: Oxford University Press, 2003).

25. See, for example, Augustine, *On the Morals of the Catholic Church against the Manichees* 15.25; *ST* IIaIIae.23.

26. C. S. Lewis, *Weight of Glory* (New York: HarperCollins, 2001), 26.

27. The seven terraces described in *Purgatorio,* cantos IX–XXVII, offer remedial punishments for each of the seven deadly sins. The punishments have the effect of lifting the weight of sin (e.g., canto XII.115–26). Similarly, in *Confessions* (e.g., Book ii.2), Augustine describes how God used his sin and its consequences as punishments to show Augustine their emptiness, a process that eventually led Augustine to conversion and freedom from those vices (Book viii.12–ix.1).

Chapter 1 Gifts from the Desert

1. Henry Fairlie, *The Seven Deadly Sins Today* (Notre Dame, IN: University of Notre Dame Press, 1979; originally published by New Republic Books, Washington, DC, 1978), viii.

2. See William White, *Fatal Attractions* (Nashville: Abingdon Press, 1992); Billy Graham, *The 7 Deadly Sins* (Grand Rapids: Zondervan, 1955); Anthony Campolo, *Seven Deadly Sins* (Wheaton, IL: Victor Books, 1987); and, with the exception of a brief introduction, Donald Capps, *Deadly Sins and Saving Virtues* (Philadelphia: Fortress Press, 1987). Os Guiness's *Steering through Chaos: Virtue and Vice in an Age of Moral Confusion* (Colorado Springs: NavPress, 2000) is a notable exception to this pattern.

3. Evagrius, *On Thoughts* 1, in Sinkewicz, *Evagrius of Pontus*; Cassian, *Conference* V.vi, trans. Boniface Ramsey, OP, Ancient Christian Writers, vol. 57 (Mahwah, NJ: Newman Press, 1999).

4. Evagrius, *Praktikos* 6, in Sinkewicz, *Evagrius of Pontus.*

5. The acronym of Latin names was GLAIT(I)AVS—*gula, luxuria, avaritia, ira, tristitia* (*invidia*—a later addition to the list)*, acedia, vana gloria,* and *superbia.* For more on the history and development of the list, see Carole Straw, "Gregory, Cassian, and the Cardinal Vices," in *In the Garden of Evil: The Vices and Culture in the Middle Ages,* ed. Richard Newhauser (Toronto: PIMS, 2005), 38; and Richard Newhauser, *The Treatise on Vices and Virtues in Latin and in the Vernacular* (Turnhout, Belgium: Brepols, 1993), chapter 6.

6. *Praktikos* VI.12.

7. The full title is *The Institutes of the Cenobia and the Remedies for the Eight Principal Vices,* trans. Boniface Ramsey, OP, Ancient Christian Writers, vol. 58 (Mahwah, NJ: Newman Press, 2000).

8. As quoted by Aquinas (in reverse order) in *ST* IIaIIae 161.6. See also *The Rule of St. Benedict,* chapter 7.

9. *Moralia on Job* 31.45.87–88, Patrologia Latina 76: 0620C–0621D.

10. For a quick overview of the history, see Paul Jordan-Smith, "Seven and More Deadly Sins," *Parabola* 10, no. 4 (1985): 34–45. Cassian describes the monk as contending in the arena against the vices, as an athlete of Christ (see, e.g., *Institutes* V.xvii–xviii).

11. See Leonard E. Boyle, OP, "The Setting of the *Summa theologiae* of St. Thomas—Revisited," in Stephen J. Pope, *The Ethics of Aquinas* (Washington, DC: Georgetown University Press, 2002), 10–11.

12. The 1587 edition; the original was completed and in circulation by the mid-thirteenth century.

13. My source for Peraldus is Siegfried Wenzel, *The Sin of Sloth: Acedia in Medieval Thought and Literature* (Chapel Hill: University of North Carolina Press, 1967), 75–77.

14. *Conference* V.xvi–xvix.

15. See Exodus 20, Deuteronomy 5, and Galatians 6, respectively.

16. For a historical development of this thesis, see Servais Pinckaers, *The Sources of Christian Ethics* (Washington, DC: Catholic University of America Press, 1995).

17. Abuses and confusions in penitential practice were no doubt a major obstacle here.

18. See, for example, Richard Foster, *Celebration of Discipline: The Path to Spiritual Growth* (San Francisco: Harper and Row, 1988); and Dallas Willard, *The Spirit of the Disciplines: Understanding How God Changes Lives* (San Francisco: Harper-SanFrancisco, 1990), and *Renovation of the Heart: Putting on the Character of Christ* (Colorado Springs: NavPress, 2002).

19. "All grace is from above, which shows even to sinners the schemes of the deceivers and which also offers assurance, saying, 'For what do you have that you did not receive' (1 Cor 4:7), so that in having received, on the one hand, we may give thanks to the one who granted the gift, and in having possession, on the other hand, we may not attribute to ourselves any boasting of honor, as though denying the gift." Evagrius of Pontus, *Vices*, Prologue. Cassian also warns, "Wherefore it is well for us both to be certified by actual experience, and also to be instructed by countless passages of Scripture, that we cannot possibly overcome such mighty foes in our own strength, and unless supported by the aid of God alone; and that we ought always to refer the whole of our victory each day to God Himself . . . I ask what could be said clearer in opposition to that impious notion and impertinence of ours, in which we want to ascribe everything that we do to our own free will and our own exertions?" *Conference* V.xv.

20. *Eulogios* 14.

21. Willard, *Spirit of the Disciplines,* 4–5.

22. David Hume, *Enquiry concerning the Principles of Morals,* 3rd ed., ed. P. H. Nidditch (Oxford: Clarendon Press, 1975), section 6, pt. 1, 199.

23. Ibid., section 8, 216.

24. David Hume, *A Treatise of Human Nature,* ed. David F. Norton and Mary J. Norton (Oxford: Oxford University Press, 2000), 2.8.7.

25. Quoted in Robert McCracken, *What Is Sin? What Is Virtue?* (New York: Harper and Row, 1966), 29.

26. In Solomon, *Wicked Pleasures,* 133–35.

27. See www.youtube.com/watch?v=JaKkuJVy2YA and www.cafepress.com/gabrielangel/1657935.

28. Solomon, "Introduction," in *Wicked Pleasures.* See also J. Shklar, *Ordinary Vices* (Cambridge: Harvard University Press, 1984).

29. *Conference* V.x.

30. The most famous of these penitential manuals was that of William Peraldus, a member of the Dominican order and a rough contemporary of Aquinas. (This work was the aforementioned *Summa de vitiis et virtutibus*). The virtues were also depicted by trees, but for Aquinas love was the "root and mother" of all the rest; while others, following the Rule of St. Benedict, showed humility as the root, with the three theological and four cardinal virtues as branches (charity being the highest). "Bearing good fruit" and being "rooted" in love are metaphors drawn from scripture (John 15:1–17; Galatians 5:22–23; Philippians 1:11; and Colossians 2:7, among others). When humility and pride were both counted as roots, the two trees retained a parallel structure, although the vices did not correspond to a consistent set of opposing virtues. Pride can also be cast as a disordered love of the self in the Augustinian tradition (of which Gregory and Aquinas are a part), so pride and love (Greek: *agapê*, Latin: *caritas*) can also play opposite "source" roles for their respective trees, with one tree rooted in self-love (over love of God), and the other in love of God (over love of self).

31. Pride thus counts as the first sin and origin of all others in two senses: it is temporally first in the human condition and a continuing source of others in the sense of being their root or first principle.

32. William Peraldus, in a popular work on the seven virtues and vices, lists sixteen "vices belonging to accidia" in no fewer than twenty-seven chapters on sloth (from the 1587 edition). See Wenzel, *Sin of Sloth*, 76.

33. *Conference* V.xvi.

34. *Praktikos* 6.

35. *Conference* V.ii.

36. Although Evagrius and Cassian included both, Gregory's list includes sadness (*tristitia*), not sloth. Aquinas's list includes sloth, not sadness; however, he defines sloth as a kind of "sorrow."

37. The earliest accounts suggested a concatenation in which one vice led to another, either beginning with carnal vices and progressing to spiritual, or beginning with spiritual vices, which, once they conquered the heart, gave way to carnal vices. Cassian preferred something along the lines of the first approach, while Gregory reversed the order, from spiritual to carnal. Aquinas offers no such internal causal relationship among all seven.

38. This work (likely written in the fourth century) is interesting for its blending of Christian virtues with Roman militaristic ideals.

39. The theological virtues (faith, hope, and love) are exceptions to this rule, since Aquinas holds that there is no such thing as believing in, hoping in, or loving God too much.

40. Thomas Aquinas, *Disputed Questions On Evil,* trans. Richard Regan (Oxford: Oxford University Press, 2003).

41. Richard Foster, *Money, Sex, and Power* (San Francisco: Harper and Row, 1985).

42. *ST* IaIIae 84.3–4.

43. Barbara Brown Taylor, *Home by Another Way* (Cambridge, MA: Cowley Publications, 1999), 67.

44. Book i.20, trans. R. L. Pine-Coffin (London: Penguin, 1961).

45. Augustine, *Confessions*, ii.VI (13), trans. Henry Chadwick (Oxford: Oxford University Press, 1991). He then expounds on specific vices and their imitation of the goodness and happiness we can find only in God: "Pride imitates what is lofty; but

you alone are God most high above all things . . . Curiosity appears to be a zeal for knowledge; yet you supremely know all . . . Idleness appears as desire for a quiet life; yet can rest be assured apart from the Lord? Luxury wants to be called abundance and satiety; but you are fullness and the inexhaustible treasure of incorruptible pleasure . . . Avarice wishes to have large possessions; you possess everything. Envy contends about excellence; but what is more excellent than you? Anger seeks revenge; who avenges with greater justice than you?"

46. There are two ways to go wrong: to direct desire at the wrong object, and to desire in the wrong manner, either excessively or deficiently. Later chapters on the specific vices will explain and illustrate this pattern in much greater detail.

47. See Boyle, "Setting of the *Summa theologiae*," 2.

48. *Institutes* XI.xvii.

Chapter 2 Envy

1. *Amadeus*, DVD, directed by Milos Forman (1984; Burbank, CA: Warner Home Video, 1997).

2. Victor Hugo, "Envy and Avarice," in *Selections, Chiefly Lyrical, from the Poetical Works of Victor Hugo* (London: George Bell and Sons, 1911), 4–6.

3. In this respect, it is unlike jealousy, which concerns protecting something (or someone) one has from being taken away. Envy, on the other hand, requires that the envier lack some desired good.

4. This is a paraphrase of Aquinas's definition (*ST* IIaIIae 36.1).

5. Francis Bacon, "of Envy," Essays of Francis Bacon, *The Essays or Counsels, Civil and Moral, of Francis Ld. Verulam Viscount St. Albans*, http://www.authorama.com/essays-of-francis-bacon-10.html.

6. *St. Augustine's Prayer Book,* rev. ed., ed. Rev. Loren Gavitt (West Park, NY: Holy Cross Publications, 1967), 117–18. Thanks to W. Jay Wood for calling my attention to this source.

7. Joseph Epstein, *Envy: The Seven Deadly Sins* (New York: New York Public Library/Oxford University Press, 2003), 90.

8. William Langland, *The Vision of Piers Plowman,* trans. Henry W. Wells (London: Sheed and Ward, 1959), passus V, 56–57. Reproduced by kind permission of Continuum International Publishing Group.

9. For an excellent articulation of this point, see Gabriele Taylor, "Deadly Vices?" in Roger Crisp, *How Should One Live?* (Clarendon: Oxford University Press, 1996).

10. Quoted by N. S. Gill, About.com: Ancient/Classical History, http://ancienthistory.about.com/cs/earlychurch/p/johnchrysostom.htm.

11. Epstein, *Envy*, 22.

12. Frederick Buechner, *Wishful Thinking: A Seeker's ABC* (San Francisco: HarperCollins, 1993), 24.

13. *The Incredibles,* DVD, directed by Brad Bird (Emeryville, CA: Disney/Pixar, 2004).

14. Epstein, *Envy*, 34.

15. *ST* IIaIIae 36.1.

16. Ibid., IIaIIae 36.1.ad 2.

17. *Chariots of Fire,* DVD, directed by Hugh Hudson (1981; Burbank, CA: Warner Home Video, 2005).

18. Thomas Williams, "Moral Vice, Cognitive Virtue: Jane Austen on Jealousy and Envy," *Philosophy and Literature* 27 (2003): 223–30. It is worth adding, however, that the envier's sense of justice and what is "deserved" by herself and others may well be deeply warped.

19. *ST* IIaIIae.28.

20. *St. Augustine's Prayer Book*, 117.

21. See the introduction for a definition and theological evaluation of this term.

22. *Little Miss Sunshine*, DVD, directed by Jonathan Dayton and Valerie Faris (Century City, CA: Twentieth Century Fox, 2006).

23. In particular, see Aaron Ben-Ze'ev, "Envy and Jealousy," *Canadian Journal of Philosophy* 20, no. 4, June 1990, 515, and "Envy and Pity," *International Philosophical Quarterly* 33, no. 1, 18. Psychologist Melanie Klein makes a similar claim about envy's inevitability and ineradicability as a human impulse (although not a possibly morally good one) in *Envy and Gratitude: A Study of Unconscious Sources* (London: Routledge, 2001).

24. As quoted in the *Encyclopedia Americana* (New York: A. B. Lyon, 1918), vol. 5, 384.

25. Robert C. Roberts, *Spirituality and Human Emotion* (Grand Rapids: Eerdmans, 1982), 69. See the updated chapter in his *Spiritual Emotions: A Psychology of Christian Virtues* (Grand Rapids: Eerdmans, 2007).

26. W. H. Auden, "Many Happy Returns," in *The Collected Poems of W. H. Auden* (New York: Random House, 1945), 71.

27. Nobel Lecture, December 11, 1979. My thanks to Terence Cuneo for suggesting this connection, and for his comments on an earlier draft of this chapter.

28. Buechner, *Wishful Thinking*, 102.

29. George Herbert, "Church Porch," st. 44 in *The Complete English Works* (New York: Alfred Knopf/David Campbell, 1995), 16.

Chapter 3 Vainglory

1. Aquinas, *On Evil* IX.1.ad 3 and IX.2.ad 9. He notes elsewhere, however, that our own glory is a good that may not be sought as an end in itself (*ST* IIaIIae 132.1.ad 3).

2. William Ian Miller, *Faking It* (New York: Cambridge, 2003), 96–97. Miller's book is an excellent and entertaining study of vainglory, hypocrisy, and other forms (virtuous and vicious) of pretending to be something we are not.

3. *Confessions*, ii.IX.

4. Ibid., i.XVIII.

5. What is common to all these forms, as William I. Miller puts it, is that we "care less that I am a moral failure than that I may be a social failure." See Miller, *Faking It*, 3.

6. Kheper Games, Inc., 2003.

7. *ST* IIaIIae 162.8.ad 2; 132.4. Aquinas acknowledges elsewhere (*ST* IIaIIae 132.3) that what the vainglorious person or his or her audience perceives or counts as an excellence may or may not be actually excellent. It is characteristic of all the vices that disordered loves distort our vision of ourselves and the objects of our love.

8. See *ST* IIaIIae 130–32.

9. *ST* IIaIIae 132.4.ad 2.

10. There are actually two related problems with ambition's excessive desire for honor: First, honor (like payment) is a good external to the activity itself. Overvaluing the honor for the sake of which one does something impairs one's ability to pursue the activity for its own sake and to appreciate its intrinsic value. Second, honor (like happiness) is something that naturally accompanies intrinsic goods pursued for their own sake—most notably, virtue. It is not something that one can acquire by direct intention and pursuit.

11. *ST* IIaIIae 132, and *On Evil* IX.

12. By contrast, it was well known to ancient Greek and Roman cultures. Aquinas has to make major modifications to the foundation of this Aristotelian virtue, since all true and perfect virtue, for Aquinas, rests on power we receive only by grace (*ST* IIaIIae 23.7).

13. I owe these labels to my former student Nathan Brink.

14. *ST* IIaIIae 132.3, *On Evil* IX.1.

15. *Confessions,* Book ii.

16. Augustine, *City of God,* trans. Marcus Dods (New York: Modern Library/Random House, 1950), Book V.12.

17. Ibid., Book XIV.28.

18. Ibid.

19. *ST* IIaIIae 132.2.

20. *On the Eight Thoughts* 7.21, Sinkewicz, *Evagrius of Pontus.*

21. Ibid., 15.

22. *Institutes* XI.xvi.

23. *On the Eight Thoughts* 28.

24. *Institutes* XI.v.

25. *Praktikos* VII.30.

26. Miller, *Faking It,* 8.

27. Westminster Shorter Catechism, Q.1.

28. *ST* IIaIIae 132.4.

29. *Confessions*, i.I. Note: Augustine references Psalm 146:5, which is Psalm 147:5 in our version of scripture.

30. Richard Foster, *The Freedom of Simplicity* (New York: HarperCollins, 1981), chapter 6.

31. Ibid., 15.

32. Ibid., 115.

33. Anne Lamott, *Bird by Bird: Some Instructions on Writing and Life* (New York: Pantheon, 1994), 116.

34. *Institutes* XI.xix.

35. Foster, *Freedom of Simplicity,* 124–25.

Chapter 4 Sloth

1. Leigh Rubin, "Rubes" (Creators Syndicate, 2003).

2. Evelyn Waugh, *London Sunday Times* (Pleasantville, NY: Akadine Press, 2002; originally published by Sunday Times Publications, London, 1962), 57.

3. Wasserstein, *Sloth.*

4. See *Institutes* X.viii–xiii, inter alia.

5. Quoted in McCracken, *What Is Sin?* 29.

6. Thomas H. Benton, "The Top 5 Virtues of Successful Graduate Students," *Chronicle of Higher Education,* September 2, 2003.

7. Josef Pieper, *On Hope* (San Francisco: Ignatius Press, 1986), 54–55.

8. Ibid., 55.

9. Morton W. Bloomfield, *The Seven Deadly Sins* (Lansing, MI: Michigan State University Press, 1967), 75; Wenzel, *Sin of Sloth,* 10; Sinkewicz, *Evagrius of Pontus,* 72.

10. *Praktikos* VI.12. Note: Evagrius references Psalm 90:6, which is Psalm 91:6 in our version of scripture.

11. *Institutes* X.xxi. See also *Conference* V, in volume 57 of the same series.

12. Ibid.

13. Originally, *acedia* and the vice of sorrow were distinguished from each other, but linked in the concatenation of vices (Cassian especially subscribed to the view that falling prey to one vice made one susceptible to the next one in the chain). Cassian and Evagrius describe sorrow's cause as excessive attachment to (or insufficient detachment from) worldly desires, pleasures, and possessions. One's religious commitment makes one unable to satisfy or attain these desires, and one feels disappointed as a result. This is the vice of sorrow. (Thus, Cassian makes much of total renunciation: the monk cannot keep even a penny of his former fortune when he joins the monastery; this in contrast to the desert fathers, who were allowed a subpoverty level of personal possessions to maintain their livelihood—e.g., basket-weaving materials.) This sorrow in turn produces resentment of one's religious vocation, which now presents itself as the major obstacle to the fulfillment of worldly desires. As such, the vocation and its demands are resented and resisted. This is the vice of sloth. Gregory will later combine sorrow and sloth under the title *tristitia,* and many in the tradition (including Aquinas) will describe sloth itself as an oppressive sorrow on the basis of this relationship between the two vices. My account of sloth, based on Aquinas's texts, also maintains the link Evagrius and Cassian first described, with excessive attachment to the "old self" making commitment to and joy in the "new self" difficult and distasteful.

14. Kathleen Norris, *The Quotidian Mysteries: On Laundry, Liturgy, and Women's Work* (Mahwah, NJ: Paulist Press, 1998), 53. See also her most recent book, *Acedia & Me: Marriage, Monks, and a Writer's Life* (New York: Riverhead, 2008).

15. *ST* IIaIIae 24.3.

16. *On Evil* XI.2, and *ST* IIaIIae 35.3.

17. Søren Kierkegaard in *The Sickness unto Death* (trans. Howard V. Hong and Edna Hong [Princeton, NJ: Princeton University Press, 1985], 67–74) describes this self as one who refuses, in defiance, not to be itself, because to be oneself would involve a relational identity—one binding the self to God. If the refusal is less conscious, *acedia* is more akin to Kierkegaard's despair of weakness (see especially 55–56). Many modern existentialist thinkers offer good descriptions of a slothlike condition, but Kierkegaard ties his description explicitly to one's identity and relationship to God.

18. *Groundhog Day,* DVD, directed by Harold Ramis (1993; Culver City, CA, Sony Pictures, 2002). This case involves love in a human–human relationship, not a God–human relationship.

19. The marriage-and-friendship metaphor is especially apt, because for Aquinas the virtue of love that flows out of our participation in God's life (called *caritas*) is defined as a *friendship* in which the lover and the beloved enjoy the fullest sense of

communion and fellowship possible between persons short of the love between the members of the Trinity. Aquinas thinks we can have this friendship with God and each other.

20. Anne Lamott, *Operating Instructions* (New York: Ballantine Books, 1994), 96.

21. This is perhaps why Evagrius describes *acedia* as one of the most oppressive of the vices.

22. Pieper, *On Hope*, 56.

23. U2, "Walk On," *All That You Can't Leave Behind* (PolyGram Intl. Music Pub., 2000).

24. For Aquinas, we love God for his own sake and love our neighbors as ourselves. Although these two loves cannot be pulled apart, *acedia* strikes primarily at the source love—our love of God—and only secondarily branches out to indifference to what love demands of us on account of our neighbors.

25. *Institutes* X.v, emphasis added.

26. Buechner, *Wishful Thinking*, 109–10.

27. *Confessions*, i.I.

28. Misery.—The only thing which consoles us for our miseries is diversion, and yet this is the greatest of our miseries. For it is this which principally hinders us from reflecting upon ourselves, and which makes us insensibly ruin ourselves." The quotation in the text concludes this passage. *Pensées*, trans. W. F. Trotter (New York: E. P. Dutton, 1958), 171.

29. *Man's Search for Meaning* (New York: Pocket Books, 1959), 129. As I explain in "The Vice of Sloth: Some Historical Reflections . . . ," and Lauren Winner suggests in her essay "Sleep Therapy," perhaps our current understanding of sloth as mere laziness occasions misdiagnosis of the vice's real symptoms (*Books & Culture*, January/February 2006), 7.

30. *ST* IIaIIae 36.3.

31. Isaac Watts, "When I Survey the Wondrous Cross" in *The Psalter Hymnal* (Grand Rapids: CRC Resources, 1987), #384.

32. *Praktikos* VI.28.

33. *On the Eight Thoughts* 6.5.

34. Debra Rienstra, *Great with Child: On Becoming a Mother* (New York: Tarcher/ Putnam, 2002), 186–87.

35. *On the Eight Thoughts* 6.5.

36. Carlos Fernandez, Chapel Resources, http://www.vanguard.edu/uploadedfiles/ Community/sfd/4_Sloth.pdf, 2/27/2007.

Chapter 5 Avarice

1. *Wall Street*, DVD, directed by Oliver Stone (1987; Century City, CA: Twentieth Century Fox, 2007).

2. *ST* IIaIIae 118.2, and *Disputed Questions on Evil* XIII.1.resp and ad 6, XIII.2 resp.

3. *ST* IIaIIae 118.1–2, and *Disputed Questions on Evil* XIII.1.

4. Ibid.

5. Perhaps there is a parallel between the joy of generosity and the joy of fasting (as Pieper notes, the tradition calls the faster's state *hilaritas mentis* [*Four Cardinal*

Virtues]). Approaching a situation without making any claims of one's own, deliberately focusing on things and others in themselves, not as *mine to consume and possess,* gives us a freedom which brings joy, contentment, detachment, and open-handedness. Elsewhere Pieper calls this outlook "transparent," because we can appreciate things and people unclouded by our own desires for them. Of course, our giving (as with all our dealings with money) should be informed by prudence—practical reason's judgment about the most appropriate response in a given situation. This is in part what keeps generosity from falling into prodigality.

6. *ST* IIaIIae 117.1.ad 3.

7. *ST* IIaIIae 117.1.

8. Ibid.

9. *ST* IIaIIae 118.6, translation adapted.

10. *ST* IIaIIae 117.5.ad 1.

11. *ST* IIaIIae 117.1.

12. *Institutes* VII.xxii.

13. James Twitchell, *Living It Up: Our Love Affair with Luxury* (New York: Simon and Schuster, 2003).

14. *ST* IIaIIae 118.1.ad 2.

15. Quoted in *ST* IIaIIae 118.4.obj.2.

16. *ST* IIaIIae 118.8, and *On Evil* XIII.3. Aquinas is using Gregory's list from the *Moralia.*

17. *ST* IIaIIae 118.2.

18. *Evangelium Vitae* I (New York: Random House, 1995), 40.

19. *Institutes* VII.xxiv.

20. *ST* IaIIae 84.3, and *On Evil* XIII.3.

21. Buechner, *Wishful Thinking*, 98.

22. *ST* IIaIIae 118.6.

23. *ST* IIaIIae 118.2.

24. Boethius, "Introduction" and Book III, Prose X, in *The Consolation of Philosophy,* trans. Richard Green (New York: Macmillan, 1962).

25. *On the Eight Thoughts* 3.3.

26. *Confessions,* ii.5.

27. *On the Eight Thoughts* 3.8.

28. *ST* IaIIae 2.1.ad 3.

29. *Christianity Today,* October 7, 1996, 27.

30. There is actually significant dispute over this claim in the Christian tradition, especially from monastic orders in which individual monks own no personal property whatsoever, although the monastery itself can own property, engage in trade for goods, and provide for its members' needs. The dispute is whether this possessionless state is a counsel of perfection, and therefore not obligatory for all, or whether it is the only way to escape from the inherently sinful desire to own possessions. Different church fathers disagreed about whether private property or ownership was a necessary evil, a neutral matter, or a good, and they disagreed about whether the desire for possessions was natural to human beings or a sinful desire resulting from the fall. My point here is simply that human beings cannot live or live well without some material goods (e.g., food, clothing, and shelter). Thus, the remedies I suggest are directed toward the virtuous handling of those goods.

31. Text by the Community of Taizé; music by Jacques Berthier (Les Presses de Taizé, 1991), in *Sing! A New Creation* (Grand Rapids: CRC, 2001), #220.

32. *Confessions*, ii.IV.

33. C. S. Lewis, *Screwtape Letters* (New York: HarperCollins, 2001), 113–15.

Chapter 6 Anger

1. Garret Keizer, *The Enigma of Anger* (San Francisco: Jossey-Bass, 2002), 10.

2. For example, *ST* IIaIIae 158.1. See also *ST* IaIIae 59.2–3 for a discussion of how passions are rightly ordered by virtue.

3. *On Evil*, 12.1.

4. *Chapters on Prayer* 13 and 24, in Sinkewicz, *Evagrius of Pontus*.

5. *Institutes* VIII.vi, also quoted in *On Evil* XII.1.obj.4.

6. *Institutes* VIII.v (emphasis added).

7. See William C. Mattison III, "Jesus' Prohibition of Anger (Mt 5:22): The Person/ Sin Distinction from Augustine to Aquinas," *Theological Studies* 68 (2007): 839–64.

8. *ST* IaIIae 46.2–3.

9. *ST* IIaIIae 158.8.

10. *ST* IIaIIae 142.2.

11. Garret Keizer, "The Enigma of Anger," *Books & Culture*, September/October 2002, 9.

12. Alan Paton, *Too Late the Phalarope* (New York: Scribner, 1996), 199; see also the story told by Keizer in *Enigma of Anger*, 35–36.

13. Pieper, *Four Cardinal Virtues*, 193.

14. *St. Augustine's Prayer Book*, 116.

15. Fairlie, *Seven Deadly Sins Today*, 108.

16. See Richard E. Barton, "Gendering Anger: *Ira, Furor*, and Discourses of Power and Masculinity in the Eleventh and Twelfth Centuries," in Newhauser, *In the Garden of Evil*; and Catherine Peyroux, "Gertrude's *Furor*: Reading Anger in an Early Medieval Saint's Life," in Barbara Rosenwein, *Anger's Past: The Social Uses of an Emotion in the Middle Ages* (Ithaca, NY: Cornell University Press, 1998).

17. Stephen Calloway and Susan Owens, *Divinely Decadent* (London: Octopus, 2001), 160–61.

18. *The Mission*, DVD, directed by Roland Joffé (1986; Burbank, CA: Warner Home Video, 2003).

19. This is a case of what the tradition calls "fraternal correction," which is an act of *caritas* (*ST* IIaIIae 33).

20. Buechner, *Wishful Thinking*, 2.

21. If anger is about justice, and justice is about our relationships with others, can we be angry at ourselves? It certainly seems psychologically possible. Although I will not discuss it here, if self-directed anger is possible, it likely depends on our ability to reflect on our own actions from a second-order perspective, in which we consider our own actions or feelings or judgments and make judgments about them from our reflective stance.

22. Martin Luther King Jr., *The Strength to Love* (1963; repr., Philadelphia: Fortress Press, 1981), 53.

23. *On Evil* XII.2 resp.

24. See also Exodus 34:6; Nehemiah 9:17; Psalm 78:38; Jonah 4:2; Numbers 14:18; Psalm 86:15; and Psalm 30:5, among others.

25. We note, of course, that some Christians have argued that it is anthropomorphic and metaphorical—scripture's concession to human limitations—to describe God as angry at all, since he lacks a body and therefore lacks passions in our sense of the word.

Chapter 7 Gluttony

1. *On Evil* 14.1.ad 2, and *ST* IIaIIae 148.2.ad 2.

2. *On the Morals of the Catholic Church* xxi, quoted in *ST* IIaIIae 141.6 sc.

3. Lewis, *Screwtape Letters*, 87–88.

4. William Ian Miller, "Gluttony," in Solomon, *Wicked Pleasures*, 33–34.

5. The Weigh Down Workshop, www.wdworkshop.com/tips.asp.

6. Buechner, *Wishful Thinking*, 35.

7. We note, however, that human gluttony is worse than animal behavior in the following way. Human beings have reason to restrain their appetites, and when we fail to exercise reason's restraint, we lack animal instincts to take over where reason has abdicated. Moreover, we can also use reason to creatively aid and abet the escalation and satisfaction of our excessive appetites, so the forms of human deviance in this sin, as with lust, are typically worse than anything we might observe in animal behaviors, as the infamous Roman vomitoriums illustrate.

8. *ST* IIaIIae 141.4.

9. *ST* IIaIIae 147.1.ad 2.

10. *On Evil* 14.1.ad 6.

11. As paraphrased by Aquinas in *ST* 146.1.

12. *QQ. Evangel.* ii.11. quoted in *ST* IIaIIae 146.1.ad 2.

13. *ST* IIaIIae 146.1.ad 2.

14. Likewise, for drinking, it requires that we are not impaired in the use of our other faculties by intoxication. Aquinas treats sobriety and drunkenness in *ST* IIaIIae 149–50.

15. This term is from Kallistos Ware, "The Meaning of the Great Fast," in *The Lenten Triodion,* trans. Mother Mary and Kallistos Ware (London: Faber and Faber, 1978), 16.

16. Foster, *Freedom of Simplicity*, 174.

17. Ware, "Meaning of the Great Fast," 16.

18. Ibid.

19. In this respect, much contemporary dieting is closer to gluttony than to virtue. The element of assumed control or willpower stands in stark contrast to the discipline of fasting, which both depends on God's power and seeks as its goal a spiritual relationship to another, not something physical or solely for oneself.

Chapter 8 Lust

1. My thanks to the following students in my Aquinas seminar at Calvin College (spring 2008), who read and suggested valuable revisions of this chapter: Brooke Levitske Brycko, Tim Perrine, Patrick Duff, Kenneth Harrell, and Daniel Williams.

The final version reflects my considered opinion on the subject of lust, not necessarily theirs.

2. *Confessions*, viii.VII.

3. Ibid., viii.XI.

4. William Gass, "Lust," in Solomon, *Wicked Pleasures*, 134–35.

5. *ST* IIaIIae 154.8.ad 2.

6. Wright, *Following Jesus*, 66.

7. Buechner, *Wishful Thinking*, 107.

8. Paul Ricoeur, *Sexualität. Wunder—Abwege—Rätsel* (Frankfurt: Rischer Bücherei, 1967, 15), as quoted in Josef Pieper, *Faith, Hope, Love* (San Francisco: Ignatius Press,1997), 266.

9. Pieper, *Faith, Hope, Love,* 265.

10. Buechner, *Wishful Thinking*, 107.

11. Put in the Greek philosopher Aristotle's terms, lust degrades a virtue friendship, in which one loves the other for his or her own sake (as one loves oneself), into a friendship of utility and pleasure, which lasts only as long as the other is able to supply the usefulness and pleasure we expect. See *Nichomachean Ethics* viii.

12. *ST* IIaIIae 142.2 and 151.1–2.

13. For the desert fathers, the goal was dampening and forbidding all sexual desire—as far as possible—since they had dedicated their bodies to God in celibacy. Their view of the body and its material needs was part of a very otherworldly program of spiritual development, whose extremes were eventually balanced by more moderate counsel on ascetic disciplines and the role of the body from (for example) St. Benedict, Gregory the Great, and Aquinas, and in some cases, even the mature thought of St. Augustine. It is an easy mistake for interpreters to take their counsel, intended for those vowing lifelong celibacy, and to confuse this with general views of well-ordered sexuality and sexual desire, which include married sex.

14. Buechner, *Wishful Thinking*, 108.

15. Plato, *Symposium,* trans. Alexander Nehamas and Paul Woodruff (Indianapolis: Hackett, 1989), 189c–94e.

16. Ibid., 192d.

17. Aristophanes' myth makes sex about the physical and psychic reunion of the lovers, leaving procreation entirely out of the picture. Seeking sexual pleasure without union to another person, for example, through masturbation, is a further step removed—it is not procreative nor does it bond persons together. While Christians disagree on the morality of sexual stimulation without a partner or sexual intercourse that seeks intimacy while deliberately blocking procreation, if it is true that sex was created to bond us with others in these ways, then there will be various degrees of distance possible from the full realization of its nature.

18. XXX Church.com, http://www.xxxchurch.com/prayerwall (February–March 2008).

19. For one example, see Justin Lookadoo, *The Dirt on Sex* (Grand Rapids: Hungry Planet, 2004), 95.

20. Madeleine L'Engle, *The Ordering of Love: New and Collected Poems of Madeleine L'Engle* (Colorado Springs: Shaw Books/Waterbrook, 2005), 3.

21. *ST* IIaIIae 154.2.obj.4.

22. Naomi Wolf, "The Porn Myth," *New York Magazine,* May 2004.

23. Solomon, *Wicked Pleasures,* 3.

24. For a variety of examples, see XXXChurch.com, www.xxxchurch.com/gethelp/ confessions.

25. Paton, *Too Late the Phalarope*, 154, 163, 200.

26. Lookadoo, *Dirt on Sex*, 97.

27. Buechner, *Wishful Thinking*, 108.

28. *Institutes* VI.ix and xx, and Aquinas, *ST* IIaIIae 151.4.

29. *Institutes* XI.xviii.

30. *On the Eight Thoughts* 2.6.

31. René Decartes, *Meditations on First Philosophy,* VI.78, trans. Donald A. Cress, 3rd ed. (Indianapolis: Hackett, 1993).

32. *Institutes* VI.xvii and xix. In this, he echoes Jesus's comments on lust and adultery in the Sermon on the Mount (Matt. 5:28).

33. Cornelius Plantinga Jr. and Sue A. Rozeboom, *Discerning the Spirits: A Guide to Thinking about Christian Worship Today* (Grand Rapids: Eerdmans, 2003), 159.

34. Steve Turner, "She No Longer Brought Him Pleasure," in *King of Twist* (London: Hodder and Stoughton Religious, 1992), 77–79.

35. Madeleine L'Engle, "To a Long Loved Love: 7," in *The Ordering of Love*, 138.

36. See also comments on lust's effects on the mind and memory on XXXChurch .com, www.xxxchurch.com/gethelp/confessions.

37. *ST* IIaIIae 153.5, *On Evil* XV.4.

38. Pieper, *Four Cardinal Virtues,* 167.

39. See Karol Wojtyla, *Love and Responsibility* (San Francisco: Ignatius, 1993), especially 130, 167, 256–57.

40. *ST* IIaIIae 23.1.

41. C. S. Lewis, *Mere Christianity,* rev. and amplified (New York: HarperCollins, 2001), 108.

42. *Flame,* directed by Rob Bell, NOOMA #002 (2002, Fringe), http://www.nooma .com.

Epilogue

1. *City of God* XV.22, 29. See Peter Brown's insightful analysis of this theme in chapter 27 of *Augustine of Hippo* (Berkeley: University of California Press, 1967), especially 325–26.

2. Traditional villains in fiction usually fit this pattern: J. K. Rowlings's Voldemort is one classic case. But many heroes typifying contemporary moral ideals, such as the self-sufficiency and self-reliance of the protagonists of American action-adventure films, also exhibit forms of pride.

3. Madeleine L'Engle, "Within This Quickened Dust," in *The Ordering of Love*, 66.

INDEX